The Year-Round

VEGETABLE

GARDENER

The Complete Guide to Growing Vegetables and Herbs Any Time of the Year

ANNE HALPIN

SUMMIT BOOKS
NEW YORK • LONDON • TORONTO
SYDNEY • TOKYO • SINGAPORE

SUMMIT BOOKS
Simon & Schuster Building
Rockefeller Center
1230 Avenue of the Americas
New York, New York 10020

Copyright © 1992 by Anne Halpin
All rights reserved
including the right of reproduction
in whole or in part in any form.
SUMMIT BOOKS and colophon are
trademarks of Simon & Schuster Inc.
Designed by Edith Fowler
Illustrations by Linda Winters
Manufactured in the United States of America

10 9 8 7 6 5 4 3 2 1
10 9 8 7 6 5 4 3 2 1 (pbk.)

Library of Congress Cataloging in Publication Data

Halpin, Anne Moyer.
  The year-round vegetable gardener: the complete
guide to growing vegetables and herbs any time of
the year/Anne Halpin.
    p.   cm.
  Includes index.
  1. Vegetable gardening.   I. Title.
SB321.H23   1992
635—dc20   *91-38154*
                                                CIP

ISBN: 0-671-70977-1
      0-671-70978-X (pbk.)

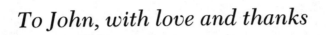

To John, with love and thanks

Acknowledgments

This book would not have been possible without the assistance and support of a number of people.

Photographer and edible landscape designer Robert Kourik supplied many of the photographs that appear in this book. Johnny's Selected Seeds, All-American Selections, and The National Garden Bureau were also most generous with photos. I thank them all.

Thanks to Linda Winters for creating the illustrations under very tight deadlines, and for her grace under pressure.

As always, my editor, Dominick Anfuso, contributed his welcome editorial expertise and guidance.

Finally, to my husband, John White, I will be eternally grateful for his unwavering belief in me, his understanding and patience during all the months I worked on the manuscript, and his ability to tolerate me at deadline time.

Contents

Introduction

Most of us have become used to eating our favorite vegetables at any time of the year. And many supermarkets and greengrocers carry fresh herbs all year round. Recent years have even seen edible flowers become available in gourmet produce shops. The idea of enjoying produce in its natural season may seem passé, a part of our less sophisticated past. But there are many pleasures to be had from homegrown produce brought in fresh from the garden at the peak of ripeness, and nobody is more aware of the satisfactions to be gained than gardeners.

In the past, a big reason people grew food was to save money. When I was in college in the early 1970s, the idea was to grow some of your own food to be more self-sufficient, less dependent on "the system." In the 1990s another great wave of food gardening is sweeping the country, and this time the concerns of gardeners have shifted again. Now more of us than ever are concerned about the quality of the food we eat, and fearful of the effects of fertilizers, pesticides, fungicides, and other products so widely used to grow it. By growing our own food, we know what goes into it. We can avoid the synthetic products if we choose, and instead feed our plants with milder natural plant foods, and kill bugs with insecticidal soaps or plant-based insecticides that break down quickly in the environment and leave no residues on our vegetables. We can have our cucumbers without the paraffin coating they receive in most supermarkets these days, and beans grown without chemical sprays. Many of us have children and worry about the long-term effects of the many environmental chemicals to which they are exposed. We want to protect them —and ourselves—as much as we can.

Fears aside, the other reason so many Americans are growing some of their own food today is the same as it has always been among gardeners—for the flavor. There is simply no way commercial operations can duplicate the taste and texture of freshly picked herbs, juicy, red-ripe tomatoes, or brussels sprouts picked after frost. Fresh food in season is a genuine treat. The harvest makes each season special, and can be a cause for celebration with friends or family, the stuff of pleasant memories. The foods somehow match the mood of the season, too. Consider the earliest spring greens, so delicate in color, texture, and often flavor. The summer garden bursts with lushness and abundance; the vegetables, herbs, and flowers are sensual delights, rich with color, and so many juicy, crunchy textures. Autumn feels more substantial, a transitional season as is spring, and the bounty of the autumn garden reflects that; we harvest the last tomatoes and eggplants from summer, along with weighty winter squashes and cabbage-family crops. Autumn is a time of gathering in, of storing the harvest. During the cold of winter we seek hearty foods, and take homegrown root vegetables from storage to make warming, comforting soups and stews. Our focus turns inward, and we cultivate some salad plants and herbs indoors.

Thus, each season has its characteristic foods, and developing an appreciation for them helps to keep life interesting. While buying strawberries at the supermarket in winter can be a special treat, if you indulge too often they won't be as special in June. And off-season produce that is shipped across the country, or from abroad, just hasn't got the quality of the homegrown, in-season item. Despite the sophistication of our agriculture industry, some foods can still be had only in season—at least that's the case if you want to enjoy them properly. Sugar snap peas, for example, are now sold frozen, but they do not come close to matching the taste and texture of snap peas fresh from the garden. And consider sweet corn; it must be freshly picked or it turns starchy and tough.

It may surprise you to learn that you can enjoy your own fresh, homegrown produce in every season of the year. But you can, and it is the aim of this book to show you how.

Careful planning is important. Most of us are not lucky enough to have greenhouses, and to make use of the techniques in this book you do not need one. You will need a cold frame and an indoor light garden to achieve maximum productivity, but even without these two special growing areas you will be able to grow and harvest at least *something* all year long.

You will need to get the earliest possible start in spring, starting some seeds indoors and getting a jump on the outdoor season with a cold frame, cloches, hot caps, and other season-extending devices. In summer, you can use shade and water to extend the harvest of cool-season crops, and later in the season you can plant for a fall harvest. In autumn, the season-extending devices come into play once again, along with the cold frame and mulch. In winter you can dig root crops that are stored in the garden under a thick mulch, grow Oriental vegetables in an insulated cold frame, force certain plants to produce crops indoors, cultivate your own mushrooms, and grow salad greens and herbs in light gardens and on windowsills.

It is important to understand your local climate in order to make the most of a multi-season garden. In the northern part of the country, the outdoor growing season can be as brief as 90 to 120 days. In these cool climates many spring vegetables will continue producing through midsummer. Warm-weather crops that cannot go outdoors until all danger of frost is past must be started indoors or limited to the fastest-maturing varieties. Some northern gardeners get the best results by concentrating most of their energy on cool-weather crops, replacing spring edibles with fall crops when they finally stop bearing in summer.

Across the middle part of the country the growing season ranges from 120 to 240 days. Two or three successive crops can be grown in the same space in these gardens. As summer crops are harvested, gardeners in the longer season areas can replace them with fall crops. But gardeners throughout this area can plant spring, summer, and fall crops in different parts of the garden.

In the warm parts of the country—the Deep South, and low elevations in the Southwest and along the West Coast—the growing season is eight to twelve months long. Hot weather comes early to these gardens, so gardeners usually do best to plant cool-weather crops to mature in fall and winter. The intense summer heat eventually exhausts most summer crops except for a few: okra, southern peas, and butter beans among them. Gardeners here often make two succession plantings of tomatoes, eggplant, summer squash, and other warm-weather favorites in order to harvest all summer.

The longer you garden, the better acquainted you will become with the climate in your area and the microclimate in your garden. You will come to understand the weather patterns and the growing environment your garden provides for the plants you grow. Of course, weather varies from year to year.

I urge you to keep a yearly journal of your garden's progress. It need not be fancy, but do keep notes on what you plant, how it performs, what weather conditions are like from day to day, or at least from week to week, when you fertilize, water, fight pests, and improve the soil. Keeping a journal requires some discipline at first, but it soon becomes an enjoyable activity. Over a period of years your journals will provide an excellent information base that will help you to plan and care for the garden.

For years I lived in a little row house with a tiny backyard. If I wanted to grow vegetables *and* herbs *and* flowers, the only way I could do it was to plant them all together. So I did, and now I will always garden that way. I like the way such a garden looks. I like that the garden is useful as well as beautiful. What I did not realize, at first, is that this kind of mixed edible garden follows the traditional concept of a kitchen garden.

This book is concerned with this sort of mixed garden, where vegetables, herbs, and edible flowers all grow together. It is aimed at gardeners whose space and time are limited, who want to grow food because they like to cook, who like to try new things, and who want a garden that is beautiful as well as functional.

All plants are pretty if you group them with care. There is no reason a garden of edibles cannot stand proudly in the front yard like a flower garden. If you design your kitchen garden with care, you don't have to hide it out back.

This year I'm moving into a new house with a half acre of land; to me that's a vast expanse. But I'll still grow herbs, flowers, and vegetables together.

How to Use This Book

This book will give you guidance in managing your garden in every season of the year. Garden design concepts and basic techniques that are used in more than one season are covered in Chapters One and Two. Highlights of the garden in each season, along with tips on planting, maintaining the garden, and other seasonal activities, are provided in Chapters Three through Six. Chapter Seven is an encyclopedia of edibles to grow, and offers information on vegetables, herbs, and edible flowers. The Appendix gives names and addresses of some of the best mail-order sources of seeds, plants, and supplies.

I have used primarily common names for the plants in this book, because few of us call vegetables by their botanical names. In Chapter Seven, however, you will also find the scientific names, given in accord with *Hortus Third,* a respected reference on plants found in North America. I have used the terms *variety* and *cultivar* informally and interchangeably, as gardeners use them in everyday speech. In reality, a variety is a variation on a plant species that appears spontaneously, and a cultivar is a variant developed under cultivation. But I have used both terms loosely, to indicate variants of particular species.

You will find the terms *cool, temperate,* and *warm climates* used to refer to broad, general regions of the Continental United States. Basically, cool and temperate climates are regions where winters are cold. Cool climates correspond roughly to USDA Plant Hardiness Zones 3 and 4, in the northernmost parts of the country. Temperate climates include zones 5 to 7, and in some cases, zone 8. Warm climates include zones 9 and 10, sometimes zone 8, and the newly designated zone 11, which is the tropical climate found in the Florida Keys and Hawaii (although this book will be of little use to gardeners in those areas). Hardiness is such an elusive concept, and even the most detailed zone map cannot possibly show all the climatological variations present in any given geographic area. It is far better to come to understand the conditions in your own garden than to rely exclusively on a zone map.

Please remember, too, that gardening is not a science. Foolproof rules for success cannot be given because there are so many variables in growing conditions, in the plants themselves, and in gardeners' observations and interpretations of what goes on in their gardens. If you read many gardening books or talk to many fellow gardeners, you know that we inevitably disagree on the fine points of our chosen passion. What works for one may fail for another. In this book I have given information based on my own experience and what I understand to be generally accepted practice. But in the garden nothing is graven in stone. Each gardener must find his or her own way; all any writer can do is point you in the right general direction.

Still, I hope you will find much useful information in this book, and some ideas that will make your food gardening easier, more fun, and more interesting.

ONE

Designing Your Garden

THERE ARE many more ways to design a garden of edibles than to set out plants in uniform, straight rows spaced widely apart. The process of planning a garden, especially a new garden, begins well ahead of planting time. In fact, you should design your garden a whole season before you want to plant it. It is important to think ahead, not only so you will know where to put the plants when the time comes, but also to prepare the soil so it has time to mellow, and so the nutrients from organic materials you add will be available for the plants. (Organic materials release their nutrients slowly, over a period of time.) Also, you have to allow time for preparing, sending, and receiving seed and nursery orders.

If you are starting a new garden, or gardening for the first time in a new location, it is a good idea to plant only annual flowers, herbs, and vegetables the first year. Wait to plant asparagus, lavender, and other perennials until you have gone through an entire year in your garden, and have a better understanding of the soil, light and shade patterns, and other environmental factors.

If you are new to gardening, or to growing edibles, make your first garden small. Gardening should be fun as well as productive, and nothing will ruin your enjoyment of the garden faster than a garden that is too big to take care of. A garden out of control not only looks weedy, unkempt, and generally sad, it is also far less productive than a well-maintained plot. It is better to grow a few plants well than many plants poorly. Be realistic about the amount of time you have to spend on gardening. Try a small salad garden, or grow some favorite herbs and greens in pots. You can always expand next year. If you can only garden on the weekend, limit the size of the garden and concentrate on low-maintenance approaches, some of which are described later in this chapter.

WHERE TO PUT THE GARDEN?

Before you can design the garden you have to decide where it's going to go. There are several things to consider when selecting a location for a garden. Understanding the growing conditions a prospective site will offer to plants is the crucial first step. Then direct your energies toward choosing plants that will grow well in those conditions. Several factors are important to consider in assessing the merits of a particular site.

LIGHT. First, pick the sunniest spot you have. A location in full sun, that receives five to six hours of direct, unobstructed sunlight each day, is best for most edibles. If you do not have a suitable garden spot in full sun, concentrate on growing plants that can tolerate some shade (see the table, Edibles for Shade). Quite a few vegetables and herbs will grow in partial shade, where they receive two to four hours of direct sun, or dappled sunlight all day. Orienting the garden so the rows or blocks of plants run east and west, with tall plants on the north side, provides maximum exposure to sun.

SOIL. A critical ingredient in the success of any garden is an understanding of the soil. Even the worst soil can be improved, but you have to know what you are starting out with in order to make changes. Good drainage is essential for practically all edibles, and for most plants in general, so do not put your garden in a low spot where puddles collect after a good rain. The perfect soil is a well-balanced loam that is crumbly, drains well while retaining adequate moisture for plant roots, and contains a good blend of sand, silt, and clay particles, organic matter, and minerals. Soils that are predominantly sandy drain rapidly and cannot hold moisture and nutrients long enough for roots to absorb all they need. Conversely, dense clay soils drain too slowly and tend to become waterlogged. Adding lots of organic matter will improve

EDIBLES FOR SHADE

The plants listed below will all tolerate partial shade. Most—not all—would prefer full sun, but will still grow and produce a decent harvest with less than five hours of direct sun a day. In warm climates many of them actually perform better if given some shade on hot afternoons.

Arugula	Chives	Nasturtiums
Asparagus	Coriander	Bunching onions
Beebalm	Corn salad	(scallions)
Beets	Cress	Pansies
Borage	Daylilies	Parsley
Broccoli	Endive and escarole	Peas
Cabbage	Hyssop	Radishes
Canary creeper	Johnny jump-ups	Sage
Carrots	Kale	Sorrel
Chard	Leaf lettuce	Spinach
Chervil	Mints	Tarragon
Chinese cabbage	Mustard	Violets

If your garden is partially shady, grow leafy greens and other edibles that will tolerate less than full sun. The raised planters in this garden contain several varieties of lettuce.

the texture and quality of either sandy or clay soils, and is the single most important step a gardener can take to grow better plants. See Chapter Two for information on organic matter and soil-building techniques.

Observing the plants that grow wild on your property can tell you a great deal about the character of the soil. Clover usually indicates a soil lacking in nitrogen, for example, pepperweed grows in alkaline soil, and quack grass indicates a wet, acid soil. Before starting a new garden, test the soil for pH and nutrient content. You can use one of the do-it-yourself test kits available at garden centers, get a test done by a private laboratory, or have soil samples analyzed through your local USDA County Extension office.

MOISTURE. The amount of moisture your garden receives is largely a function of your climate, and the availability of the moisture to plants is dependent upon the soil type. If your soil is sandy and drains too quickly, work in lots of organic matter to help it retain more moisture. If your soil is heavy and slow to drain, work in organic matter to improve drainage. If the drainage is extremely poor, you would do best to construct raised beds on top of the existing soil. Make the beds at least one foot deep and fill them with a blend of topsoil, compost or leaf mold, composted manure, and builder's sand or peat moss. Edge the beds with stone, brick, or wood (be sure the wood is treated with a preservative that is nontoxic to plants), or simply slope the sides.

AIR. Good air circulation is important in preventing plant diseases, but too much wind can snap stems and damage crops. Tall plants may need staking or other means of support. If your location is very windy,

ROBERT KOURIK

install a windbreak. Position the windbreak on the side of the garden from which the prevailing winds blow. The windbreak can be a fence of an open construction, such as a picket fence, that allows air to pass through, or it can take the form of plants, such as a row of evergreen shrubs. The windbreak should be far enough away from the garden that it will not cast shadows on the plants.

Designing Your Garden 21

Pick a spot for your garden that has the best combination of conditions. Also, locate the garden as close to the house as you can, to make it easy to go out and pick fresh ingredients for dinner. California landscape designer Robert Kourik, who specializes in edible landscapes, always advises gardeners to site the garden no farther from the kitchen than they can throw the kitchen sink. Your garden can become as convenient a source of fresh food as the refrigerator if you put it close to the house. And with a bit of creative design, the garden will be so pretty that you will want to look at it often.

Edible gardens are not maintenance free. If you have to pass through the garden whenever you enter or leave the house, or if you see it every time you look out the kitchen window, you will find it hard to ig-nore the weeding and other regular care your plants need to perform their best.

Traditionally, vegetable gardens have been planted in rows, like miniature farm fields. Farmers, of course, plant in widely spaced rows that enable them to plant, plow, and harvest with the help of machines. For lack of a better model, backyard gardeners patterned their plots after farmers' fields. But the old single-row method is not necessarily the best way to lay out a kitchen garden, although many gardeners still prefer it. Single rows certainly do not make the best use of space. Consider some alternatives to single rows when designing your edible garden, for more ornamental results. You can plant in square or rectangular beds, with the plants staggered or equidistant from one another in the beds. Or curve the beds, or make them round, or geometric in shape. Or take those rows, widen them into bands, and curve them into borders similar to a flower border. Set the plants in blocks, or drifts, or clumps, or complex mandala patterns.

A garden of edibles need not be a rectangle laid out in rows. A circular island bed set in a lawn can hold food as well as flowers. Place the tallest plants in the center of the bed. This garden contains tomatoes, dill, and lettuce, and is edged with nasturtiums.

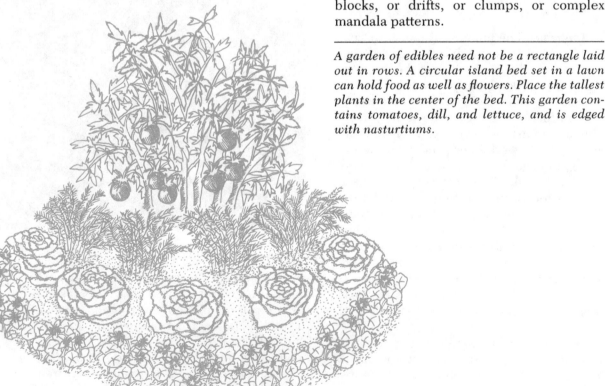

Another option is to plant edibles in a curved border, borrowing the shape of a classic perennial border. Tomatoes, spinach, and curly parsley are one interesting combination.

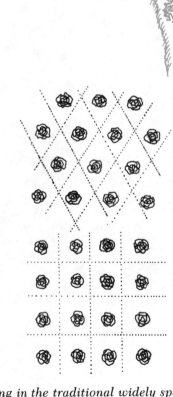

SAVING SPACE IN THE GARDEN

If you are pressed for space, as so many of us are, there are numerous ways to take maximum advantage of the space you do have available. First, concentrate on building the richest, most crumbly soil and plant in intensive beds. In intensive beds, plants are placed close together in equidistant patterns that make more efficient use of space than do single rows. Close planting does not mean crowded, however; the leaves of adjoining plants should not quite touch when the plants are full grown. Intensive planting can be especially valuable in summer in warm climates, when the leafy cover shades the soil, helping to keep roots cooler, slow

A food garden can be any shape you want it to be, from a formal square to a flowing freeform. Architect's templates can come in handy for designing creatively shaped garden beds.

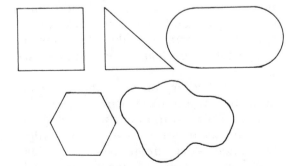

Planting in the traditional widely spaced single rows wastes a lot of room. Two ways to make more efficient use of garden space are to plant in a staggered pattern based on a diagonal grid, above, or to set plants equidistant from one another in all directions, below.

the evaporation of moisture, and keep down weeds—like a living mulch. But only top-quality soil can support so many plants. Soil with the necessary fertility and tilth is often easiest to achieve in raised beds. Bed spacings are given for individual plants in Chapter Seven.

Another way to save space is to train vining crops to grow vertically on a trellis, grow netting, or other support. Pole beans and peas are natural climbers, but sprawling vines like cucumbers and squash can also be trained upward. You will have to fasten the stems loosely to the supports at intervals, with long twist-ties, soft yarn, or string. If the plant produces large, heavy fruit, like melons or winter squash, support each one with a cloth sling so the weight does not break the stem. The vertical method also works for indeterminate tomato varieties; pinch off all the suckers and train the main stem up the support. Vertical plants make a handsome screen and an effective backdrop for lower-growing plants. They also make harvesting easier—you don't have to crawl around on the ground hunting for the vegetables. Put vertical crops and other climbers on the north side of the garden where they will not cast shade on lower plants.

You can augment the harvest of the main garden with plants growing in containers on a patio, deck, or porch. Many herbs, salad greens, and edible flowers are especially well suited to container growing. Containers offer the ultimate in convenience—your favorite herbs can be literally right outside the kitchen door—and also dress up the entrance to your home. More and more miniature, dwarf, and compact varieties of vegetables are being introduced to the market, and they are ideal for container growing.

In fact, whether you grow them in containers or in the main garden, compact varieties of plants, and plants that are naturally compact in form, save lots of garden space. Small salad greens take up far less space than zucchini and cucumbers, which

A good way to save space is to plant compact varieties of cucumbers and other vining crops, and train the vining stems to climb a trellis. This gardener did both, planting a "bush" cucumber in a pot and training its shorter vines on a small trellis.

Save space in a small garden by training climbing crops to grow vertically. Train indeterminate varieties of tomatoes on a single stake, pruning away nonfruiting stems, like the one indicated by the arrow at left. Cucumbers, squash, and melons will happily climb a trellis if you attach the vines at intervals, and provide support for large, heavy fruit.

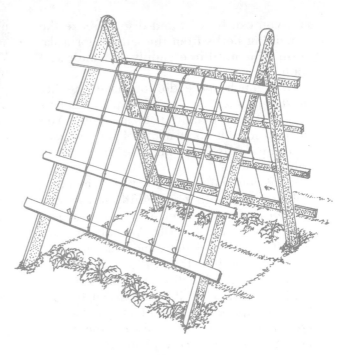

spread out all over the place. But if you cannot live without those cukes and zukes, plant bush varieties that require only a fraction of the space. Many of the baby vegetables that are such delectable treats in summer (see Chapter Four for information) can be grown in significantly less space than their full-sized counterparts.

Finally, you can interplant small, fast-growing crops among larger, slow-growing crops.

DECIDING WHAT TO GROW

Deciding what to plant is the most fun part of planning any garden. This is a time for wish fulfillment; however small your garden or elementary your gardening skills, you will be able to grow at least a few of your favorite foods or culinary herbs. In choosing from the universe of plants presented in catalogs those that you want to have in your garden, start by asking yourself several questions.

First, what do you like to eat? The purpose of a kitchen garden is to grow food, and if you and the members of your family don't like to eat what you grow, it's a waste of the food, and the space, time, and resources it took to grow it.

Which herbs do you use often in cooking? I cannot stress enough the rewards of growing your own herbs. You will find, as I have, that once you have cooked with fresh herbs they will become indispensable in your kitchen. And freshly picked leaves and sprigs are vastly superior to the limp bunches of stems you find in the supermarket. For maximum flavor and the best texture, pick herbs when you are ready to use them. When the weather turns cool in fall, you can harvest and dry or freeze the remaining herbs from the garden for a flavorful, chemical-free supply of winter seasonings.

How much space do you have? Reality must unfortunately intrude upon the process of garden planning at some point. You need to consider how many plants your garden can really accommodate and start to trim your wish list.

What new things can you try? I am a firm believer in planting something new in the garden each year, even if it is just a new variety of an old favorite. We all have our favorite crops, of course, and space must always be found for them. But to keep alive your spirit of adventure and expand your gardening horizons it is important to continue to experiment with plants you haven't grown before. There is always something new to learn, and new plants to discover. Besides, growing new things is fun, so reserve just a little bit of space for it every year.

One good way to choose reliable varieties to try in your garden is to look for vegetables and flowers that have been designated as All-America Selections winners. All-America Selections oversees the evaluation of new varieties of vegetables and flowers grown from seed in a network of trial gardens all over the United States. The varieties that perform the best are named AAS winners. When you see this designation in seed and nursery catalogs and on plant identification tags, you know the variety has been demonstrated to grow well under average garden conditions.

LAYING OUT THE GARDEN

When the plants have been selected, the final step in developing a garden plan is figuring out where to put them. This is where a plan of the garden on paper is essential. You need not work up a precise architectural rendering of your garden beds—a simple sketch will do. But drawing the garden before you plant it will let you change parts of the layout that don't work *before* you have done any planting, so you will end up with a design that really pleases you. To facilitate alterations, do your drawing in pencil, or use tissue paper overlays, or make photocopies of the basic sketch without plants to design different planting schemes.

There are several factors to take into account when laying out a garden. First, what does the plant need to grow? Plants that need full sun should not be planted next to taller plants that will shade them. Plants needing rich soil should be grouped in a part of the garden where you have worked especially hard to build fertile soil. Surround plants with others whose environmental needs are similar.

Since you want the garden to be attractive as well as functional, consider the visual characteristics of each plant—its height, growing habit, leaf shape and size, color, and texture. Aesthetic considerations are discussed further below.

You will also need to think about crop rotations, in which plants are moved to a different location in the garden each year to prevent the buildup of soilborne disease organisms in one spot. Members of the cabbage family, for example, should not be planted in the same spot more than once every three years.

You may also want to practice companion planting, placing certain plants together because they are said to enhance one another's growth, or because one may repel pests that prey on the other. Finally, you can interplant smaller, fast-growing crops among larger, slower-growing plants to make more efficient use of garden space. By the time the big plants need all the space, the smaller ones can be harvested and out of the way.

USING FOOD PLANTS IN ORNAMENTAL WAYS

To create a kitchen garden that is pretty as well as practical, you can employ most of the same principles used in designing flower gardens. Consider the ornamental qualities of the vegetables, herbs, and edible flowers in your garden as you think about where to place the plants. You need to place the plants according to what they look like, in addition to their environmental needs, and try to combine plants that look good together.

Imagine the garden as a painting, with the space divided into foreground, middle ground, and background. Planning a succession of plant heights with short plants in front and tall plants in back creates an illusion of greater depth, much like the pictorial space in a painting. Staggering the plant heights also allows you to see all the plants in the garden. If the garden will be viewed primarily from one side, place the smallest plants in the front and the tallest plants in the back. If the garden is an island bed that can be seen from all sides, put the tallest plants in the center of the bed and work outward to place the smallest plants around the outer edges of the bed. Because the tall plants will cast shadows during some part of the day, use leafy greens and other shade-tolerant plants as the lower plants in an island bed.

As a backdrop you might use pole beans —lavender-flowered purple beans, and scarlet runner beans with their brilliant red blossoms and deep green leaves are especially handsome. Or consider planting peas, with their white flowers and graceful tendrils. Or you could train cucumbers to grow vertically on a trellis at the back of the garden. The other way to get height is to grow tall plants such as okra or corn. Put the tallest plants on the north side of the garden so they will not cast shade on lower-growing plants.

In the middle ground of the garden go all the branching and bushy, massive plants: tomatoes, peppers, eggplant, bush beans, head lettuce, cabbage, and chard, for example. Many herbs are also medium-height plants, and their often-delicate textures can create an attractive complement to the bolder, bigger leaves of the vegetables.

To create an illusion of greater depth and allow all the plants in the garden to be visible, stagger plant heights as you would in a flower garden, putting the shortest plants in the front and the tallest plants in the rear. This garden contains, front to back, marigolds, carrots, eggplant, daylilies, and pole beans.

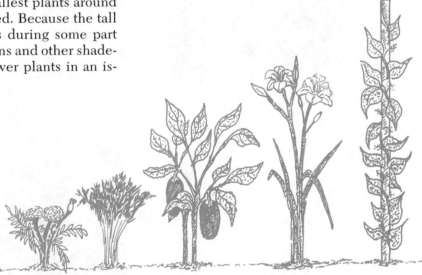

Unusual varieties of favorite crops can add unexpected bursts of color to the garden. Two decidedly untraditional sweet pepper varieties are Corona, above, which turns orange when it ripens, and Islander, right, which turns deep purple.

The foreground contains compact plants —leaf lettuce and other small salad greens, beets, carrots. Edge the garden with the smallest, shortest plants. Thyme, dwarf marigolds, dianthus, and curly parsley all make handsome edgers.

You may tend to think of a kitchen garden as being pretty much all green. But there are myriad colors and textures to work with in the edible garden. Consider first of all the many shades of green: lime and chartreuse, blue greens, gray greens, sparkling emerald, deep forest green, and pale, near-white icy greens. There are brilliant yellow squashes and peppers, softer yellow wax beans, rich golden calendulas. Consider the arresting red violet of red cabbage, the dusty lavender of purple kohlrabi, the deep purple of snap beans, the rich, glossy violet of eggplant. Blue is contributed by borage and pansies, pink by dianthus and bee-

balm. Vibrant reds can come from tomatoes, scarlet runner beans, peppers, or pineapple sage. The palette of the kitchen garden is as rich and varied as that of the flower garden, if you are aware of it. The table, Edibles by Color, offers a listing of vegetables, herbs, and edible flowers by color.

Textures, too, are amazingly varied and can be used to great effect in the kitchen garden. Contrast the bold shapes of chard, eggplant, and cabbage with the curly, frilly foliage of parsley, cress, and kale, or the delicate, feathery leaves of dill or asparagus.

All you need to do is regard your vegeta-

EDIBLES BY COLOR

RED/PINK

Scarlet runner beans	Chive blossoms	Okra
Beebalm	Dianthus	Peppers
Beets (stems, leaf veins)	Scented geraniums	Radicchio
Brussels sprouts	Flowering kale	Pineapple sage
Cabbage	Lettuce	Tomatoes
Chard	Nasturtiums	

PURPLE

Basil	Cauliflower	Lavender
Purple snap beans	Eggplant	Pansies
Sprouting broccoli	Kohlrabi	Violets

YELLOW/ORANGE

Wax beans	Marigolds	Summer squash
Calendulas	Mustard flowers	Winter squash
Canary creeper	Nasturtiums	Squash blossoms
Garland chrysanthemums	Pansies	Tomatoes
Lemon cucumbers	Peppers	

WHITE

Sprouting broccoli	Dianthus	Kohlrabi (pale green)
Cauliflower	Eggplant	Summer squash
Chard (stems)	Garlic chive blossoms	Violets
Cucumbers	Flowering kale	

BLUE

Borage	Hyssop
Chicory blossoms	Rosemary

Okra has lovely cream-colored flowers, and this variety, Burgundy, has reddish purple pods as well.

The textures of edible plants are many and varied. This variety of dill, Fernleaf, has lacy foliage rather resembling a fern.

bles and herbs in a different way. Forget about the harvest, for now, and look at the plants from an aesthetic perspective. Once you are aware of their visual qualities you will be able to mix and match them in a garden that provides beauty in the landscape as well as delicious food for the table —a most satisfying combination.

Another way to design an interesting garden is to plan around culinary themes. You might want a salad garden, or a garden of ingredients for Mexican or Oriental cooking. See the table of Plants for Theme Gardens (page 32) for some ideas.

COMPANION PLANTING

Companion planting is the practice of mixing plants in the garden according to the effects they have on one another. Companion planting is a folk art that has been practiced by gardeners for centuries. Mentions of good and bad plant partners can be found in the great medieval herbals, and even as far back as the works of Pliny. Few of the tenets of companion planting have been tested scientifically, and of those that have, some have been disproven and others found to have some merit. But the folklore surrounding companion planting persists, and many organic gardeners still practice it. I have had mixed results in my own garden over the years. But you may want to give it a try; if it doesn't work there's no harm done, and if it does work your garden will be that much better for it.

According to tradition, some plant companions are supposed to repel pests or disease organisms to which other plants are susceptible; planting the two together could thus have a protective effect on the intended victim. Some plants are thought to enhance one another's growth, others to hinder it by secreting toxic or irritant substances into the soil (an effect known as allelopathy). Some plants make good neighbors because they have complementary rooting patterns; a shallow-rooted crop can be placed next to one with deep roots, so the two do not compete for the same water and nutrients. Similarly, you can combine plants according to their light requirements, planting lower-growing, shade-tolerant crops in the shadow of tall sun lovers.

Following is a rundown of the traditional companion qualities of some popular vegetables, herbs, and edible flowers for gardeners who want to try their luck.

Anise is a host plant for beneficial wasps, which are attracted to its flowers. Plant it close to coriander but away from carrots.

Asparagus. The ferny foliage makes a nice backdrop for flowers and other plants. Good near basil, calendulas, parsley, and tomatoes. Keep it away from onions.

Basil is a good companion for tomatoes and asparagus.

Beans. Useful because they fix nitrogen in the soil. Plant near corn, squash, and members of the cabbage family. Marigolds help repel Mexican bean beetles.

Beets. Plant near the cabbage family, leafy greens, garlic, and onions. Do not plant with beans.

Borage grows well near tomatoes and spinach. Its flowers attract bees.

Cabbage family (broccoli, brussels sprouts, cabbage, cauliflower, kohlrabi). All cole crops love herbs; plant with dill, mint, hyssop, rosemary, chamomile, and sage. Also compatible with beets, cucumbers, lettuce, onions, radishes, potatoes, marigolds, and nasturtiums. Cabbage can be the centerpiece of a small round bed, ringed with low herbs (such as thyme and dwarf purple basil) and marigolds or nasturtiums.

Caraway. The flowers host beneficial wasps.

Carrots. Grow near tomatoes, cucumbers, beans, chives, onions, lettuce, radishes, peas, or sage. Keep them away from dill.

Chamomile. The flowers attract beneficial insects but the roots are invasive like mint, so be careful. You may want to plant in a bottomless wood box sunk in the soil. Does well near onions, cucumbers, thyme, sage, and other aromatic herbs.

Chervil. Likes to grow near radishes. Its flowers host beneficial insects.

Chives. Plant near carrots, tomatoes, and lettuce. Keep away from peas and beans.

Cucumbers. Plant near radishes, beans, the cabbage family, peas, tomatoes, marigolds, nasturtiums, and oregano. Keep away from sage.

Dill. Grow near cabbage-family members, onions, and lettuce. Does not like carrots or tomatoes. The flower heads attract beneficial insects.

PLANTS FOR THEME GARDENS

SALAD GARDEN

Arugula
Carrots
Chives
Corn salad
Cress
Cucumbers

Kohlrabi
Lettuce, assorted varieties
Nasturtiums
Pansies
Sugar snap peas
Peppers

Radishes
Sorrel
Spinach
Tomatoes
Violets

MEXICAN GARDEN

Black beans
Lima beans
Pinto beans
Coriander

Corn
Marigolds
Onions
Bell peppers

Chili peppers
Summer squash
Winter squash
Tomatoes

ORIENTAL GARDEN

Chinese celery cabbage
Mustard cabbage
Garlic chives
Garland chrysanthemums

Coriander
Oriental cucumbers
Oriental eggplant
Mustard greens

Bunching onions (scallions)
Snow peas
Daikon radishes

CONTINENTAL GOURMET GARDEN

Asparagus
Flageolets (shell beans)
Haricots verts (snap beans)
Baby carrots
Celeriac
Chervil

Corn salad
Cornichon cucumbers
Endive
Belgian endive
Leeks
Petits pois (peas)

Rosemary
Shallots
Sorrel
Summer squash
Tarragon

ITALIAN GARDEN

Arugula
Basil
Romano beans
Romanesco broccoli
Sprouting broccoli
Chicory

Italian eggplant
Escarole
Fennel
Garlic
Oregano
Flat-leaf parsley

Sweet frying peppers
Radicchio
Thyme
Tomatoes, paste types
Zucchini

Eggplant is good near beans, tarragon, thyme, and marigolds.

Fennel grows well with thyme and sage; its flowers host beneficial insects. Avoid planting fennel next to coriander, bush beans, caraway, kohlrabi, or tomatoes.

Garlic and **hyssop** are supposed to repel many different pests from many kinds of plants.

Lettuce does well near cabbage, beets, carrots, chives, garlic, and onions, and will grow in partial shade cast by pole beans, peas, and tomatoes. Lettuce does not like to grow near broccoli.

Mint flowers attract beneficial insects. Contain the invasive roots by planting in bottomless wood boxes. Mint is reputed to repel a variety of insects.

Mustard likes beans but is antagonistic to turnips.

Nasturtiums. A trap crop of aphids, and repels numerous other pests. Good companion for beans, peppers, and cabbage-family members.

Onions. Plant near beets, carrots, lettuce, potatoes, and the cabbage family. Keep away from sage and peas.

Parsley likes asparagus, corn, and tomatoes.

Peas do well near tomatoes, eggplant, lettuce, spinach, peppers, corn, radishes, cucumbers, carrots, and beans. Keep them away from onions and garlic.

Peppers. Grow near carrots, onions, marigolds, basil, marjoram, or oregano. Keep them away from eggplant, tomatoes, kohlrabi, and fennel.

Radishes. Interplant with beans, lettuce, cabbage, or tomatoes. Good companion for chervil, peas, parsnips, onions, carrots, cucumbers, or squash. Does not like hyssop.

Sage. Plant near cabbage, carrots, tomatoes, or marjoram. Keep away from cucumbers. The flowers attract bees.

Spinach. Good companion for borage, eggplant, cabbage-family members, peas, onions, marigolds, nasturtiums, beans, or oregano. Antagonistic to potatoes.

Squash. Plant with beans, corn, sunflowers, marigolds, nasturtiums, radishes, or mints. Keep away from potatoes.

Thyme. Grows well near cabbage-family members. The tiny flowers attract bees.

Tomatoes. Plant near asparagus, cabbage, carrots, cucumbers, onions, peppers, marigolds, calendulas, beebalm, basil, borage, parsley, and sage. Interplant with arugula,

---

Peppers and marigolds make good companions in the garden, and look attractive planted together, as well.

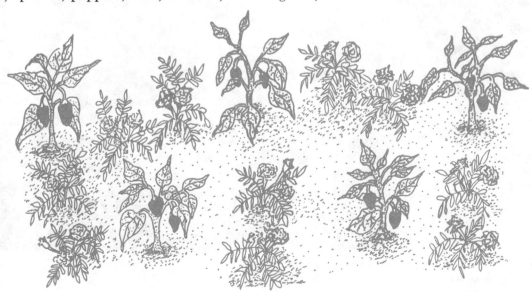

Marigolds are versatile in companion planting schemes; they make good partners for a host of different plants.

leaf lettuce, cress, and other small, fast-growing plants. Keep away from corn, dill, fennel, kohlrabi, and potatoes.

WORK-SAVING STRATEGIES

Most of us work full-time, and between our work and our families it is difficult to find time for gardening. If your gardening is limited to the weekend, or to a few stolen hours here or there during the week, you must strive to decrease the garden's maintenance needs as much as possible.

Probably the most important labor-saving technique of all is to mulch the garden. Mulching slows the evaporation of moisture from the soil, so plants need less frequent watering, and also helps keep down weeds, so you will have fewer weeds to pull.

Keep the garden small, and rotate crops each year to help minimize pest and disease problems.

Another strategy is to plant crops that require less maintenance—that can tolerate some drought and that can go for several days without picking even during their peak harvest times. Many herbs fit the low-maintenance category, as do a lot of the edible flowers. Avoid growing vegetables that need special care, such as cauliflower, or that are very moisture sensitive, such as cucumbers. Instead, grow plants that do not require constant upkeep, that can tolerate a bit of dry weather, that are not usually prone to a lot of pest problems in the garden. Some good candidates for a low-maintenance garden include arugula, asparagus, bush beans, beebalm, beets, cabbage, carrots, canary creeper, chard, chervil, chives, collards, cress, dill, escarole, fennel, leaf lettuce, nasturtiums, okra, parsley, peas, peppers, radishes, spinach, bush summer squash, determinate varieties of tomatoes, and violets.

PLANNING AHEAD

Garden planning is not a once-and-done process; each year brings a new garden, and a new plan. Planning for next year's garden begins with an assessment of this year's results. Which crops were successful, and which performed poorly, or failed entirely? Keeping a garden notebook throughout the season makes it easy to keep track of plant performance. Which new plants do you want to try next year? What do you want to repeat?

Plan for next year's crop rotations, moving all the nonperennial crops to a different spot in the garden from where they grew this year. In general, where a root crop grew this year, plant a leaf or fruiting crop next year; where a heavy feeder grew this year, plant a light feeder or leguminous soil builder next year. It is especially important to rotate members of the cabbage family, because all are susceptible to clubroot and various other nasty diseases. Do not plant any cabbage-family member where it or any other family member has grown more than once in three years.

Seed and nursery catalogs come pouring through the mail slot in winter, when about the only gardening activity in many places is that which is going on indoors. Most of us love to page through the catalogs and make endless lists of all the swell things we want to grow in our next garden. By all means go ahead and indulge yourself. But before you fill out your seed and plant orders, work up a new garden plan to see where all these marvelous plants will fit in your garden. You will probably have to trim your wish list to fit within the limitations of available space, time, and funds. But life requires of us many compromises, and you will still find yourself with a garden full of plants, and plenty to harvest.

TWO

Gardening Techniques

THIS CHAPTER introduces the basic techniques and cultural practices you will use throughout the year in your outdoor and indoor gardens. Methods for starting seeds, transplanting, improving soil, watering, and controlling pests and diseases are covered here, along with information on cold frames and other plant protection devices to extend the growing season. Cultural practices that are most used at particular times of year are covered in the seasonal chapters. For example, Chapter Three, The Spring Garden, contains information on using phenology to gauge outdoor planting times, hardening-off seedlings, and extending the harvest of spring crops into summer. Chapter Four discusses strategies for conserving water in summer. If you are in doubt about where to look for information on a particular subject, consult the index or table of contents. For specific information on individual plants, consult Chapter Seven.

STARTING SEEDS INDOORS

Although most people think the gardening season does not begin until spring, when outdoor planting begins, you can get a jump on the season by starting seeds indoors in late winter. Some plants, such as peas, are difficult to transplant, and are best sown directly in the garden where they are to grow. But many plants transplant readily and are good candidates for sowing indoors. Starting your own seeds indoors of lettuce, broccoli, cabbage, or tomatoes, for example, can gain you weeks of growing time. Generally, northern gardeners can start seeds of easy-to-transplant crops, warm-season vegetables, and tender herbs and flowers to get an advance on spring. Gardeners who live in warm climates where springtime cold snaps are not a problem can find it beneficial to start seeds for the fall and winter garden indoors, out of intense summer heat, where they can exercise more control over the seedlings' environment.

If you haven't got the time, space, or interest in starting seeds indoors, buy transplants at a local garden center or nursery. You will be more limited in your choice of plants, but you will save a month or more over planting seeds outdoors.

It isn't difficult to start seeds indoors, and the experience of getting your hands into some soil and watching the tiny plants begin to grow can make it easier to get through the long, dark days of February when it seems like spring will never come. Along with the arrival of seed and nursery catalogs, and the noting of Groundhog Day, starting the first seeds for the outdoor garden is a sign that spring is indeed on the way.

You don't need a lot of sophisticated equipment to start seeds indoors. All you need, basically, are a source of light, containers for planting, and some planting medium.

CONTAINERS
FOR STARTING SEEDS

Containers can be anything from clay flowerpots to wooden nursery flats to peat pots to old margarine cups. The only requirements are that the containers be clean —sterile, if possible—and that they have a drainage hole or holes in the bottom. I often use small clay pots because I have them around, but I've also started plants in various kinds of peat pots, peat pellets, Styrofoam drinking cups, margarine cups, and assorted other things. A tremendous array of containers for starting seeds is on the market. If you find that local garden centers don't have what you want, you can order from one or more of the mail-order companies listed in the Appendix.

Peat pots are very convenient because they can go right into the garden with the seedlings. They are made of compressed peat and wood fiber, and many kinds have

fertilizer added. You can find peat pots with round or square sides, in some cases with tapered sides. A choice of 2½- or 3-inch diameter is available. Some peat pots have drainage holes, but they aren't really necessary because the peat is porous. Peat pots need to be thoroughly moist before you use them, or the sides of the pot will absorb moisture from the growing medium, and could cause it to dry out. When you transplant seedlings in peat pots to the outdoor garden, tear the sides of the pots to make sure roots will not be confined, and make sure the top edge of each pot is completely below the soil.

Peat pellets look like dried tablets of peat when you buy them. When you add water, each pellet expands into a small container about 2 inches high, already filled with potting medium. Plant one seed in each container.

You can also buy peat planting cubes that are actually a blend of compressed mosses and vermiculite with a depression in the top where you plant the seed. These cubes contain fertilizer. To use them, set them in a tray or flat and moisten thoroughly before planting. When the young seedlings outgrow the cubes, transplant them to six-packs or individual pots.

A somewhat similar type of material for containers is pressed wood fiber, which is molded into rectangular boxes. A standard size is 7½ by 5½ inches, by 2¾ inches deep. The boxes have drainage holes in the bottom. Each box accommodates several seedlings, but you will have to block the soil before transplanting the youngsters to individual pots or out to the garden. (See Transplanting, later in this chapter, for information on blocking out seedlings.)

The standard nursery flat is still the seed-starting container of choice for many gardeners and nurserymen. A flat is, simply, a shallow wooden box 22 inches by 12 inches, by 2½ inches deep, with drainage permitted through the cracks between the slats of wood forming the bottom of the box.

Many gardeners like to start seeds in plastic containers. Plastic containers are lighter in weight than clay pots, they do not allow moisture to evaporate through their sides, and if made of heavy enough plastic they are reusable. The most convenient plastic pots for starting seeds are 2¾ or 4 inches square, with tapered sides that make it easy to unpot seedlings for transplanting. Set the pots in a plastic tray to make it easy to water the plants and move them around.

Many commercial growers now start plants in compartmentalized plastic containers called six-packs, market packs, or cells. These cells give each seedling its own growing space, eliminating the need to block out seedlings before transplanting. One company offers packs with an outer measurement of 11 inches by 22 inches by 2½ inches deep, with the inside divided into twelve small or six larger compartments. Another company offers 14-by-9-inch packs with depths of 2 or 2½ inches and compartments measuring 1½ by 1½, 2 by 2, 2 by 2½, 2½ by 2½, or 2½ by 3¼ inches. The cells sit inside plastic trays. Seedlings that grow quickly and are planted out early can be grown in the smaller cells. Slower-growing seedlings that will be indoors longer are planted in larger cells. Bear in mind that any of these cells are intended only for seedlings. Larger plants will quickly become rootbound in the limited space.

The plastic trays that hold the market packs have no drainage holes, so do not plant seeds directly in the trays unless you first punch in some drainage holes. You can turn these trays of cells into propagating units with the addition of a clear plastic cover to help hold humidity. Mail-order suppliers sell covers that fit the size trays they sell. These plastic cells are not generally reusable because they are made of thin plastic that is easy to tear or crumple during transplanting. Unless you recycle them you may have ecological concerns about using them. However, six-packs of a heavier grade of plastic are available for gardeners who want a reusable product.

Reusable six-packs should be disinfected before you plant in them a second time. Wash them in soapy water, rinse, and dip them in a solution of one part liquid chlorine bleach to nine parts water.

From England comes equipment for starting seeds in little individual blocks of soil, not contained in pots. A simple tool operated by plunger action forms the growing medium into small blocks of soil, each of which can accommodate a single seedling. Soil blockers come in a couple of different sizes and cost about $15 to $20. Some have an attachment that makes a depression in the top of each block. The advantage to planting in soil blocks is that roots can grow freely, and it's easy to see when a plant's roots have outgrown their space. There is also no used pot to discard or sterilize before reusing. The disadvantage is that the cubes have to pretty much stay in one place until the seedlings are ready to transplant, or you run the risk of crumbling the cubes.

Plastic trays can be had in a range of sizes and are intended primarily to hold market packs or pots. Most trays thus come without drainage holes, although some have embossed areas that can be easily drilled out if you want to plant directly in the trays. Of course, if you plant in the trays you will have to find something to set underneath them to catch runoff water.

Some plastic trays have inserts to hold individual square plastic pots. You water in the bottom of the tray. These trays are called "self-watering," which they're not in a literal sense, but they do cut down on watering time.

Many plastic trays can be purchased with domed covers of clear plastic that help hold humidity around the plants. Some of the covers have butterfly vents that you can open when humidity gets too high and you notice condensation. You will find trays and vented covers sold together as propagating units. They come in several sizes. You can also make your own cover from a piece of plastic, but you will need to drape it over wire hoops or some other supporting framework to keep it from touching plant foliage.

One rather sophisticated unit has a compartmentalized planting tray, a water reservoir and capillary matting for automatic bottom watering, and a plastic greenhouse cover. The unit comes in two sizes, one for smaller seedlings like lettuce and broccoli, and a larger size for bigger seedlings like those of peppers and tomatoes.

PLANTING MIXES
FOR STARTING SEEDS

To produce the best results, a medium for germinating seeds must first of all be sterile, free of pathogens that can attack delicate seedlings and cause diseases such as damping-off. The medium must be able to hold moisture, for seeds need to absorb substantial amounts of water before they can germinate. In addition, a germination medium should be light and porous in texture, with plenty of air pockets in which tender new roots can grow. It is difficult for young roots to push their way through a dense, compacted medium, and such struggles result in weak, stunted plants.

Seed-starting media can contain soil or not. Soil contains nutrients that will nourish the young plants, but it also contains microorganisms that can cause problems for seedlings. To kill harmful bacteria and other pathogens soil must be sterilized or at least pasteurized before it can be used in germination media. You can pasteurize soil in your oven, but it creates an unpleasant odor and it is a fair amount of work. It is easier to start seeds in a soilless medium in which all the ingredients are sterile when you buy them.

The five most common ingredients used in germination mixes are peat moss, finely milled sphagnum moss, perlite, vermiculite, and sharp (builder's) sand. Peat and sphagnum contribute organic matter and water retention to the medium. Sphagnum moss has the additional benefit of a fungi-cidal, germicidal action (it was used on World War I battlefields to dress wounds) that helps fight off disease pathogens. It can be incorporated into the medium or spread over the top in a thin layer after planting. Perlite and vermiculite help to lighten and aerate a seed-starting mix, as well as aiding in water retention. Sand adds porosity and improves drainage. Although it's been said many times, I must stress here the importance of using builder's sand instead of beach sand. Beach sand has very fine particles that are apt to compact, and it also contains salts that could damage your young plants. If you get your sand at a building supply store or lumberyard, it is best to pasteurize it before you use it. You may also be able to find packaged, sterilized sand intended for use in planting media.

Relatively new ingredients for planting mixes are water-retentive polymers that are mixed with soil or germination media to increase the ability of the growing medium to hold water. (Burpee sells a product called Water-Grabber; see Appendix for address.) These additives are said to be especially useful for plants in outdoor containers, in which soil dries out quickly from hot sun and wind. I have not tried these gels myself, but have heard mixed reviews from other gardeners.

You can buy premixed packaged germination media or blend your own. Most of the commercial media contain fertilizers, which eliminates the need for you to feed the seedlings yourself for their first six to eight weeks—by which time you may be ready to transplant them out to the garden. However, the fertilizers may actually overstimulate very young seedlings, causing them to grow too quickly and thus weakening them. Such seedlings will have a harder time making the transition into the garden than will more compact, sturdier plants. If you fertilize the seedlings yourself you can start with a very weak solution and gradually increase to a half-strength formula as the plants grow. The decision is one of convenience versus control for the gardener.

If you opt to mix your own seed-starting medium, there are several classic formulas you can use. The recipe I use was developed years ago at Cornell University and consists of equal parts peat, perlite, and vermiculite. Another mix, created at the University of California, contains equal parts peat moss and sharp sand. Many growers add small amounts of all-purpose fertilizer to these mixes. But since seeds contain enough food to nourish the seedlings as the first roots and shoots develop, you can wait to start fertilizing until the tiny plants break through the soil surface. Then mist the seedlings once a week with a solution of seaweed concentrate, fish emulsion, or another foliar feed diluted to one-quarter or one-half of the recommended strength. After a couple of weeks, increase the dosage to one-half the recommended strength.

GROWING SEEDLINGS INDOORS

Some seeds need absolute darkness to germinate, while others must have bright light. But most seeds are less demanding of darkness or light than has generally been thought. Horticulturists at Park Seed Company have experimented with many kinds of seeds and found that most will germinate just fine if they are simply placed on top of the medium and very lightly pressed down or covered with additional medium.

Some seeds—those of parsley and peas, for instance—will germinate more willingly if you soak them in lukewarm water for several hours before planting. Read seed packets carefully before you plant to be sure you are planting correctly. The seeds of many woody plants need a period of cold temperatures, or alternating periods of cold and warmth, before they will germinate. Luck-

ily, the seeds of most edibles are far less complicated in their requirements.

The first step in the planting procedure is to moisten the germination medium. The medium should be evenly damp but not soggy when you plant. Premoistening the medium is especially important if it contains peat moss. When moist, peat moss absorbs and holds water like a sponge, but when dry it actually repels water. If you planted your seeds in a dry peat-based medium and then watered them, the water would simply roll off the surface. The best way to dampen a peat-based medium is to pour on some water and work it through with your fingers.

Fill the seed-starting containers with moist medium to slightly more than ½ inch from the top. Place the seeds on top of the medium; sow large seeds individually, and broadcast tiny seeds (like those of lettuce) as evenly as you can over the surface of the medium. Mixing tiny seeds with an equal volume of fine sand makes them a bit easier to handle. Or place the seeds in a folded piece of paper and tap them out slowly.

It is important to sow with a light hand. Thickly sown seeds produce masses of tightly crowded seedlings that are difficult to thin, more prone to damping-off and other problems, and weakened by the intense competition for moisture and nutrients. Press the seeds gently into the medium. If you like you can sift a thin layer of milled sphagnum moss on top of the seeds to protect them from pathogens.

Next, water to settle the seeds into the medium. It's best to water from the bottom to avoid disturbing the seeds. Set the containers in a pan of room-temperature water and leave them there until the surface of the medium feels moist. You could instead mist the seeds, but it takes a lot of misting to thoroughly moisten a flat or pot full of medium; bottom watering is easier. Keep the planting medium constantly moist (but never soggy) until the seeds germinate. Poking your finger into the containers each day is the best way to tell when it's time to water.

An easy way to keep germination and growing media evenly moist is to set the containers on top of capillary matting. The matting conducts water from a reservoir to remain continuously and evenly moist; it provides steady bottom watering for the containers. All you have to do is make sure the reservoir never runs dry. Capillary matting comes in several widths and is sold by the inch.

As soon as you plant a batch of seeds, take a minute to label the containers with the type of seeds planted there and the date of planting. It is amazingly easy to forget which seeds you put in which flats, and to mix up different varieties of the same crops. Labelling is well worth the effort. You can use commercial plant labels, Popsicle sticks, or pieces of masking tape stuck to the sides of the containers.

Many seeds germinate best when the soil is warm. The old-fashioned way to provide bottom heat for seeds was to set the containers on top of the family refrigerator. A more reliable, controlled way is to purchase heating mats or tape. Rubber heating mats are sized to fit under flats or trays. Some models heat soil to a standard temperature (70 to 75°F), while others raise the temperature of the soil about 15°F above the ambient air temperature. If you are starting seeds on windowsills you might use heating tape instead of mats. The 3-inch-wide tape is encased in Mylar and is sold in 2-foot lengths. If you are lucky enough to have a greenhouse, you can install special heating cables underneath the soil in the benches to provide the necessary warmth.

LIGHT SOURCES

When your seedlings break through the soil surface they will need as much light as you can give them. That light can come from either natural or artificial sources.

If you have bright windowsills with an unshaded eastern or southern exposure, by all means use them. Unless your windowsills are very wide, as they sometimes are in older homes, they won't be able to hold a standard nursery flat. But you can use smaller containers on the sill. South-facing windows get the most light but they also collect the most heat. If you live in a warm climate, a southern exposure may be too hot for seedlings and an eastern exposure would be better. But if you live up north, a southern exposure, if you have it, is probably the best choice.

If the surfaces near your seedlings are reflective, the plants will receive the maximum possible amount of light. White walls and windowsills are more reflective than darker-colored surfaces. You can line the sills with aluminum foil, or place a foil-covered panel between the plants and the room to bounce light back onto them. Now on the market and available in some seed catalogs is a collapsible three-sided cardboard box lined with foil, that was designed specifically to increase the light available to windowsill seedlings. It is called The Lighthouse, and comes in two sizes. A light-colored sidewalk or driveway immediately outside the window will reflect more light into the room than will a brick or macadam surface.

Windowsill gardeners can take advantage of some specialized pieces of equipment for growing seedlings. A mini-greenhouse unit designed to fit on a windowsill is 20 inches long by 4 inches wide. It has a white plastic tray 5 inches deep, and a domed lid of clear plastic with a vent to help you control humidity. If you are really short of space you can stack several of these units, but light will then be admitted only through the sides of the lids.

You can also purchase an indoor greenhouse unit that consists of a plant tray with a built-in-wick watering system, and a high vinyl top supported by a collapsible aluminum frame. If you can't keep this unit by a window, you can get a fluorescent light fixture and a timer that fit inside it.

LIGHT GARDENS

Electric lights, when properly used, will produce seedlings just as healthy as those grown in natural light. In fact, electric lights are in some ways better than natural light, because you can provide the optimum daylength (number of daylight hours each day), and the lights can be positioned directly above the plants, allowing them to grow straight and tall without the frequent turning of containers that is necessary for plants on a windowsill receiving most of their light from one side. You can set up a light garden in a convenient place where it will be out of your way—in a spare room or the basement, for example.

A light garden can be as basic or as elaborate as you want it to be. You can devise your own setup or purchase a free-standing unit complete with shelves, lights, and planting trays in a choice of finishes. Probably the first decision you will make, however, is what kinds of lights to use.

Plants depend heavily on light in the blue, red, and far-red bands of the spectrum for good growth. Blue wavelengths support leaf development, promote bushy growth, and regulate respiration; the red and far-red wavelengths promote general growth and flowering.

Fluorescent lights are most often used in indoor light gardens because they stay cool when lit. Incandescent lights get very hot and can burn foliage. Cool white fluorescent tubes are the cheapest and easiest to find, and they provide the most light. As their name implies, though, most of that light is from the shorter wavelengths, and you will need to supplement the lights with a source of red for optimum growth. You can use incandescent lights to supply red wavelengths, but because of their heat you will have to position them some distance away from the plants. That means the light intensity will be lower and the lights will have to stay on longer each day. This is probably the least efficient combination of lights to use.

A better solution is to use a combination of cool white and warm white fluorescent tubes, although there are some drawbacks to this approach, as well. Warm white fluorescent tubes are hard to find in many hardware stores and building centers, although you can order them from mail-order suppliers of light-gardening equipment (see Appendix). Also, you must mount the lights far enough above the plants so the wavelengths of the two lamps mix. This will reduce light intensity and you will have to leave the lights on for a few extra hours each day. Wide-spectrum or daylight fluorescents supply a broader range of wavelengths than either warm white or cool white tubes, and will serve adequately.

The best source of light for plants are the fluorescent lamps specially designed for gardening. Gro-Lux tubes provide lots of red and blue light, but they cast a weird purplish glow that visually distorts the colors of the plants and gives a rather eerie feeling to a room. They are also expensive. But if your seedlings are down in the basement the strange color of the lights won't matter.

A more recent introduction to the market, the Vita-Lite Powertwist, also contains the important wavelengths but does not alter the appearance of the plants beneath them. These lamps are also rather costly.

According to the people at Indoor Gardening Supplies, a mail-order supplier, the most efficient setup for light gardening uses 4-foot-long, 40-watt fixtures. The ballasts are more efficient than those of smaller fixtures, and 40-watt lamps put out more light per watt than 15- or 20-watt lamps.

The smallest, simplest fixtures for light gardens are designed to sit on a tabletop. The reflector and a 24-inch tube are mounted on two arms, one at either end of the lamp. The fixture can be moved up and down on the arms to adjust the height of the light as plants grow.

If you are the ambitious type, or if you

want to have a light garden inexpensively, you can put together the various elements on a larger scale than the tabletop model. You will need, first of all, a flat surface on which to set containers of plants; a sheet of heavy-duty plywood set atop sawhorses will suffice. Buy as many 48-inch light fixtures as you will need to light the growing area, along with the fluorescent tubes of your choice. To allow the distance between lights and the tops of plants to be kept constant as the plants grow, you will have to be able to adjust the height of the lights or the growing surface. Light fixtures can be suspended on chains that can be raised or lowered. Or you can place your growing surface atop stacks of books or wooden blocks that

can be removed one level at a time as plants grow.

If you would like your light garden to take up less floor space, you can mount light fixtures on the undersides of the shelves of a utility shelving unit.

For most gardeners, a setup using four 40-

A simple, versatile light garden can be made from a workbench or potting bench. Mount a two-tube fluorescent fixture under the top of the bench to light the bottom shelf, and suspend another fixture above the bench. Set containers of seedlings on the bottom shelf atop books or boards or upended pots to bring them close to the lights, and gradually lower the containers as the plants grow taller. Suspend the upper light fixture on chains to make its height adjustable.

watt tubes should provide plenty of space for indoor gardening efforts. When you plan your light garden, keep in mind that a single fluorescent tube will illuminate an area roughly 6 inches wide, and a two-tube fixture will light an area about a foot across.

There are a variety of ready-made light garden units in a range of styles and prices on the market for gardeners prepared to spend a little money. One mobile unit consists of a white-enameled aluminum frame with two shelves, mounted on wheels. Each shelf holds an adjustable 48-inch fluorescent fixture with single or double tubes. You can buy the unit complete with light fixtures, or purchase just the frame and install your own lights. Larger units have three or four shelves and come complete with plant trays in a choice of sizes. Some of these light gardens are designed especially for starting seeds and are sized accordingly. For many of these light gardens you can get a clear plastic tent that will help hold in humidity.

GROWING PLANTS UNDER LIGHTS

There are several advantages to growing plants under lights. For one thing, the plants receive a consistent amount of light every day because there are no cloudy days in the light garden. You also control the day-length, and can make sure your plants receive the optimum number of light hours each day.

To keep your light garden functioning at peak efficiency, keep the lights clean. Dust the fixtures and bulbs every couple of weeks, and give the fixture a good cleaning with a damp cloth whenever you have to replace a bulb. Always use fixtures that have reflectors. To maximize the efficiency of the ballasts, use preheat or rapid-start tubes. Fluorescent tubes grow dimmer as they age. To make sure your plants are getting enough light, it's a good idea to change the tubes when they develop dark rings at the ends; don't wait until they burn out.

Young seedlings need all the light you can give them. As a general rule, position them so the tops of the plants are about 4 inches below the center of the fluorescent tubes, and leave the lights on for twelve to sixteen hours a day. When the plants grow larger—reaching a height of about 6 inches or more—you can place them a bit lower, with their tops 6 to 10 inches below the lights.

When plants are not getting enough light their stems are spindly and elongated, and they appear to be stretching toward the light. In a windowsill garden the stems will curve toward the window. Leaves will be small, stunted, and far apart on the stems. The color will look pale and washed out.

Healthy seedlings are sturdy and compact. They stand up straight, their leaves are firm and closely spaced along the stem, and their color is a deep, vibrant green.

Electric lights reduce humidity in their vicinity by 5 to 10 percent, and you will probably need to increase the humidity to a more desirable level for your plants. There are several ways to do this. You can place a humidifier near the light garden, or set the plant containers on top of pebble trays. These are shallow plastic trays with a layer of pebbles in the bottom. Keep an inch or two of water in the bottom of the tray. The containers sit on top of the pebbles, and they should be above the water level—this is not a method of bottom watering. The evaporation of water from the trays makes the air more humid right around the plants. A third way to boost humidity is to mist the plants once or twice a day with room-temperature water. If you opt for misting, be sure to leave the lights on for at least two hours afterward so the foliage dries. Wet leaves in a dark place are prone to rot, mildew, and fungus attack.

Along with humidity, plants indoors also need plenty of air circulation. Good ventilation is important to prevent mildew and fungus diseases from setting in, and to make sure plants are getting plenty of carbon dioxide, which fuels photosynthesis. (As most of us learned in high school science class, plants respire through pores in their

SEED STORAGE TIMES

Seeds of many plants can be kept from year to year if stored in cool, dry conditions. Here is a storage method that has worked for me: Put seed packets in a glass jar with some powdered milk or silica gel to absorb moisture. Screw on the cap tightly and place the jar in the refrigerator.

Some gardeners like to grow open-pollinated and heirloom varieties and collect and save their own seeds. Home gardeners can also help maintain the gene pool for breeders to draw on in the future by growing varieties that are no longer sold commercially. If you are interested in learning more about this work, and getting in touch with other gardeners who save seeds, contact The Seed Savers Exchange, P.O. Box 70, Decorah, Iowa 52101. Send them a self-addressed stamped envelope to receive information on the group's activities and publications.

Can be stored five years or longer: beets, cucumbers, mustard, tomatoes

Can be stored three to five years: asparagus, beans, cabbage, carrots, celery, chicory, endive, okra, peas, peppers, radishes, spinach

Can be stored one to two years: corn, lettuce, parsley, parsnips, salsify

Start with fresh seeds every year: onions and their relatives

leaves, taking in carbon dioxide and giving off oxygen and water vapor.) A small fan placed near the light garden will keep the air moving. But don't give the plants too much of a good thing; keep them away from drafts, especially cold ones.

Temperature needs for indoor seedlings vary with the type of plant. Vegetables for spring and fall crops, such as lettuce and other salad greens, cabbage and its relatives, Oriental greens, and radishes, will grow best in cool temperatures of 60 to 65°F. Warm-weather vegetables like tomatoes, eggplant, cucumbers, and squash, along with most herbs, like a bit more warmth—65 to 70°F. If the temperature is too warm, plants will be weak and spindly.

SOME TIPS
ON STARTING VEGETABLES
UNDER LIGHTS

Put containers of vegetable seeds in a warm (70 to 75°F) place until germination occurs. Cover the containers with newspaper or plastic to hold in humidity. Remove the cover for an hour or so each day to let in some fresh air, or you may find yourself growing fungus instead of vegetables.

Some gardeners like to presprout vegetable seeds before sowing them. Presprouting can speed germination for seeds that tend to be slow to sprout. To presprout seeds, soak them for several hours or overnight, then put them on a wet paper towel, roll up the towel, and hold it together with a rubber band at both ends. Place towel and seeds in a plastic bag with a few air holes punched in it, and close it tightly. You can also test the viability of seeds stored from last year by this method. Leave the bag in a place away from direct light until the seeds sprout, then remove the seeds and plant them. Handle the seeds with care (the tiny root sprouts are very fragile) and plant them a bit more shallowly than the planting depth recommended on the seed packet.

Generally speaking, spring and fall crops are easiest to start from seed indoors, because they mature quickly (needing to spend less time indoors before moving to the outdoor garden) and they can tolerate less heat and light. But summer crops that need a long, warm growing season, like tomatoes, are also good candidates for indoor starting, especially in northern climates where summer comes late and departs early. Most vegetables like a drop in temperature at night when they are started indoors.

Keep young vegetable seedlings 3 to 4 inches from the lights and give them twelve to sixteen hours of light a day. Feed young seedlings with a liquid fertilizer (fish emulsion works well if you can tolerate the fragrance indoors) diluted to half the recommended strength, once or twice a week.

TRANSPLANTING

You can transplant most vegetable seedlings when they have developed their second set of true leaves. The true leaves are the leaves characteristic of the mature plant. The very first leaves a seedling develops are its cotyledons, or seed leaves, which in most plants do not look like the mature leaves. If the seedlings become crowded before they have developed their second set of true leaves, you can transplant them at an earlier stage or thin excess plants by

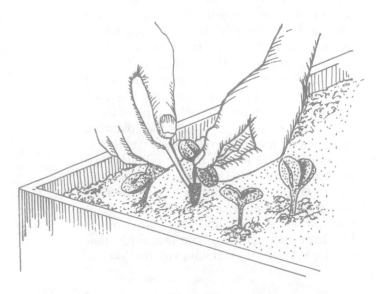

snipping off the stems with a manicure scissors. Handle tiny seedlings (or any seedlings) carefully, supporting under the root ball and lifting them by their leaves, not the stems. A useful tool for lifting tiny seedlings from the soil is a wooden tongue depressor or Popsicle stick with a small notch cut in one end. Place the notched end of the stick into the soil next to the plant and lift up, taking some soil as well as the plant.

When plants have one or two sets of true leaves and are getting bigger, they need a richer growing medium. To gradually increase the amount of nutrition your plants are getting, instead of transplanting them from the germinating medium to a very rich soil mix, you could transplant them twice: first to an intermediate mix and then after a few more weeks to a richer medium. To a basic seed-starting mix such as equal parts of peat, perlite, and vermiculite, add one part potting soil for an intermediate mix and add two parts sieved compost or one part each compost and potting soil for a richer medium.

Transplant the seedlings into individual containers or compartments in market packs, or give them more space in a flat. Transplant seedlings or plants that have a branching, upright growth habit slightly deeper than they were in their previous container. Vegetables that grow from a single crown (such as lettuce) are best transplanted to the same depth; if you inadvertently bury the crown, the point where the leafy top joins the roots, plant growth will be hindered or the crown could even rot.

After transplanting, plant tops should be 6 to 10 inches below the lamps in a light garden, and lights can remain on twelve to sixteen hours a day. The seedlings will stop growing for a few days after transplanting, and will be able to take up less water until the roots become established in their new

When transplanting a tiny seedling, support it under the roots and hold it by the leaves, never by its delicate stem.

home. Keep the plants out of direct sun and away from the lights for a couple of days and cut back on watering, and they should recover quickly from the shock of transplanting. Then return the plants to the windowsill or light garden and resume watering. Unless the plants are in a rich growing medium, feed them with a weak solution of liquid fertilizer every two weeks.

The next step will be to move the plants out to the garden when weather conditions are suitable and the plants are large enough. Information on when to transplant individual crops can be found in Chapter Seven.

Before seedlings go out to the garden they must be gradually acclimated to the outdoor environment through a process known as hardening-off, which is described in Chapter Three. Seedlings growing in undivided flats should also be "blocked" to separate their root systems and start each plant producing new feeder roots. About ten days before you plan to transplant the seedlings to the garden, use a sharp knife to cut the soil in the flat into squares, as if you were cutting a sheet cake, so that each plant is standing in a block of soil about 3 by 3 inches.

Preparing the Soil for Outdoor Planting

A good garden starts with good soil. A dark, crumbly loam that drains well but retains some moisture, is rich in organic matter and nutrients, and has a pH in a range acceptable to most plants is the ideal garden soil. Unfortunately, few of us are blessed with such soil, but any soil can be improved. The first step is to understand what kind of soil you have.

If you have never gardened on this site before, by all means do a soil test. Your local USDA County Extension office will analyze soil samples (they will give you instructions on collecting the samples, too), or you can purchase a do-it-yourself test kit. There are also private laboratories that perform soil analyses. A soil test should show you the pH and content of the major nutrients—nitrogen, phosphorus, and potassium—as well as various trace minerals. Some tests also give you a reading on the organic matter content.

Fertility and pH are not the only important things about soil. Understanding your basic soil type is essential in understanding what sort of conditions it offers to plants. There are three main soil types, determined by the sort of particles that compose them.

Most soils were formed by the breakdown of rocks, and the type of rock determines the qualities of the soil. The three primary mineral particles of which soils are made are sand, silt, and clay. Soils also contain organic matter (from plant and animal remains) and various minerals.

Sandy soils contain a high percentage of sand. Sand particles are large, and such soils have a light, loose texture, making them easy to dig and quick to drain. Sandy soils can be worked quite early in spring, since they do not hold much moisture, but they can be problematic in summer, when it can be difficult to keep them moist enough for plants. When I moved to Long Island I gardened in sandy soil for the first time in my life, and found that I had to water my garden every day in the height of summer (unless it rained), or the plants did not get enough moisture. Since sandy soil drains so quickly, it follows that it also allows nutrients to pass through quickly. Adding lots of organic matter to sandy soils gives them more body, improves their water-retention capacity, and contributes some nutritional value. You will also need to feed plants with compost, seaweed concentrates, rock powders, manures, and other organic fertilizers, or with a balanced all-purpose organic fertilizer. Root crops generally grow well in sandy soils, where the light texture allows the roots to penetrate easily and grow long and straight. Relatively light feeders such as spinach, lettuce and other leaf crops, and herbs are also well suited to sandy soils, as are members of the cabbage family.

Clay soils have a large proportion of clay particles, which are very tiny and tightly packed together. As a result, such soils are dense, heavy, and slow to drain. Although clay soils may contain adequate nutrients, they dry out very slowly in spring and may become waterlogged and compacted if not handled properly. I grew up in Pennsylvania and spent much of my life gardening in clay soil, and it was never easy. I remember jumping on top of the shovel to try to force it into the ground when I was starting a new garden. And every spring there were stones to remove, and lumps and clods to break up. The advantage of clay soil is that it needs less watering in summer. Adding organic matter to clay soil lightens the texture (organic matter particles are larger than the tiny clay particles), helps aerate the soil, and improves drainage. If the soil is very heavy, you will have to dig in organic matter for several years before the soil becomes crumbly enough to produce good root crops. Planting of early crops like peas and onions will have to be delayed until the soil dries out enough to be workable.

If you live in the North and your soil is heavy clay, gardening in raised beds will allow you to get into the garden earlier in spring. Beds in which the soil is built up 8 to 12 inches above the level of the surrounding soil will drain faster and warm up more quickly in spring than the ground around them. Add lots of compost or other organic matter to the soil in the beds to lighten and loosen the texture.

Loam soils are the best for gardening. They contain a mixture of sand, silt, and clay particles, are crumbly in texture, drain well while still retaining adequate moisture for plants, and are naturally fertile. A true loam is a gardener's blessing. These soils can support all kinds of crops, even heavy feeders like corn and potatoes.

A fourth type of soil, known as muck or peat soil, is less common. Muck soil is very rich in nutrients and organic matter, having been formed from plant and animal remains that decayed underwater.

No matter what type of soil you have, soil building is a continuous process, even in long-established gardens. I do not believe it is possible to add too much organic matter to your soil. Work in lots of compost, composted manure, peat moss, seaweed—whatever is readily available in your area. It is best to dig in organic matter and natural fertilizers several months before planting, to give the soil microbes a chance to start working on the material and making nutrients available for plants. It is especially important to apply uncomposted animal manures well in advance of planting time, because fresh manure heats up as it decomposes and can burn plant roots.

If your garden is very large, an easy way to add organic matter is to plant a green-manure crop the season before planting your garden crops, and till it into the soil a month or two before planting the garden. Green-manure crops are usually legumes, which fix nitrogen in the soil, or grasses. Alfalfa, clover, and rye grass are three examples.

COMPOST AND FERTILIZERS

Compost is the best soil conditioner there is. It adds organic matter and nutrients to the soil, improving its texture, fertility, drainage, and water retention. And composting allows you to give back some of what you take from the earth, by recycling plant wastes and, if you wish, some of your household garbage. You can never have too much compost. I believe compost and organic fertilizers are the best ways to build rich soil for the kitchen garden.

The philosophy behind organic gardening is to feed the soil rather than the plant, because healthy, fertile soil will yield healthy, productive plants. When you add a variety of natural materials to the soil, plants get nutrients in small, continuous doses, rather than the single large dose supplied by synthetic or chemical fertilizers. Also, organic materials supply trace elements and other substances in addition to the major nutrients. Scientists tell us that nutrients are nutrients, and plants use them the same way no matter where they come from. This may well be true; certainly as a nonscientist I'm in no position to argue the logic. But I don't believe science can tell us everything, nor do I believe gardening is a science. I am the most unscientific of gardeners, and to me natural fertilizers simply seem kinder and gentler, closer to what nature provides to plants in the wild. I am not going to go into the old organic-versus-chemical arguments. I use organic materials in my own garden and get good results with them, and see no reason to switch to chemical products, especially in a kitchen garden. But each gardener must make his or her own choice.

These days a whole host of natural fertilizers is available. Read the labels carefully and look for products that are made from natural materials, not just labelled "organic." Organic sources of nitrogen include animal manures, cottonseed meal, fish products, dried blood, bonemeal, and clover or legumes grown as cover crops. Potassium can be supplied by bonemeal, rock phosphate, and colloidal phosphate. Potassium comes from greensand, granite dust, or wood ashes. Trace elements can be contributed by seaweed and algae products. In addition to individual materials, gardeners can also purchase preblended natural fertilizers.

No matter what you use for fertilizer, one thing all gardeners should do is make compost. It is easy to make, especially if you use materials readily available to you. If you have lots of leaves in fall, for instance, you can compost them into leaf mold.

Constructing a compost pile according to certain guidelines will allow materials to decompose quickly and odorlessly. A properly made compost pile does not smell bad. Finished compost is brown and crumbly, with an earthy smell. Here's how to make it.

In the bottom of a pen or bin, put a few inches of branches or brush to let air circulate underneath the pile. Put down a 2- to 4-inch layer of green plant debris or household garbage (use vegetable peelings, coffee grounds, and eggshells, but do *not* use meat products, fats, oils, or pet wastes. Follow with 2 to 4 inches of dry material, preferably chopped or shredded into small pieces: dry leaves, straw, pine needles, or dry plant material, for example. It is okay to compost weeds, as long as they have not yet gone to seed; weeds with seeds will be spread throughout the garden with the compost. If you wish you can put a 1- to 2-inch layer of manure or soil on top of the dry material. Repeat the layers, moistening each layer as you build—the material should be moist but not soggy. You can use a compost activator if you wish; they contain bacteria to help get the decomposition process underway, and several are on the market.

Turn the pile with a pitchfork at least once a week to mix the materials and keep the decomposition process going. The center of the pile should become hot. When turning, put material from the outer edges of the pile into the center. If the pile seems dry, water it. The compost should be ready to use in a month or two.

Add ½ to 1 inch of compost to the garden every year after the soil is in good shape, to maintain good quality.

WATERING

All plants need water to grow, and to produce a good harvest all gardeners have to give their plants water to supplement rainfall, at least once in a while. The trick is to know how much water to give the plants, and to get it to them as efficiently as possible, to conserve this precious resource. The most important point to keep in mind is that to grow the strongest plants, it is best to water deeply and only when plants need it. Frequent light waterings cause plants to develop lots of shallow feeder roots that are very susceptible to drought. Watering less often—say once or twice a week—but more deeply encourages roots to grow deep into the soil, where they will be more likely to find water during dry weather. How often plants need water depends upon the plants themselves, the type of soil in which they are growing, and climate and weather conditions. The old dictum to give the garden 1 inch of water a week does not hold true for all gardens in all places. A seaside garden where the soil is sandy and the sun is strong will need more than an inch of water per week. A garden in dense, clayey soil in a cool, cloudy climate will need less.

The best way to tell when your garden needs water is to poke a finger into the soil. When it is dry more than a couple of inches below the surface, it is time to water. Do not wait to water until your plants all go limp; it means they are in water stress. Some plants will look flaccid in the middle of a hot afternoon and perk up again later in the day; that does not necessarily indicate water stress. But if plants are wilted in the morning or evening they are in trouble. Water-stressed plants suffer growth setbacks and will produce later and sparser crops than plants receiving adequate moisture.

The traditional way to water has been to sprinkle the plants with a hose. That gave rise to automated sprinkler attachments, which can be connected to timers. This sort of overhead watering is the least efficient way to water. It uses the greatest amount of water, because the water must filter down through the leaves to reach the soil, and a substantial amount is lost to evaporation in the process. Also, it is not always beneficial to wet plant foliage; wet leaves at night invite mildew and fungus diseases. On the plus side, overhead watering cleans foliage and helps cool plants in hot weather. If you must water with a conventional hose, do it in the morning or late afternoon so less water is lost to evaporation, and so foliage dries before dark. Or get a bubbler attachment for the end of the hose and lay the hose on the ground, moving it to different parts of the garden.

A better method is to deliver water directly to the root zone where it is needed. Soaker hoses and drip irrigation systems are two ways to water at ground level. Soaker hoses are made of canvas or fiber, and allow water to seep slowly from pores all along their length. The hoses connect to one another and to an outdoor faucet that you need turn on only partway. Lay them through the garden early in the season while the plants are small. A drip irrigation system can be put together from lengths of narrow plastic hose with small holes along its length. The tubing is put together with couplings and can be connected to a timer for automatic operation. Drip irrigation systems are installed under the soil surface. There are systems for container gardens as well as in-ground gardens. The equipment is rather expensive, and requires a fair amount of labor to install, but drip irrigation is effective and convenient, and does not detract from the appearance of the garden. If you use an automatic timer, the system will water your garden when you cannot be home to do it.

If your garden is small, you can water plants individually by dipping water from a bucket.

Plants in containers, because they are growing in such a small volume of soil, need to be watered more often than gardens in the ground. In hot weather you will need

Water in this garden is supplied by a drip irrigation system—the most efficient way to water.

ROBERT KOURIK

to water daily or perhaps even twice a day to give plants the moisture they need.

Strategies for conserving water in the garden are discussed in Chapter Four.

CONTROLLING PESTS AND DISEASES

The best way to control pests and diseases is to prevent them in the first place. Although you cannot keep pests and diseases from invading your garden, there are several things you can do to discourage them, and to help your plants withstand the damage when they do attack.

Practice good sanitation: keep the garden clean. Plant debris provides hiding places for bugs to overwinter and lay their eggs, as well as sites for disease organisms to take hold. You can spread disease organisms from plant to plant just by working in the garden. Avoid working around plants—especially beans—when they are wet. Don't smoke in the garden, particularly around tomatoes and other solanaceous plants; if you smoke at all, wash your hands before working in the garden. If you have to remove diseased plants or parts of plants, wash your hands when you finish, and sterilize any tools you've used. Dip the tools in a solution of one part liquid chlorine bleach to nine parts water.

Use good cultural practices. Healthy, well-nourished plants will be better able to withstand attacks by pests and diseases when they do occur. Build your soil every year to provide the best possible growing medium. Make sure there is an adequate supply of nutrients for plants, but do not overfeed them. Overfeeding stimulates weak, rapid growth that is highly susceptible to pest damage. Do not overwater plants, but do water when necessary; both water-stressed and overwatered plants will be weakened.

When possible, plant varieties that are resistant or tolerant to the pests and diseases common in your area. Breeders are introducing more and more resistant varieties, and some old-favorite varieties, such as Marglobe and Rutgers tomatoes, are now available in improved forms that have some resistance to disease. Read carefully the descriptions in seed and nursery catalogs to find out which varieties have resistance or tolerance.

Rotate plants through the garden, planting them in different parts of the garden each year, to prevent the buildup of disease organisms in the soil. Rotating crops also helps foil insect pests; if a pest lays eggs near a favorite host plant and that plant is no longer nearby when the eggs hatch, the pests may not be able to find their target. Rotations help keep soil nutrients from being depleted, too, when you follow one plant with another that has different nutritional requirements. The easiest rotation pattern is to follow a heavy feeder with a light feeder, and then in the third year with a soil builder (see the table, Nutrient Needs of Vegetables). Do not plant any member of the cabbage family where any other cole crop has grown more than once in three years. In fact, members of most plant families should be rotated in this way. Companion planting is another technique that may prove helpful; it is discussed in Chapter One.

Floating covers can be laid over young plants to keep pests off them. These covers let in light, air, and water but keep bugs from getting at the plants. Covers are especially effective in keeping out the flies that lay eggs that hatch into borers and grubs.

As you gain experience you will learn when to expect annual onslaughts of pests like potato beetles and squash borers. Keeping a garden journal is an invaluable memory aid. Major pest populations tend to arrive in the garden around the same time each year. If you know when to expect pests, you can time plantings to avoid them, planting earlier or later so the crop is not at the most critical stage of growth when the pests show up.

Watch your plants carefully throughout the season and take action whenever you notice the first signs of pests or disease. Problems are easier to solve while still in their early stages. If you wait too long to act it may be too late to save the harvest.

Use natural and plant-based controls that break down quickly after they are applied and do not linger in the environment. One of the most useful products I've found is insecticidal soap. It has proven very effective in my garden against aphids, whiteflies, flea beetles, and other small pests, and it does not harm birds, bees, and butterflies. Plant-based insecticides include rotenone, pyrethrum, ryania, and sabadilla. Diatomaceous earth controls soft-bodied pests, and *Bacillus thuringiensis* is effective against cabbage worms and other caterpillars. If Japanese beetles are a problem, use milky spore disease to kill the grubs that winter over in your lawn.

Most of these organic controls must be

NUTRIENT NEEDS OF VEGETABLES

It is important to be familiar with the nutrient needs of the plants you grow in order to plan crop rotations, and also to gauge fertilizer needs. This table summarizes the requirements of the most commonly grown vegetables.

HEAVY FEEDERS

Asparagus	Corn	Okra
Beets	Cucumbers	Parsley
Broccoli	Eggplant	Radishes
Brussels sprouts	Endive, escarole	Spinach
Cabbage	Kale	Squash
Cauliflower	Kohlrabi	Tomatoes
Collards	Lettuce	

LIGHT FEEDERS

Carrots	Mustard	Shallots
Chard	Onions	Turnips
Garlic	Peppers	
Leeks	Potatoes	

SOIL BUILDERS

Beans and peas actually build soil, by fixing nitrogen

reapplied after rain, but the extra effort seems a small price to pay for the peace of mind they afford.

If slugs and earwigs plague your garden, you may wish to forgo mulching the plot. Mulches offer ideal hiding places for these creatures. Put out bait or traps to catch them, and empty the traps every day. Here's a good way to catch earwigs: crumble a sheet of paper and put it in a tin can. Place the can upside down on a short stake in the garden near the plants under siege. The earwigs should crawl up into the paper to hide during daylight hours. Remove the paper in the morning and burn it or seal it inside a plastic bag and put it in the garbage.

It is also a good idea to become familiar with the predatory insects that eat the pests. Learn to recognize ladybugs, parasitic wasps, lacewing larvae, and other beneficial insects. When you see them in your garden, leave them alone. You can also purchase them to release in your garden.

As far as diseases go, practicing cleanliness and rotation to prevent them is the best approach. If you notice a disease problem, remove the affected leaf or plant part. If more symptoms develop, pull up the entire plant and put it in the garbage. Do *not* put diseased plant material in the compost pile; even a hot pile will not get hot enough to destroy disease organisms. You can use fungicides and other products in the garden to fight disease if you wish; I prefer not to use them in my own garden. Remember, you are growing these plants for food.

COLD FRAMES AND OTHER SEASON-EXTENDING DEVICES

Using season extenders will allow you to get your garden started earlier in spring, stretch the harvest of spring crops into summer, prolong the harvest in fall, and even do some winter gardening. One of the most useful devices you can have is a cold frame.

A cold frame is a sturdy boxlike structure with a glass or plastic cover that lets in sunlight. Light is converted to heat inside the cold frame, and the soil and air are warmed. In the cold frame you can start spring plants, especially hardy ones, several weeks before their usual outdoor planting date. You can use the cold frame to harden-off transplants, overwinter hardy fall plants, and grow some leafy crops from seed during the winter. In summer you can remove the lid and use the cold frame as a nursery to start plants that will go into the main garden later on.

You can purchase a cold frame, or build your own. A simple homemade cold frame can have sides made of scrap lumber, bricks, cement blocks, or, for a temporary setup, even bales of hay. Use an old storm window for the top. If you opt for a wood frame, treat the wood with a preservative that is not toxic to plants.

Site the cold frame where it receives full sun all day, if possible. The frame should face south, and the back should be slightly higher than the front so the lid is on a slant, to let the maximum amount of sunlight into the frame. If the spot you choose is buffeted by prevailing winds, install a windbreak. Probably the best location for a cold frame is with the north side (the back) against the wall of a shed, a garage, or the house—this provides the maximum protection, and is especially helpful if you want to use the frame to grow winter crops.

The soil in a cold frame must be light and porous, with excellent drainage, but rich enough to nourish the plants. Since the cold frame is a limited space, you can blend a special soil mix to use in it, just as you prepare growing mixes for potted plants. One good recipe to try is a mix of one part topsoil, one part composted manure, one part sand or vermiculite, and two parts leaf mold or compost.

It is important for the cold frame to have good ventilation so that temperatures do not rise too high inside and damage plants. Ventilation is also essential to let out excess moisture and provide air circulation, which in turn helps prevent damping-off and other diseases. Ventilate the cold frame by opening the lid partway on sunny days. Some commercially available cold frames come with devices that raise and lower the lid or open vents automatically to maintain temperature. Keep in mind, though, that too much fresh, cold air can shock plants and dry them out. You have to strike a balance.

Gardeners in cold climates may want to insulate the cold frame for winter use (see Chapter Six for directions), or turn it into a hotbed. To make a hotbed you can install electric heating cables under the soil in the cold frame (the frame must, of course, be

You can construct a simple, functional cold frame from scrap lumber and old storm windows. Be sure the back (north side) is a bit higher than the front so the glass top is angled toward the south for maximum sun exposure.

located near an electrical outlet). First, excavate the soil to a depth of at least 3 inches. Lay the cable in loops on top of the soil (the loops of cable must not touch one another), and cover with an inch of soil. On top of that lay a piece of hardware cloth or window screening. Then put down at least 6 inches of your prepared soil mix. Remember to allow enough space above the soil level for plants to grow without touching the lid.

OTHER SEASON-EXTENDING DEVICES

There are lots of simple structures and devices you can use to protect plants from early or late frosts and unseasonably cold weather, either individually or in groups.

Various sorts of materials can be used to cover a group of plants, or an entire bed or row. A cloche is a sort of miniature greenhouse that consists of two pieces of glass held together at the top with a special alu-minum clip, to form a tent. You buy the clips and supply your own glass. The clips, named Rumsey clips after their inventor, were developed in England. Other fittings made of heavy-gauge wire can be used to add upright sides to the glass tent, to gain extra height; the cloche then resembles a little glass barn. A standard size cloche is 24 by 22 inches, by 19 inches high.

There are also several kinds of covers you can use on rows or beds. You will need to hold covers other than floating covers off of plants with a series of plastic or wire hoops, or another kind of frame. Anchor the sides with pegs, U-shaped pins, or rocks.

Two popular types of plant covers are floating covers made of a spun polyester fabric called Reemay, and a polypropylene-nylon mesh known as Agronet. Both materials are very light in weight, and simply lay lightly on top of the plants; the plants push up the covers as they grow. Both materials admit light, moisture, and air, but afford protection from birds, light frosts, and egg-laying flies, caterpillars, and other pests. The covers also keep out bees, and pollination can be affected. The solution is to remove the covers, at least during the day, when plants are in bloom.

Plastic row covers can be used to create a sort of mini-greenhouse right in the garden. They are very useful in large row gardens (you could also make your own covers for beds), where they extend the growing season in spring and fall, and help give warm-season plants an early start. These covers are made of clear polyethylene 4 mm thick. Polyethylene is used because it allows plants to respire; other plastics would suffocate them. Stretch the plastic over hoops or a frame to make a tunnel or a tent. For the ventilation that is necessary on sunny days, cut slits in the top or roll up the sides of the tunnel. In my area, commercial growers of strawberries use plastic row and bed covers in spring.

Devices that protect individual plants are best used only at night, put in place late in the day and removed in the morning. These devices are very easy to use—you just set them in place—but they tend to overheat on sunny days, and they can't hold all that much heat at night. However, in a small garden or for a few favored plants they can come in quite handy.

You can purchase cones made of heavy waxed paper to use as hot caps, or make your own; use plastic milk jugs with the bottoms cut out, upside down peach baskets, or the bottom half of a half-gallon milk carton with holes punched in the sides for ventilation.

An interesting device that is said to work quite well is called Wall-O-Water. It is a plastic teepee with double, channeled walls that are filled with water. During the day the water absorbs heat and warms the air around the plant. At night the water releases its heat slowly; the temperature inside the teepee remains warmer than the outside air temperature and plants do not freeze.

For tips on using season-extending devices at different times of year, see the appropriate seasonal chapters.

THREE

The Spring Garden

In SPRING the world is full of a sense of new growth and fresh beginnings. Although according to the calendar the new year begins in the depths of winter, to many of us spring *feels* like the start of a new year. After a winter spent indoors, when we seem to retreat deeper inside ourselves while the weather is cold and the days are short, the coming of spring brings us back outdoors and out of our lethargy. We want to feel the sun on our faces, breathe the fresh air, and watch as buds swell and tender shoots push up through the ground.

Gardeners watch the weather anxiously, waiting for outdoor planting to begin. We observe what the local flora and fauna are doing, watching for natural indicators that tell us more surely than any calendar when winter is gone and spring has truly come. There is a science of using natural indicators to monitor weather conditions from one year to the next, called phenology. Understanding a bit about phenology can come in very handy for a gardener. If you know how to time your planting by the natural indica-

tors around you, you will lose far fewer plants to late cold snaps and other vagaries of the weather. The USDA can tell you the *average* date of the last frost in your area, but frost dates can vary by several weeks according to yearly weather conditions and the microclimate in and immediately around your garden. Phenological indicators are a more reliable guide to gauging planting times from year to year.

PHENOLOGY

Phenology is the study of events that occur in regular cycles during the lives of plants and animals. The term comes from the Greek words meaning "science of appearances." The phenology of perennial plants in the local landscape is closely related to temperature and daylength, and you can use plants as natural indicators of when

58

conditions are right for planting various crops. Plants usually don't start to grow until the weather is warm enough for them. In a cold, wet spring they will get a later start, and so should your garden plants.

Make notes in your garden journal on when trees, shrubs, and wild plants in your yard start to grow, leaf out, form buds, and burst into full bloom; also keep running notes on weather conditions. After several years your journals can begin to help you choose the best indicator plants in your neighborhood.

You can also use phenology to predict the annual arrival of pest populations in your garden. When a major infestation occurs, look around and make notes of plants in the landscape that are in bloom, at a particular height, or at another readily observable stage in their development. If after several years the plant is always at the same stage when the pests arrive, you may be able to use it to predict when they will come.

Farmers and gardeners have been using phenology for thousands of years. It was familiar both in China and ancient Rome. Hesiod wrote that it was time to plant when the cranes migrated. In Colonial America, the Indians in New England planted their corn when the oak leaves were as big as a mouse's ear (the advice is still valid today).

All plants are sensitive to climate and weather conditions, but indicator plants are the most reliable and predictable in their performance. Indicator plants are different in different places. For example, on Long Island where I live, cabbage root maggots arrive when the forsythias are in bloom, but in upstate New York they come when a common weed, yellow rocket, flowers. Farmers and market gardeners who routinely spray for pests could use phenology to cut back on the amount of pesticides they apply, and spray only when it is most necessary.

Probably the most widely used indicator plant is the lilac. Lilacs are good indicators because their annual development is very regular and easy to observe, and because they grow in most of the United States. When lilacs first begin to leaf out, that is, when the widest part of the first emerging leaves goes beyond the bud scales that had enclosed the leaf buds, it is safe to plant hardy, cool-weather plants like peas, lettuce, spinach, and calendulas. When lilacs are in full bloom, that is, when all of the flowers on 95 percent of the plant's flower clusters are fully open, it is safe to plant tender, warm-weather plants such as corn, tomatoes, and basil.

Becoming attuned to the cycles of local plants and animals is a rewarding, enjoyable experience for gardeners, linking us more closely to the natural world of which we are a part.

PLANTING BY THE MOON

Another venerable tradition for gardeners with an astronomical bent is planting in accord with phases of the moon. Planting by the moon has survived for seemingly eons as part of garden folklore, and many gardeners still swear by it today. The theory behind planting by the moon is that as the moon governs the ocean tides, so does it influence the movement of the fluids within plants (and also, presumably, within our bodies). For those who want to experiment, here is a very basic description of how it works.

The simplest way to plant in harmony with the moon is to plant crops that grow above the ground when the moon is waxing, and plant roots and bulbs when the moon is waning. A slightly more detailed scheme keys gardening activities to the phases of the moon. When the moon is young, between new and first quarter, it is best to sow or transplant leafy plants and crops that bear their seeds on the outside of the fruit, like strawberries and corn. When the moon is between first quarter and full, plant crops that carry their seeds inside the fruit:

The Spring Garden 59

squash, cucumbers, tomatoes, peas, and beans, among others. From full moon to last quarter, plant root crops. From last quarter to new moon do not plant anything. Instead, direct your energies to weeding.

Moon gardeners can also assign gardening tasks by the phase of the moon, and can also take into account which zodiacal sign the moon is in. It can all become rather complicated. Ed Hume, the proprietor of a small seed company in Washington, puts out an annual garden almanac that lists moon phases and signs, and gardening chores to be done under each, for the entire year. If you are interested in gardening by the moon, you may want to order a copy of this booklet. Send $1.50 to Almanac, Ed Hume Seeds, P.O. Box 1450, Kent, WA 98035.

SPRING COMES TO THE GARDEN

The first signs of life in the kitchen garden are perennials returning from last year, and self-sown seedlings from some of last year's tender plants. Established clumps of chives begin to show new growth very early in the season. Second-year parsley will start to grow, too, and asparagus spears will start to push through the ground. Hardy annuals sown last fall begin to grow when the worst frosts are over. When the weather gets a little warmer, the first edible flowers start to bloom, just in time for the earliest harvests of newly planted salad greens. Violets, pansies, and Johnny jump-ups are all candidates for the springtime salad bowl. If you let some of your dill go to seed last year, watch for the feathery little seedlings in mid-spring.

You will have plenty of opportunity to notice all this renewed growth in spring because you will be spending lots of time outdoors planting the garden. Spring is a hectic time—there are seeds to sow indoors at the very start of the season, and seedlings to watch over for weeks thereafter. The garden must be readied for planting, and seeds sown outdoors and transplants set out. There are also—unfortunately—weeds to pull. And there is also a surprising amount of food to harvest and enjoy in spring.

PLANTING GUIDE

This table offers guidance on when to plant edibles indoors and out, and whether plants transplant easily or are better sown directly in the garden where they are to grow.

Plant name	Weeks before planting out to start seeds indoors	Weeks before or after last frost to set out	Ease or difficulty of transplanting
ARUGULA	—	6–8 weeks before, and every 2–3 weeks thereafter	Easiest to direct-sow.
ASPARAGUS	12–14	Set out plants 6 weeks after last frost. Set out crowns as soon as soil can be worked.	Dormant crowns transplant easily.
BASIL	7–10	1–2 weeks after	Easy

PLANTING GUIDE

Plant name	Weeks before planting out to start seeds indoors	Weeks before or after last frost to set out	Ease or difficulty of transplanting
LIMA BEANS	—	2–4 weeks after, when soil has warmed	Direct-sow; do not transplant well.
SHELL BEANS (OTHER THAN LIMAS)	—	1–2 weeks after	Direct-sow; do not transplant well.
SNAP BEANS	—	1–2 weeks after	Direct-sow; do not transplant well.
BEEBALM	8–10	Sow or transplant after heavy frost, while soil is still cool. Or sow in summer for transplants in early fall. Or sow in early fall.	Seeds, plants, or divisions all work well.
BEETS	4	2 weeks before, or as soon as soil can be worked; repeat every 2–3 weeks until midsummer. Sow anytime in frost-free climates.	Transplant carefully to minimize root disturbance. Direct-sow if possible.
BORAGE	—	When danger of frost is past	Does not transplant well; direct-sow if possible, or transplant only when young.
BROCCOLI	6–8	2 weeks before to 2 weeks after. Sow seeds in late spring or early summer for fall harvest.	Easy
BRUSSELS SPROUTS	4–6	2 weeks before to 2 weeks after, or start in spring and set out plants in early summer for fall harvest. In zones 8–10 plant for winter crop.	Easy
CABBAGE	6–8	3 weeks before to 2 weeks after for early and mid-season varieties. Direct-sow late varieties in late spring to early	Easy

PLANTING GUIDE

Plant name	Weeks before planting out to start seeds indoors	Weeks before or after last frost to set out	Ease or difficulty of transplanting
CABBAGE (continued)		summer for fall harvest. Zones 9 and 10 sow in fall for winter harvest or early winter for spring harvest.	
CALENDULAS	6–8	Direct-sow or transplant after last heavy frost, while weather is still cool and light frost may occur. Sow in fall in warm climates.	Easy
CANARY CREEPER	—	Direct-sow after last heavy frost, while soil is cool and some light frost may still occur.	Transplant with care; direct-sow if possible.
CARROTS	5–6	2 weeks before; every 2–3 weeks thereafter	Transplant with care to minimize root disturbance; direct-sow if possible.
CAULIFLOWER	6–8	2 weeks before to 2 weeks after. Or sow in midsummer for fall harvest.	Easy
CELERIAC	8–12	2 weeks before, when danger of hard frost is past	Easy
CHARD	4	2 weeks before last frost date	Transplant with care to minimize root disturbance; direct-sow if possible.
CHERVIL	—	2–3 weeks before; for continuous supply, sow every 3 weeks until weather turns hot. Sow again in late summer for fall harvest, or in fall to germinate in spring.	Does not transplant well; direct-sow. Also grows well indoors.
LEAF CHICORY	—	Early spring or 60 days before first fall frost	Direct-sow; transplants may bolt early.

PLANTING GUIDE

Plant name	Weeks before planting out to start seeds indoors	Weeks before or after last frost to set out	Ease or difficulty of transplanting
WITLOOF CHICORY	—	Sow early to midsummer to have roots by fall for indoor forcing in winter.	Direct-sow if possible.
CHINESE CABBAGE	4–6	Direct-sow 90 days before first fall frost, or set out transplants 4–6 weeks later; or sow indoors in early spring and plant out 2–3 weeks before last spring frost.	Easy
CHIVES AND GARLIC CHIVES	4	Start indoors in dark place with temperature of 60–70°F. Plant out 2 weeks after last frost date.	Seeds germinate very slowly but seedlings transplant well. Easier to start with divisions from established clump, or nursery plants. Can also grow indoors.
CLARY	—	Sow in spring; plants bloom second year. Or divide established plants in spring or early fall. Often self-sows.	Start from seed or divisions; established plants may self-sow.
CORIANDER	—	1–2 weeks after last frost. Zones 9 and 10 sow in fall.	Direct-sow; does not transplant well.
CORN	—	1–2 weeks after	Direct-sow; does not transplant well.
CORN SALAD (MACHE)	—	Direct-sow in early spring and again in late summer for fall crop. May self-sow.	Direct-sow; grows quickly.
CRESS	—	4 weeks before last frost, or 4 weeks before first fall frost. Grow indoors over winter.	Grows so quickly, not worth starting indoors.
CUCUMBERS	2–3	1 week after last frost	Transplant with care to minimize root disturbance; best to direct-sow.

PLANTING GUIDE

Plant name	Weeks before planting out to start seeds indoors	Weeks before or after last frost to set out	Ease or difficulty of transplanting
DAYLILIES	—	Plant in spring; divide established clumps in fall.	Plant divisions or nursery plants; transplant well.
DILL	—	1–2 weeks after last frost. For continuous supply of leaves, sow every week until midsummer. Or sow in fall for harvest next year. May self-sow.	Direct-sow if possible; can be hard to transplant.
EGGPLANT	8–10	2–4 weeks after last frost, when soil has warmed	Easy
ENDIVE, ESCAROLE	4–5	2 weeks before to 2 weeks after last frost	Easy
FENNEL	—	1–2 weeks after last frost; for continuous supply sow every 3 weeks until midsummer.	Direct-sow; does not transplant well.
GARLIC	4–6	2–4 weeks before last frost. Plant cloves as soon as soil can be worked, 4 weeks before last frost. Or plant in early fall for crop next spring.	Easy. Easiest to grow from cloves.
SCENTED GERANIUMS	—	2–4 weeks after, when danger of frost is past	Best to start from cuttings or nursery plants; seeds slow to germinate. Can also be grown indoors.
HYSSOP	—	Plant in early spring.	Direct-sow; or start from cuttings or divisions of established plants.
KALE	6–8	3 weeks before to 4 weeks after; or plant midsummer, 90 days before first frost, for fall crop.	Easy. Also easy to direct-sow.

Arugula, chives, and Johnny jump-ups grow together in a tiny salad garden in spring.

Pansies start blooming while the weather is still cool and add a bright flash of color to spring salads.

ANNE HALPIN

Opposite, fresh basil brings the taste of summer to pasta, pesto sauce, grilled baby vegetables, and other dishes. You can plant green or purple basils, as shown here, or basil with a touch of cinnamon, licorice, lemon, or clove in its leaves.

COURTESY NATIONAL GARDEN BUREAU

The lilac is a dependable guide to determining safe planting times for tender crops in spring.

Garden peas are among the earliest crops planted outdoors in spring. For the best flavor, harvest right before cooking to preserve the maximum sugar content.

Violas, pansies, and Johnny jump-ups are pretty in the spring garden, and edible, too, with a bland, mild flavor that contains a faint suggestion of mint.

COURTESY JOHNNY'S SELECTED SEEDS

COURTESY NATIONAL GARDEN BUREAU

Nasturtiums make a pretty edging for a garden of edibles, especially if you have a location in full sun where the soil is not too rich in nitrogen.

A food garden doesn't have to be planted in rows. In this garden, blocks of edibles form an attractive pattern. Shown here are, front to back, cabbage, lettuce, and calendula.

ROBERT KOURIK

Grow edibles in pots on a sunny deck or patio to supplement the harvest from the main garden. Or place a few pots of favorite herbs and vegetables right outside the kitchen door for quick access.

Some herbs can be used as groundcovers, like the woolly thyme shown here.

COURTESY JOHNNY'S SELECTED SEEDS

Lemon Gem and Tangerine Gem marigolds, shown here, have a citrusy flavor.

The summer garden in all its lush exuberance is a cornucopia of flavors, colors, scents, and textures.

Sun Drops squash, shown here, and other summer squash varieties, are delectable when picked young. The fruits develop quickly; for baby vegetables, pick while the flower is still attached to the young fruit.

ROBERT KOURIK

COURTESY ALL-AMERICA SELECTIONS

Paths make all the parts of a large garden accessible. Here, narrow beds of herbs and flowers near the house are separated from one another by lawn and a brick path. The "tree" is actually an herb—lemon verbena—an amazing sight for gardeners who live outside the warm climates where the plant can survive outdoors year-round.

Lavender surrounds a bed of other edibles in this California garden.

BOTH PHOTOS: ROBERT KOURIK

Bronze fennel has delicate, soft leaves of a bronzy green with a purplish cast. From a distance the plant is a fuzzy haze of foliage, a beautiful addition to the summer garden.

PLANTING GUIDE

Plant name	Weeks before planting out to start seeds indoors	Weeks before or after last frost to set out	Ease or difficulty of transplanting
FLOWERING KALE	6–8	Sow indoors in early to late spring; plant out or direct-sow while soil is still cool and light frost may still occur. In warm climates direct-sow in late fall.	Easy
KOHLRABI	6–8	On last frost date to 4 weeks after	Easy
LAVENDER	—	2–4 weeks after last frost	Start from nursery plants or cuttings; seeds hard to germinate.
LEEKS	8–10	6 weeks before to last frost date; or plant in fall.	Easy
LETTUCE	4–6	4 weeks before to 4 weeks after last frost; direct-sow as early as soil can be worked; or plant mid to late summer for fall. Sow summer lettuce around last frost date. Start autumn/winter varieties in late summer to early fall.	Easy
MARIGOLDS	2–3	Direct-sow or transplant out 2–4 weeks after last frost. Zones 9 and 10 sow in fall for winter flowers.	Easy
MARJORAM	6–8	1–2 weeks after last frost	Start from nursery plants or divisions; difficult to germinate.
MINTS	—	Anytime in spring	Easiest to start cuttings or nursery plants. Plant in containers or bottomless boxes to confine roots.
MUSTARD	4–6	3 weeks before to 3 weeks after last frost	Easy

PLANTING GUIDE

Plant name	Weeks before planting out to start seeds indoors	Weeks before or after last frost to set out	Ease or difficulty of transplanting
NASTURTIUMS	2–3	Sow after last heavy frost, 1–2 weeks before last frost date. Zones 9 and 10 sow in fall for winter flowers.	Direct-sow if possible; does not usually transplant well. Also grows indoors.
OKRA	6–8	4–6 weeks after last frost	Direct-sow if possible; does not transplant well.
BULBING ONIONS	4–6	4 weeks before to 3 weeks after last frost	Easy
BUNCHING ONIONS	4–6	2–3 weeks before to 4 weeks after last frost	Easy
OREGANO	—	1–2 weeks after last frost	Plant nursery plants or cuttings; seeds difficult to germinate.
PANSIES	8–10	Sow indoors in winter; plant out after heavy frost, or in midsummer and keep in cold frame all winter. Zones 9 and 10 sow in early fall for winter flowers.	Easy
PARSLEY	4–6	Plant out 2–3 weeks before to 2 weeks after last frost. Or direct-sow when soil temperature is 50°F or more. Slow to germinate.	Direct-sow if possible; doesn't always transplant well.
PEAS	—	2–4 weeks before last frost, or as soon as soil can be worked in spring	Direct-sow; do not transplant well.
PEPPERS	10–12	2–4 weeks after last frost, when soil has warmed	Easy
PINKS (DIANTHUS)	6–8 for annuals; 8–10 for perennials	Direct-sow annuals or transplant perennials in early spring, after last heavy frost, 1–2 weeks before last frost date. Or	Easy, but do not bury crowns.

PLANTING GUIDE

Plant name	Weeks before planting out to start seeds indoors	Weeks before or after last frost to set out	Ease or difficulty of transplanting
PINKS (continued)		sow perennials outdoors in early fall.	
POTATOES	—	Plant seed potatoes 1–2 weeks before last frost.	Use seed potatoes; plant directly in garden.
RADICCHIO	—	Direct-sow in late spring, to 3 weeks after last frost.	Does not transplant well.
RADISHES	—	As soon as soil can be worked, 4–6 weeks before last frost, or 60 days before first fall frost	Direct-sow; grow so quickly they're not worth starting indoors.
ROSEMARY	—	2–3 weeks after last frost	Start with nursery plants or cuttings; difficult to germinate.
SAGE	—	4 weeks after last frost	Start from nursery plants or cuttings; slow to reach harvest size from seed.
SHALLOTS	—	Early to late spring; or indoors in winter	Start from sets.
SORREL	—	Sow in mid-spring, when soil temperature is at least 60°F; or in fall.	Direct-sow.
SPINACH	4–6	1–4 weeks before last frost; or plant in late summer for fall harvest.	Transplant with care to minimize root disturbance; direct-sow if possible.
SQUASH	4	2–4 weeks after last frost, when soil has warmed	Transplant with great care to minimize root disturbance; best to direct-sow.
TARRAGON	—	2–3 weeks after last frost	True French tarragon does not produce seeds; start from nursery plants or cuttings.
THYME	10–12	3–4 weeks after last frost	Easy
TOMATOES	6–8	2–4 weeks after last frost	Easy

PLANTING GUIDE

Plant name	Weeks before planting out to start seeds indoors	Weeks before or after last frost to set out	Ease or difficulty of transplanting
TURNIPS	—	2–3 weeks before last spring frost; or 8–10 weeks before first fall frost	Easiest to direct-sow
VIOLETS	—	Around last frost date	Start with plants or divisions.

WHAT TO PLANT INDOORS IN SPRING

By March everybody's ready for spring. And in warmer climates outdoor planting is underway. But for those of us farther north, the weather in March is usually unsettled, and gardening efforts are focused indoors. Although you may already have planted some seeds in February, this month is a good time to start many plants indoors or in the cold frame. The table, Planting Guide, gives information on planting times for a number of edible plants.

In the first week of March most of us can start seeds of head lettuce, other salad greens, early varieties of cabbage, broccoli, cauliflower, brussels sprouts, annual flowers, and a number of herbs. In mid-March it's time to start eggplant, peppers, and tomatoes. Later in the month gardeners in the North, where the outdoor growing season is short, can try their hand at winter squash, melons, and cucumbers. These plants are difficult to transplant successfully, but they need a long frost-free growing season. There are some early-maturing varieties that are recommended for northern gardens, but if you want to grow some of the traditional favorites, you may have to start them indoors in order to get a harvest before the first fall frost. To improve the odds, start seeds of these crops in peat pots or soil blocks so that their roots will suffer minimum disturbance during transplanting.

By late March the seedlings you started in February may be ready to transplant to larger containers. Continue to transplant as seedlings become ready throughout April, too.

PREPARING FOR PLANTING OUTDOORS

In spring, as soon as the soil is ready to work, it is time to dig the garden. The classic test for determining whether soil is ready to work is to squeeze some into a ball in your hand. When you open your fingers, if the soil ball sticks together, the soil is still too wet. Digging now could cause compaction. But if the soil ball falls apart, the garden is ready for digging.

Garden soil should be loose to a depth of at least a foot. For the very best tilth, you can double-dig. That involves removing the soil to the depth of a spade (about a foot), then loosening the subsoil with a spading fork. Double-digging is backbreaking work, and if hard labor is not your idea of gardening, you can probably skip it. In most soils it is not essential. But do be sure to dig and turn over your soil to a depth of at least a foot. Break up any large lumps and clods, remove any sizable stones, and rake the surface smooth.

PLANTING OUTDOORS IN SPRING

Onions and peas are usually the first crops to be planted in spring. Where I grew up in Pennsylvania, old-timers used to watch for the "onion snow"—the last snowfall of the season, usually in March, after which it was considered time to plant onion sets in the garden. In some areas, the traditional date for planting peas is St. Patrick's Day (or St. Joseph's Day, March 19, if you're of Italian descent). So strictly do some gardeners adhere to these dates that they can be seen putting in their peas even in the driving rain . . . or snow. Although I'm all for getting an early start in the garden, I don't believe in planting under adverse weather conditions. If the soil is too wet and cold the seeds won't germinate anyway. Although they grow best in cool weather, peas actually cannot withstand serious frost and prolonged subfreezing weather. It makes more sense to wait a week or two, if necessary, until the weather settles and the soil is in better shape before you plant.

In late March or early April, or four to six weeks before the date of your last expected frost, provided the weather is not unusually cold, a number of cool-weather crops can go into the garden. You can direct-sow peas, radishes, spinach, and kale, and plant garlic, onions, and shallots from cloves and sets. You can plant lettuce if you protect it with hot caps or row covers (see Chapter Two for information). It is also time to start hardening-off some of the seedlings growing indoors, to prepare them for planting in the outdoor garden. Broccoli, brussels sprouts, cabbage, kohlrabi, and leeks can all

THE FASTEST-MATURING VEGETABLES

To get the quickest harvest from spring crops, check seed catalogs to find the varieties of each crop that mature fastest. Also bear in mind which vegetables in general will grow to harvestable size fastest. The following plants will be ready for harvest in approximately the number of days given for each. This is the number of days from sowing of seeds to the start of the harvest.

Arugula: 35 days
Beets: 55 to 60 days
Broccoli (early varieties): 55 days
Chard: 60 days
Garden cress: 20 days
Kohlrabi: 60 days

Leaf lettuce: 45 days
Mustard: 45 days
Peas (early varieties): 55 days
Radishes: 25 days
Scallions: 40 days
Spinach: 50 days

be readied for transplanting. If you have a cold frame, put the containers of seedlings there and harden them off as explained later in this chapter.

If the weather has been wetter and colder than usual this year, and you haven't been able to prepare the soil for planting these early crops, you can resort to artificial means to warm up the ground. Cover the planting area with a sheet of clear plastic for a week. At the end of that time, if you have had some sunny weather, the soil should be warmer and drier, and if you are lucky, ready for planting.

If you're adventurous, you can try planting some seeds that would not normally go into the garden for a few more weeks (beans, perhaps) and cover the area with a plastic tent or tunnel. Use a sheet of heavy-duty transparent polyethylene and support it on a framework of lath strips, plastic tubing, or wire hoops. You can gain a few weeks on the outdoor growing season this way. It's a gamble dependent on the weather, but worth a try and has great brag value when it works.

By late April or early May, or two to four weeks before you expect your last frost, you can plant Swiss chard, more lettuce, garden cress, arugula, sorrel, chervil, beets, carrots, mustard greens, celeriac, endive, escarole, more radishes, and parsnips. Bear in mind that kohlrabi and other cabbage relatives are all subject to the same pests and diseases. Planting them all in the same part of the garden will make it easier to plan for the annual crop rotations that help avoid disease problems, but it will also make it easier for pests to find all the foods they like.

Intrepid gardeners eager for the taste of the first squash or cucumbers can try sowing some seeds now and covering each hill with a hot cap or plastic tent (see Chapter Two for more information on hot caps). You could also gamble on a couple of tomato plants, and set out hardened-off seedlings in the cold frame or in the garden under hot caps or cloches.

By now your peas will be up, and garlic and onions planted a month ago will also have sprouted.

Around the first week of May you can begin to harden-off seedlings of tender plants—tomatoes, peppers, eggplant, cucumbers, and squash—to prepare them for their transition to outdoor life. These plants cannot tolerate any frost, so wait at least a week after your last frost date to plant beans, okra, tomatoes, and sunflowers. The tenderest crops of all should wait one additional week before planting. This very tender group includes lima beans, cucumbers, eggplant, peppers, and both summer and winter squash. Basil is the tenderest of the herbs, and can go into the garden with this last group of vegetables. All these plants need temperatures of at least 70°F in order to really get growing. If nighttime temperatures drop below 40°F you are likely to see damage to the tender leaves.

SPRING PLANTING IN WARM CLIMATES

Peas, onions, lettuce, and other cool-weather crops are grown in winter throughout much of the South and Southwest. By spring the harvest is well underway. As soon as the danger of frost is past in March, sow seeds of beans, corn, squash, and cucumbers directly in the garden. Set out tomato and pepper transplants. A few weeks later (early April in many gardens) set out eggplant and okra. This is also a good time to plant nasturtiums and other tender flowers, along with basil, rosemary, marjoram, summer savory, and other tender herbs.

THE SPRING HARVEST

The first harvests from the spring garden are snippings of leaves here and there from chives and salad greens. You can also eat the leaves of seedlings thinned from rows or beds of beets, lettuce, arugula, cress, sorrel, and other greens. If you can let the seedlings grow until they're several inches tall before thinning, the harvest will be worthwhile, and you will have a nice handful of tender young leaves to add to a late April or early May salad. If you are a salad lover, spring is an ideal time to grow *mesclun*, a French style mixture of salad plants that are planted together and harvested young. The Cook's Garden (see Appendix) sells several different *mesclun* mixes.

By the middle of May, if the weather cooperates, you can probably start to cut the first spears of asparagus, and pull the first radishes. Harvest asparagus by cutting the spears close to the ground with a sharp knife. You may also have some small scallions to harvest as you thin your onions. By the end of May, four weeks after the last frost, salad greens will be producing in earnest, along with radishes, chives, and

How to Pick the Best Plants at the Garden Center

When confronted with a sea of little green seedlings at the garden center, how do you decide which ones to buy? Here are some helpful tips. Above all, remember that bigger is not necessarily better. Large seedlings will have a harder time making the transition to the garden, and their growth will likely be set back after transplanting. Big plants have also probably outgrown their little nursery containers, and will be weakened by lack of moisture and nutrients. They will undoubtedly be rootbound, too.

Instead of looking for the biggest plants, look for seedlings whose leaves are a good green color, and firm in texture, whose stems are stocky and straight. Look for compact size, with the leaves close together on the stems.

Avoid buying seedlings with yellowish leaves, or leaves with a purplish cast (unless you are buying a red- or purple-leaved variety, of course). Don't buy plants with insects or insect eggs on the undersides of the leaves. Shaking the plant gently will show you if there are whiteflies—they will fly up like a little cloud around the plant. Check the axils of the leaves (where leaves join stem) for aphids and other pests. Don't spend your money on spindly, floppy plants that haven't gotten enough light, or flaccid, wilted plants that are water stressed.

Follow these guidelines and you will soon learn to recognize the healthiest plants at the garden center.

The healthy, stocky seedling on the left is a much better choice at the garden center than the pale, lanky specimen on the right.

parsley, and spinach will be getting started, too.

By mid-June you may be able to pick the first fresh peas, if you got them into the ground by the end of March, and the first leaves of Swiss chard will be ready. The harvest of salad greens and radishes continues, along with scallions, if you planted enough extra onion sets to allow for both early scallions and mature onion bulbs later on.

In warm climates the spring harvest comes earlier. Gardeners in these areas will be picking lettuce, arugula, Swiss chard, and other greens, and pulling radishes, beets, and carrots in early and mid-spring. Peas and spinach that were planted in winter are also harvested in spring. Asparagus will be finished in many gardens by the end of April. The last harvests of all these crops are made before the weather really gets hot in late spring.

Early potatoes and corn are also ready for harvest later in spring.

EXTENDING THE HARVEST

Most leafy spring crops—leaf lettuce, spinach, arugula, and other greens—stop producing and bolt to seed when the hot weather and long days of summer arrive. To extend the harvest and get the maximum production from these leafy crops, make sure they receive plenty of water, and give them some shade. You can provide shade

Shade netting can help postpone bolting and extend the harvest of spring crops into summer. The netting allows air and water to get to plants while cutting down on the amount of hot sunlight.

by covering the rows or beds with agricultural shade netting of polypropylene. The netting lets in air and moisture while reducing the amount of sunlight striking the plants by as much as 50 percent. At this time of year, less sunlight means less heat, which is the critical factor in keeping many leaf crops from bolting. Drape the netting over plastic or wire hoops, or some other framework, to keep it from weighing down delicate leaves. This netting can be ordered from several of the suppliers listed in the Appendix.

HOW TO HARDEN-OFF SEEDLINGS

Seedlings that begin their lives indoors or in a greenhouse need time to adjust to the cold conditions of the outdoor garden in spring. The process of gradually acclimating seedlings to outdoor weather is known as hardening-off. Basically what you do is expose the plants to increasing amounts of outdoor weather over a period of days until they are able to withstand the nighttime low temperatures and bright sunlight without suffering any ill effects.

Hardening-off is important, because seedlings damaged by the cold will at best be set back in their growth. At worst they can be killed, and all your weeks of careful tending will have been in vain.

Approximately fourteen to twenty days before beginning the hardening-off process, begin to pamper your seedlings a bit less. The idea is not to stress them, but just to start toughening them up a bit. Allow a bit more time between waterings; not so long that the plants wilt, but so that the soil dries out to a greater depth and roots are forced to reach for water. This will encourage the roots to grow downward, as they will have

to out in the garden to survive during dry spells, and also to create a sturdy anchor for the plant. Also stop fertilizing the plants at this time.

A cold frame, if you have one, is a great place to harden-off seedlings. Place the containers of plants in the frame and open the cover for a longer time each day (follow the same procedure to harden-off seedlings you seeded directly in the cold frame). Open the cover for about two hours the first day, and leave it open two to three hours longer each succeeding day over a period of seven to ten days. The last night leave the cover open all night. By this time the seedlings should be ready to brave the rigors of the garden. Of course, the lid of the cold frame should remain closed during bad weather. If you get rain, or even some late snow, extend the hardening-off period by several days.

If you do not have a cold frame, you can harden-off seedlings by moving them outdoors during the day and bringing them back indoors after the appropriate length of time. Try to put them in a sheltered place during inclement weather; an outdoor porch with a roof makes a good location. And keep the plants protected from strong winds at first, too, until their stems are tougher. Follow the same timetable suggested for hardening-off plants in a cold frame.

No matter where you harden-off your seedlings, don't forget to water when they need it. A couple of days into the hardening-off process, fertilize the seedlings with a solution of seaweed concentrate or fish emulsion diluted to one-half the strength recommended for normal use. This nutrient boost will help the plants fight off transplant shock.

If the weather is poor when it's time to transplant—rainy, windy, or unseasonably cold—wait until it settles before setting out the young plants. Postponing transplanting a few days or a week won't make much difference to you, and could make all the difference to your plants. Harsh weather conditions may set back the new transplants and delay the harvest further than waiting to plant until growing conditions are more hospitable.

When the seedlings have been hardened-off and the weather is favorable, transplant them according to the directions given in Chapter Two.

MAINTENANCE ACTIVITIES IN THE SPRING GARDEN

Besides starting new plants, there are other garden chores to be done in spring. Early in the season (March in many places) prepare for spring planting by spreading a layer of compost, adding whatever fertilizers are necessary, and tilling the soil when it has dried out enough to be workable. If you started a compost pile late last fall, turn it as soon as it thaws out. As you remove winter mulches from your garden beds, put the mulch on the compost pile.

Think ahead to meeting the needs of the earliest crops you will be planting. Peas will need supports to climb on, and it is best to install the trellises, stakes, netting, or tripods before you plant the seeds. If your garden is in a windy location, young plants will benefit from a windbreak installed on the side of the garden facing into the prevailing winds.

If you have an established asparagus bed, cut off any old stalks remaining from last year before the new spears start to push. This is also the time to weed and fertilize the bed, and cultivate lightly and carefully to avoid disturbing the roots. In northern gardens, it is a good idea to mulch asparagus beds so the earliest new spears will not suffer any frost damage.

If your weather turns cold, protect young seedlings with hot caps, cloches, or covers at night. Protection is especially important for tender seedlings (such as cucumbers) that you planted a week or two early. If you are growing members of the cabbage family, make sure all the plants have cutworm collars. Cutworms, the larvae of a fly, are small worms about an inch long that attack the stems of seedlings, chewing through them near the base. If cutworms are at work in your garden you will come out one morning to find what were perfectly healthy seedlings lying flat on the ground. It is particularly annoying that the worms do not eat the plants after mowing them down. Cutworms are especially fond of the cabbage family. But placing a simple collar of cardboard or tar paper used for roofing around each plant will keep cutworms from getting to them. The collar should extend about an inch below the soil surface and rise a couple of inches above it. Make them from paper cups with the bottoms removed, or cut apart cardboard milk cartons horizontally into bands. Or cut strips of tar paper and staple the ends together to make rings.

If you have a fireplace or wood stove, you will find a number of uses for wood ashes in spring. If you have planted onions, you may want to scatter wood ashes around them to keep onion maggot flies from laying eggs. Wood ashes also keep root maggots from carrots and radishes. Some gardeners claim that topdressing potatoes with wood ashes improves their flavor.

Early spring is the time to prepare garden paths for the season, too. If you don't have permanent paths of brick or stone in your garden, spread straw on pathways or lay down boards to keep your shoes clean. If you place bricks or wood blocks under the ends of the boards to lift them off the soil surface, they will last longer without rotting, and will also not provide a hiding place for slugs and earwigs.

Even in spring it is important to be sure plants have enough moisture. During dry weather keep your plants well watered. New transplants need to be watered every day unless it rains, until their roots begin to

There are lots of ways to provide support for peas and pole beans. Four options are, left to right, a collapsible metal frame covered with grow netting, a circular maypole-type arrangement, a corridor of stakes and string, and a tripod of tall wooden stakes.

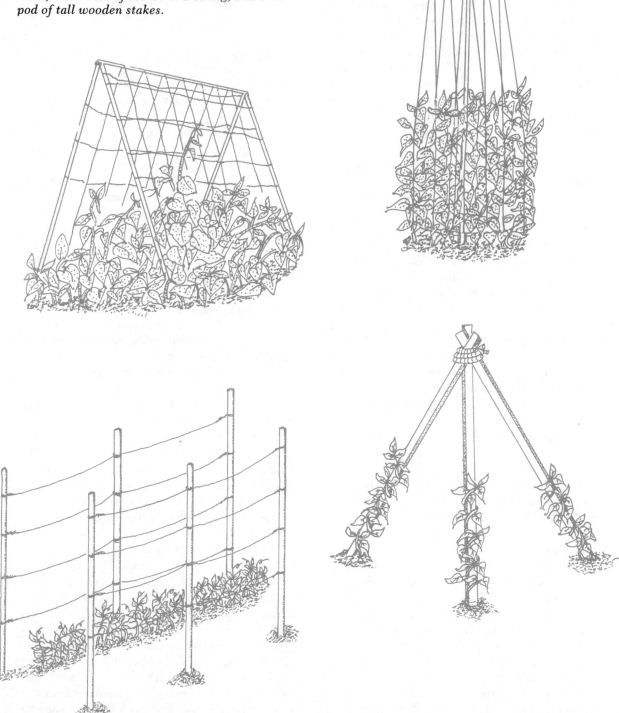

grow. When the plants become established in the garden and have started to grow, you may want to mulch them to conserve soil moisture.

By sometime in April, depending on your location and this year's weather conditions, peas, onions, and garlic will all have started to grow. This is a good time to decide on a succession crop to follow the peas when they are harvested.

As spring progresses, keep an eye on areas where you have planted seeds, and thin young seedlings as needed. If you thin several times as plants grow, you can eat the larger thinnings of beets, salad greens, and onions in salads. Thinning continues throughout the season as new crops are planted, until plants reach their final spacing distance. Keep an eye on onions and if you spot any seed heads on the tops of stalks snap them off so the plants put their energy 705into producing bulbs.

In mid-spring, northern gardeners can harden-off seedlings of warm-weather vegetables to prepare them for planting out near the end of May. This is also the time of year when cabbage butterflies lay their eggs, so dust plants in the cabbage family with *Bacillus thuringiensis* to prevent the laying of eggs that will hatch cabbage worms.

Spring is the time to divide mature plantings of perennial herbs such as mints, thyme, and oregano.

By late spring garden maintenance is in full swing. Monitor moisture levels and water during dry spells. Inspect plants carefully and often for signs of pests or diseases and take appropriate action immediately if you notice problems. Holes in leaves, raggedy, chewed edges, and fine webbing in leaf axils all indicate the presence of insects. Aphids gather in the leaf axils, and numerous bugs lay their eggs on the undersides of leaves. Yellowing, brown spots, moldy patches, and withering of leaves are all indications of disease problems.

Weeds are happily growing now, too, so keep them pulled or they will compete with your garden plants for nutrients and moisture. Make sure all plants that need stakes or other supports have them.

SPRING GARDENS IN WARM CLIMATES

In warm-climate gardens spring is farther advanced, and the maintenance schedule picks up speed sooner than in the North. Tender plants are out in the garden in March or April in warm climates, and temperatures are rising steadily. Watering is essential in spring, and mulches should be in place in Florida and other areas where spring weather is often dry. Incorporating plenty of organic matter into the soil also helps to hold moisture for thirsty plants.

Be sure tomatoes have stakes or cages. Tomatoes often suffer from blossom-end rot in southern gardens because of fluctuating moisture levels and temperatures in the soil. A good layer of mulch will help avoid the problem, as will careful attention to watering, and sidedressing or foliar feeding with a well-balanced fertilizer.

Inspect your plants carefully and often for signs of pests and diseases, and take immediate action if you notice any problems. Gardens are especially susceptible to disease in hot, humid climates where the air is often heavy and still, so be vigilant.

As spring progresses, provide shade and extra water for lettuce and other leafy crops to extend the harvest period.

After harvesting early crops (onions, shallots, garlic, peas, radishes, beets, carrots, spinach, lettuce, and Swiss chard), clean up the beds or rows that contained them. Replant with tomatoes, eggplant, and other tender crops, or use summer's intense heat to do some soil-building instead. Work lots of compost and composted manure into the soil and let it mellow over the summer to prepare this part of the garden for fall planting. This is a good time to plan your fall plantings and prepare seed orders.

Late in spring, when cucumbers and squash are in bloom, warm-climate gardeners may need to help pollination along because the weather is too warm for bees. Use an artist's paintbrush to transfer pollen from male to female flowers, or just rub a male flower with ripe (loose) pollen against the pistils in female flowers. Female flowers have a swelling at the base that becomes the fruit; male flowers do not have this swelling. If you are training cucumbers, squash, and other vining crops on a trellis to save space, do not use a wire trellis; the metal may get hot enough in the intense sun to scorch the plants' delicate tendrils.

FOUR

The Summer Garden

FOR MOST OF US, summer is a time of lushness, growth, and bounty. In the garden it is the most sensual of seasons, rich with colors, scents, and flavors. Late salad crops still lend their smooth or ruffled leaves of lime, deep emerald, or bright green to the garden palette. They are joined in summer by herb foliage in an array of textures, from feathery dill and caraway to spiky chives and garlic chives to frilly parsley to tiny-leaved thyme. The jewellike tones of edible blossoms and the ripening fruits of tomatoes, eggplant, and peppers add grace notes of color to the symphony of greens. The fiery reds, golds, and russets of nasturtiums foreshadow the hues of fall, while the cool blue blossoms of borage seem to reflect the summer sky above. Bean pods grow long and fat on the vine; squash and cucumbers ramble around their garden beds or clamber up trellises. The heady aromas of basil and rosemary mingle with the sweet scents of dianthus and lavender, and all are intensified on a hot, humid day when the air is still.

Summer is a time of heat, of long, languid days. For gardeners, though, summer is anything but lazy and hazy; it is the busiest time of year in all but the hottest climates. We are busy planting, harvesting, weeding, and watering. But working in the garden is a pleasure, and in summer it's a joy to be outdoors, especially in the morning and early evening, when the heat is not so intense.

THE SUMMER HARVEST

In early summer there are still lettuce, spinach, arugula, cress, and other salad crops to

The variety of scallop or pattypan squash shown here, Peter Pan, can be picked young as a baby vegetable, or left to grow to 4 or 5 inches across. Unlike most other scallop squashes, which have creamy white skin, this variety is light green.

The Summer Garden 79

BABY VEGETABLES

Recent years have seen baby vegetables become the darlings of food fashion; they have shown up in gourmet produce shops and on the menus of trendy restaurants on both coasts. Despite their trendiness, baby vegetables do have a great deal to recommend them. Their flesh is tender and succulent. Their seeds are smaller and less noticeable than those of larger, older vegetables. You don't need to peel them; the skins of carrots, beets, and eggplants, which are usually removed from larger vegetables, are much more tender when they are young. Baby vegetables cook quickly and look pretty when served. Some of them, in particular some of the squashes and lettuces, can be prepared as single servings for individual diners.

Baby vegetables capture the taste of summer and add yet another item to your kitchen repertoire. When you grow them yourself you can be assured of peak quality. You can harvest the vegetables right when you're ready to prepare them, eliminating the shipping and storage time that can rob commercially available vegetables of texture and flavor. You will also save money; baby vegetables are quite expensive to buy. Miniature scallop squash, for example, sells for about $7 a pound where I live.

To grow the best baby vegetables, you need the plants to grow fast, and produce their harvest quickly. Give them the very best growing environment you can. Provide loose, crumbly soil that is rich in organic matter and nutrients. Make sure the plants get lots of sun and plenty of moisture. When the harvest begins, keep up with it. Check the garden every day. Baby squash is picked from one to three days after the flowers are pollinated. Do not leave any vegetables to mature on the plants, or growth will slow down. Directions on harvesting individual vegetables are given in Chapter Seven. Here are some varieties to grow for baby vegetables.

BEANS

Camile
Dandy
Finaud
Triumph de Farcy

BEETS

Dwergina
Little Ball
Spinel

CARROTS

Little Finger
Minicor
Parmex
Sucram

EGGPLANT

Easter Egg
Little Fingers
Purple Pickling
Slim Jim

LETTUCE

Baby Oak
Little Gem
Sucrine
Summer Baby Bibb
Tom Thumb

PEPPERS

Canape

SQUASH

Aristocrat
French White Bush
Gold Rush
Peter Pan
Seneca
Sunburst
Sun Drops

TOMATOES

Gem State
Gold Nugget
Pixie Hybrid
Red Cherry
Sundrop
Tiny Tim

TURNIPS

Tokyo Market

pick. These leafy plants will keep producing longer if you give them some shade, especially around noon when the sun is at its hottest. Northern gardeners are picking peas in early summer. As the hot weather settles in, these early crops give way to Swiss chard, beans, cucumbers, and the first zucchini of the season. The first tomato is an annual highlight for many gardeners. There are also shallots and, later on, onions. Baby vegetables are a special treat in summer.

Some standard vegetables when picked small and young, such as beets and zucchini, are more tender, more delicate in texture and flavor than when left to mature fully. And there are more and more vegetable varieties specially bred to be ready for harvest when still small. Many of these diminutive cultivars are perfect for growing in containers or small gardens where space is limited. The selection includes, for example, Little Fingers eggplant, Sun Drops squash, Little Gem lettuce, Parmex carrots, and Gem State tomatoes. See the box, Baby Vegetables, for more on these summertime treats. Chapter Seven contains information on small varieties of individual vegetables.

Another special delight in summer are the exquisite flavors of freshly picked herbs. Chives, basil, thyme, parsley, rosemary, marjoram, chervil, oregano, tarragon, dill— what a great pleasure it is to pick a few leaves or sprigs of favorite herbs to toss into salads, chop up into vegetables dishes and pasta sauces, or sprinkle over grilled fish and meats. For me, the taste of fresh herbs is the taste of summer itself. Although now we can buy small bunches of fresh herbs in the market year-round—or grow them ourselves on winter windowsills—the flavor is somehow never quite the same as when you pick the herbs right outside your door on a summer day.

And flowers lend their special qualities, too. Think of a tossed salad bright with the colors of chive blossoms. A cooling glass of iced tea with refreshing blue borage blossoms floating in it. A creamy soup with a few nasturtium blossoms adrift on top. Edible flowers lend a distinctive touch to summer cooking.

Here is a rundown of some of the highlights of the summer harvest. The important thing to keep in mind is to keep vegetables picked as they mature. Big, leathery beans and zucchini left to become the size of baseball bats make poor eating and also rob water from developing fruits that need it. On flowering plants, dehead flowers as they fade, even when you can't use them all in the kitchen, to keep the plants blooming longer. Many annuals will bloom all summer if you keep dead flowers picked off so they can't set seed, and even perennials will bloom longer when deheaded regularly.

In early summer, the first beets and Swiss chard will be ready to harvest if you got them planted early. Beets and chard planted in April will be big enough to eat beginning around the middle of June. You can keep picking Swiss chard all summer and into fall. Leaf lettuce and other salad greens will also still be harvestable in early summer. The leafy harvest will continue longer in cool climates and in gardens where the plants are given plenty of water and some shade as the weather gets hot. Heat-resistant varieties such as Oak Leaf can be kept going through much of summer, especially in the North.

Midsummer will bring the first harvests of leaf lettuce planted in spring, parsley started from seed in May, and some cabbage-family members. Spring-planted broccoli is harvested in midsummer, with side shoots ready for picking about two weeks after the main head is cut. Cauliflower is ready to harvest when the heads are full, firm, and tight, before the curds turn ricey. Cauliflower needs to be blanched in early summer to keep the developing heads nice and white; see Chapter Seven for details. Early varieties of cabbage are ready to pick when the heads are full and round, but before they split open. If you are growing a miniature variety, look for mature heads to

Common thyme, above, tumbles over bricks edging this small garden. Its tiny summer flowers can be eaten right along with the aromatic leaves.

Coriander, or cilantro, below, is an essential ingredient in Mexican and Chinese dishes. Its flowers attract bees to the garden.

be about the size of softballs. Kohlrabi planted early in spring is also ready for harvest in midsummer. All these crops taste best if you can harvest them before summer reaches its peak. If summer weather tends to heat up early where you live, you will probably do better if you plant the cabbage family in mid to late summer to mature in fall when the weather is cooler.

The carrot harvest begins in mid to late summer, depending on the variety and when you planted. But carrots are one crop that need not be harvested as soon as they mature. You can leave them in the ground all summer long—even into winter if you mulch them—and dig as needed.

If you planted turnips in spring you can dig them in midsummer. Or plant them in midsummer to harvest in fall.

Summer is the season when fruiting crops come into their own. Beans are picked from mid to late summer, depending on the variety. Snap beans will be ready sooner than limas, which need a fairly long, warm growing season to develop properly. The annual inundation of summer squash begins in midsummer, too. At this time of year gardeners desperate to cope with an avalanche of zucchini have been known to make zucchini pickles and zucchini bread, not to mention gifting friends, neighbors, and relatives with the bounty of the vine. If you planted prudently and find that you are not overwhelmed with excess squash, you may want to take advantage of the fact that picking the squash when young will boost the productivity of the plants. Letting the fruits grow bigger before you pick them will slow down production. For an interesting change, pick some squash blossoms (male flowers, if you don't want to reduce fruit production) and stuff or batter-dip and fry them.

Solanaceous crops (members of the nightshade family) are the other stars of the summer garden. This clan includes eggplant, tomatoes, peppers, and potatoes, the first three of which are picked from mid to late summer into fall, when the weather turns cool. The plants will produce right up till frost, but some varieties, especially of tomatoes, lose flavor and decline in quality when the weather cools down.

If you are growing cucumbers, check them often from midsummer on to find developing fruits. Pick them while they are still a good green color, before they turn yellowish or white. Older cukes have bigger seeds and tend to be bitter and not as juicy and crunchy as younger fruits picked at their peak. If you are growing the cucumbers on a trellis to save space, check regularly to make sure all the vines are still fastened to their supports. If you find some crawling across the ground or growing at a crazy angle on the trellis, gently pick them up or unwind them, straighten them out, and fasten them to the support with soft yarn or loose twist-ties. Gardeners with the space and inclination to grow sweet corn

Red-ripe, juicy tomatoes are still the pride and joy of most vegetable gardeners, an incomparable summertime delight.

and potatoes will be able to dig some new potatoes in mid to late summer, and pick corn in late summer and early fall.

The herb harvest continues all summer. Snip leaves as needed. Picking off developing flower heads of dill will postpone bloom and prolong the foliage harvest, but sooner or later the plants will go to seed, no matter what you do. If you collect the seeds (see Chapter Five for instructions), leave a few flower heads to drop their seeds in the garden; chances are good that you will have volunteer seedlings early next spring.

As summer draws to a close, northern gardeners can extend the harvest into fall by covering tender plants on cool nights. In addition, succession planting, and planting some varieties with slower maturation times, will give you the longest possible harvest of your favorite summer vegetables. In some high-altitude gardens, frost can come as early as the end of August. Keep harvesting vegetables as soon as they are ready in late summer to get them out of the way of a surprise early frost.

If frost comes early in your garden, late summer is the time to cut down your herb plants and dry or freeze them for winter storage. See the section in Chapter Five on Harvesting and Storing Herbs, and Chapter Seven under the specific herb, for more information.

If you are growing onions, start watching for the tops to fall. When two-thirds of them have fallen, push the rest down. It will soon be time to dig the bulbs. See Chapter Seven for details.

THE SUMMER HARVEST IN
WARM CLIMATES

In the Southeast and other warm climates, the summer harvest comes earlier. Gardeners in these areas are picking snap beans, summer squash, corn, and cucumbers in early June. Later in the month eggplant, tomatoes, peppers, okra, and lima beans are ready. Keep harvesting and watering all these plants to keep them producing as long as possible. By August the weather is too hot for most vegetables to grow well, and most gardening efforts are aimed at preparing for fall planting. Okra and eggplant, though, hold up well in hot weather and keep producing until fall in many gardens.

FEASTING ON FLOWERS

Flowers are pleasing to the eye, of course, but some of them please our palates as well. The jewellike colors of some of our favorite flowers can dress up a summertime salad or garnish a special dessert. Eating flowers is nothing new; people all over the world have been doing it for thousands of years. The ancient Romans ate roses. So did Arabian people; rose water flavors a confection known as Turkish Delight. Rose petals and violets can be candied, brandied, or chopped and sprinkled over desserts. The Elizabethans enjoyed candied violets, and ate salads made of flowers because they believed flowers were easier to digest than greens. Chrysanthemums are popular in Japan; there is even a special type, known as *shungiku*, which is grown expressly for consumption. The tea that, along with madeleines, transported Marcel Proust's memory back to his childhood was made from the flowers of the linden tree. The petals of calendulas can be used as a substitute for costly saffron (which is itself made from the dried anthers of a species of crocus). Nasturtium leaves and flowers taste like watercress, and add a peppery zing to salads. Alice B. Toklas was known to make a salad of nasturtiums and chervil dressed with oil and lemon juice. Nasturtium seed pods can be pickled like capers. Daylily and gladiolus blossoms can be stuffed like squash blossoms, or daylily buds can be dipped in batter and fried (in China they are known as golden needles). Pansies and Johnny jump-ups don't offer much in the way of flavor, but they are a pretty—if bland-tasting—garnish. Violets can be candied (brush the petals with beaten egg white, then dust them with very fine granulated sugar) and used to decorate cakes and other desserts. Carnations, lavender, and other fragrant blossoms can be used to make flavored oils, waters, vinegars, wines, butters, jellies, and ice creams.

From the herb garden, borage flowers can be sprinkled over salads or floated in glasses of iced tea. They have a fresh flavor, something like cucumber. Tiny thyme blossoms can be tossed into salads, sprinkled over fish, and used right along with the thyme leaves. Chive flowers have a very mild onion flavor and a pretty purplish pink color. The beautiful, starry white flowers of garlic chives have a bit of garlic to them.

Edible flowers include beebalm, borage, calendulas, carnations, chamomile, chives, chrysanthemums, daylilies, dill, forget-me-nots, garlic chives, scented geraniums, gladioli, hollyhocks, honeysuckle, hyssop, Johnny jump-ups, lavender, lilacs, dwarf marigolds, marjoram, nasturtiums, oregano, pansies, pineapple sage, roses, squash blossoms, thyme, and violets.

Nasturtiums have a mildly peppery flavor similar to that of watercress. They add zing to salads and sandwiches, and can be chopped and blended with softened butter for a colorful spread.

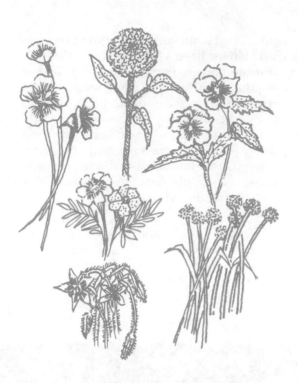

Edible flowers delight both the eye and the palate. A few to grow in your kitchen garden are, clockwise from top, calendula, pansy, chive blossoms, borage, marigold, and nasturtium.

marigolds, monkshood, narcissus and daffodils, oleander, periwinkle, German primroses, snow-on-the-mountain, sweet peas, and wisteria. Do not eat *any* flower unless you know that it is safe.

To prepare edible flowers for the table, pick them in the morning, if possible, when they are fresh and firm. Handle them very gently. Wash them carefully in cold water. If the flowers have prominent stamens and pistils, remove them—they usually taste bitter. Cut off the stem right at the base of the flower. Refrigerate the flowers until you are ready to use them; most will keep for several days in the refrigerator.

Recipes for using edible flowers are easier to come by than they used to be. Two of my favorite sources of information on preparing edible flowers (and other garden produce) are *Recipes from a Kitchen Garden,* volumes 1 and 2, by Renee Shepherd (available from Shepherd's Garden Publishing, 7389 W. Zayante Rd., Felton, CA 95018), and *Cooking from the Garden,* by Rosalind Creasy (Sierra Club Books, 1988).

SUMMER GARDEN MAINTENANCE

There are some cautions to keep in mind, though, if you decide to add flowers to the menu. Some flowers are highly poisonous, and several can even cause death. Never use those flowers in the kitchen. Use only homegrown blossoms, and grow your flowers organically. Many florist flowers have been treated with pesticides or chemical preservatives that should not be ingested. Following is a list of flowers that should not be eaten: anemones, datura, autumn crocuses, azaleas and rhododendrons, bleeding heart, buttercups, Christmas roses, clematis, daphne, delphiniums, Dutchman's breeches, four o'clocks, foxgloves, hyacinths, lily-of-the-valley, lupines, marsh

One of the most essential elements in maintaining a healthy garden in summer is sufficient water. Garden plants need plenty of water to fuel their growth and mature their crops. Most parts of the United States are subject to at least occasional dry spells in summer, and in some regions, like southern California and the desert Southwest, drought is an annual occurrence. Water shortages are expected to become more widespread and frequent in the years to come, as supplies of unpolluted groundwater decrease. *All* gardeners should become concerned with water conservation now.

There are a number of ways to conserve water and make more efficient use of water, and all of us should practice them, even if we are not yet feeling a shortage.

One of the best defenses against drought is a well-prepared soil, and organic matter is the key. A soil containing lots of organic matter is able to hold moisture while still draining well and not becoming waterlogged. The particles of organic matter absorb water like little sponges, retaining it for plants without allowing it to puddle in the soil and suffocate plant roots. Prepare your garden soil according to the guidelines given in Chapters Two and Three.

Plants can survive drought better when they are growing at a steady, even rate, and are adequately nourished but not overfed.

Avoid overfertilizing in spring, which causes plants to grow too quickly and weakens them.

To catch and hold runoff water for large plants, make a shallow depression in the soil around the base of each tomato, pepper, and eggplant, and other large plants in your garden.

Plant only as much as you need. Watering and feeding plants whose crops will eventually rot in the garden because you overplanted is a waste of resources. If you live where summers are dry, plant more crops to mature in spring and fall, and grow less in summer when you will have to water frequently. Be mindful of which plants are

CRITICAL WATERING TIMES

No matter what you are growing—vegetables, herbs, or edible flowers—there are some times when all plants need water. First, water drills or other planting areas immediately before you sow seeds of any plant. Unless conditions are very dry, try not to water again until seedlings emerge, to avoid disturbing the seeds. If you must water during the germination period, use a fine-rose attachment on a watering can, or a fine spray from a hose. Indoors, water containers of germinating seeds from the bottom.

New transplants also need water during their first couple of weeks in the garden. Water all new transplants every day that it doesn't rain.

Following is a rundown of critical times to water vegetables.

Asparagus: water after the harvest is over, when the fernlike foliage is growing.

Beans, peas: water when plants begin to bloom, and when pods start to develop right through the harvest period.

Broccoli, cabbage, cauliflower, and kale: these cabbage-family members need water regularly throughout the growing season. For broccoli, cabbage, and cauliflower water is especially critical when heads are developing. Brussels sprouts need less water once established in the garden.

Corn: needs water when tasselling and as cobs develop.

Eggplant, peppers: need water regularly throughout their growing season.

Fruiting crops (tomatoes, squash, cucumbers): water is important during flowering and fruit development.

Leafy crops (lettuce, spinach, Swiss chard, salad greens): need regular water throughout the growing season.

Onions, garlic, shallots: water regularly when bulbs are enlarging. Stop watering onions when tops fall.

Root crops (beets, carrots, radishes, parsnips, turnips): water only when soil starts to really dry out, every 2 to 3 weeks.

Leeks: need regular watering throughout the growing season.

able to tolerate dry, hot conditions; examples include nasturtiums, blue corn, and some special varieties of beans and summer squash.

Be intelligent about watering. Water plants during the critical times in their growth (see box), instead of simply watering once or twice a week all season. New transplants establishing roots, and larger plants with shallow root systems, are most in need of regular watering. When you do water, water deeply so plants develop long, deep roots that can seek out water well below the soil surface. Shallow watering encourages plants to grow feeder roots close to the soil surface, where they can suffer damage from heat and drought, which will weaken the plants and reduce their productivity. Overhead watering from sprinklers and hand-held hoses is the least efficient method. Instead, deliver water directly to the roots, where it is needed, by installing a drip irrigation system or inexpensive soaker hoses in your garden.

Water in the morning or early evening. When watering in the evening, do it early enough that leaves will dry before dark. Wet leaves at night invite disease problems. If you water during the hottest part of the day, much of the water will be lost to evaporation. In addition, water droplets on leaves can act like lenses to focus the sun's rays and actually burn foliage. When watering tender crops, if possible let the water warm up to air temperature before giving it to these crops. If you live in a hot climate where the summer sun is quite intense, do not let your garden hose sit out in the sun all afternoon and then use it to water the garden—the water passing through it, at least initially, may be hot enough to damage plants.

How often to water varies with the weather, soil type, and type of plants being grown. The old rule of making sure the garden gets an inch of water a week is a generalization. A better guideline is to poke a finger into the soil every day or two when it hasn't rained, as described in Chapter Two.

When the soil feels dry a couple of inches below the surface, it is time to water. Some places are drier in summer than others, and some soils drain faster than others. This test will let you water when *your* garden needs it.

Recycle household water for garden use whenever possible. Set out buckets to catch water that drips from window-mounted air conditioners and from rain gutters. You might even try an old-fashioned rain barrel, although unless you empty it often it will provide a perfect breeding ground for mosquitoes. If you have a dehumidifier, empty its collection bucket into the garden instead of pouring the water down the drain.

You can also recycle water used for bathing and laundry (called greywater), as long as you use detergents that contain no boron or chlorine. Another consideration is whether the soap residues (which are alkaline) will raise the pH of your soil. Most edibles like slightly acid soil, so test the pH if you are recycling greywater in your garden. In southern California, where drought is a persistent and growing problem, greywater management is rapidly gaining importance. It is only a matter of time before we face similar problems in the eastern part of the country. A helpful book on the use of greywater is Robert Kourik's *The Greywater Handbook* (to order a copy send $6.00 to Edible Publications, P.O. Box 1841, Santa Rosa, CA 95402).

Mulches are very helpful in conserving soil moisture. Organic mulches also help keep the soil cooler and the surface texture looser, protecting the bare soil from the baking rays of the sun. Save your grass clippings to use in summer mulches. See Work-Saving Strategies in Chapter One for information on using mulches. In northern gardens, plants that like lots of warmth may do better without mulch. You should also be aware that mulches offer swell hiding places for slugs and earwigs. If you have problems with these pests, you may want to avoid mulching. Or you could put out traps to lure them out of the garden.

Speaking of pests, summer is prime time for garden pests. The best defense is, first of all, constant vigilance. No matter what the culprit, if you catch an infestation in its early stages it will be easier to control. Inspect your plants every day for signs of pests and their damage. Tiny holes in leaves, raggedy edges, and chew marks are some signs that pests are present. Also look for a sticky sap on leaves and stems, or fine webbing between leaves and stems. Learn to recognize aphids, whiteflies, spider mites, squash borers, cabbageworms, potato beetles, and other summer pests. After a few years you will learn which pests are most prevalent in your vicinity. Look for the insects themselves on tender new shoots, in leaf axils, and on the undersides of leaves. Some insects lay their eggs on the undersides of leaves, too. Shaking plants gently will show you if whiteflies are present—they fly around the plant like a little cloud when disturbed.

Before taking any combative measures against bugs you see in the garden, make sure that they are pests. A number of insects are actually beneficial in gardens, helping to keep pest populations under control. Learn to recognize ladybugs and green lacewings, whose larvae consume pest insects. Parasitic wasps, such as ichneumon and trichogramma wasps, are also valuable. All of these helpful predators can be purchased for use as biological controls.

When you do have to actively fight garden pests, try the least drastic measures first. Chapter Two outlines basic methods of pest control. Because this is a garden of edibles you will probably want to concentrate on organic methods of pest and disease control. Wash aphids and whiteflies off plants with a strong spray of water from a hose. Use insecticidal soap on persistent aphids, flea beetles, spider mites, whiteflies, and other small bugs. Handpick and destroy larger pests such as potato beetles and cabbageworms if not too many are present.

If cutworms are a problem in your garden, put cutworm collars (described in Chapter

Three under Maintenance Activities in the Spring Garden) around seedlings of eggplant, peppers, and tomatoes.

When checking the garden for pests watch for disease symptoms, too. If you spot any, take immediate action as described in Chapter Two. Remember, when you must pull up and dispose of diseased plants, do not under any circumstances put them on the compost pile!

Weeding, especially if your garden is not mulched, is the other maintenance activity that continues all summer. Weeds generally slow down in hot, dry weather, but in a wet year they will grow like crazy all summer long. When you weed, try to pull out the roots, not just break off the tops. Roots left in the soil will grow a whole new crop of weeds. Weeds are easiest to pull when they are small, and when the ground is loose and moist. Don't weed immediately after a rain, though. Walking on wet soil can compact it, and working around wet plants can spread disease organisms from one to the other. Let the plants dry off, and let the soil dry partially, too, before you weed. It is also easy to pull weeds growing up through mulch—the mulch keeps the soil nice and loose.

There are various sorts of tools you can buy to make weeding chores easier. The quickest way to clear a large area of weeds is with a hoe. The drawback is that hoeing chops off the weed tops but does not remove many of the roots, and the weeds will grow back. Regular cultivation, though, will keep the weed problem at bay, and is good for overall soil health. If your garden is planted in single rows, with a fair amount of space between the rows, you will probably want to use a hoe. There are a number of styles available: you can choose a narrow or wide blade, a model with a gooseneck handle and a triangular, pointed blade, or an oscillating or "scuffle" hoe, which has four slender blades joined into an open square, and the entire assembly moves back and forth as the hoe is pushed and pulled across the ground.

For small gardens various sorts of hand

tools are available for weeding. Small claw-type cultivators will get rid of shallow-rooted weeds. There are weeding tools with blades in the form of an open U or V, and something called a Cape Cod weeder, which has a knifelike blade with a bent tip. Trowels with long V-shaped blades are useful for removing weeds with long taproots. And there are also knives with flat, hook-shaped blades for weeding between paving stones and bricks. You can also, of course, pull up weeds by hand.

However you do your hand weeding, I recommend that you buy a foam-rubber kneeling pad to use while you're working in the garden—I have found mine to be invaluable when I am spending several hours a day weeding my own garden and those of my clients.

If you live where dry summer winds can be a problem (many midwestern gardeners must contend with these conditions), be sure your garden is well mulched. Gardens on exposed sites will also benefit from a windbreak—a line of trees or shrubs planted in the direction of the prevailing winds, or an open-weave fence on the windward side of the garden are two possibilities.

If you go away for a week's vacation in summer, weed, water deeply, and make sure a thick layer of mulch is in place before you leave. If you will be away longer than a week, try and arrange to have someone look after the garden for you.

Watch newly planted parts of the garden and thin any plants that need it. For example, spring-planted parsnips usually get thinned in early June. Also, be sure pole beans and other climbing plants have the necessary supports. Put stakes or cages for tomatoes in place when you set out transplants—it's easier to do when plants are small. As plants grow, make sure growing stems are kept fastened to the supports.

If you have a compost pile, remember to turn it and mix the contents every week or so (at least once a month), and make sure the pile stays moist but not soggy.

Plants growing in containers must be watched carefully all summer. The soil in containers dries out quickly in hot weather, especially when it is windy and/or the humidity is low. You will have to water once or even twice a day, depending on the size of the container. This frequent watering leaches out nutrients, so you will need to fertilize container plants about every three weeks with a soluble fertilizer.

Here's a tip for cold-climate gardeners: to get a longer season for tender vegetables and herbs, try planting them in pots and setting the pots in front of a south-facing masonry wall that is white or light in color. The wall will reflect extra warmth from the sun onto plants.

Give vegetables a midsummer boost with a foliar feeding of seaweed concentrate, fish emulsion, or manure tea. Heavy feeders will appreciate a monthly feeding. Be sure to feed fruit-bearing crops (tomatoes, eggplant, squash, peppers, and cucumbers) when the fruit is forming.

If you are growing nonhybrid and heirloom varieties and you plan to save seeds to plant next year, give that some thought right now, at the height of the growing season. Look over your plants, and put tags on the most vigorous and productive specimens, and plan to save seeds from those plants when they mature.

It is important to keep spent blossoms picked off of nasturtiums, pansies, and other edible flowers to keep them blooming. If you let the flowers mature and go to seed, the plants will stop blooming, or at least produce fewer flowers. Regularly deadheading pansies can keep them blooming throughout most of the summer in moderate climates (even though they are known as cool-weather flowers), especially if they get plenty of water. Keeping flowers pinched off basil and dill will prolong the production of good foliage (as well as providing additions to the salad bowl). Pinching back the tops of basil and other multi-stemmed herbs also promotes bushier growth from more side shoots.

Summer is a good time to build a cold frame if you do not already have one. See Chapter Two for directions. When deciding where to put the cold frame, bear in mind that the sun will move south in the sky in fall and winter, and try to put the cold frame in a place where autumn and winter sunlight will be unobstructed, even if that location has some shade now. It is best to put the cold frame close to the house—right against a south-facing wall is ideal, because the frame will be sheltered from the north. You could also excavate an area for a cold frame, and build an earth berm against the north side to insulate it.

If you already have a cold frame, and used it to start seedlings for summer crops, it is time to renew the soil. After all the plants have been transplanted to the garden, dig out the top 4 to 6 inches of soil from the cold frame. Mix the soil with compost and composted manure, and refill the frame (put any leftover soil mix in the garden). Rake the surface smooth and the cold frame will be ready when you need it in fall. You can also use a cold frame as a nursery bed for replacement plants in summer, as long as you leave it uncovered.

Follow a similar soil-building procedure in the garden as well. After the harvest is completed in a section of the garden, remove the plants, spread a layer of compost and/or composted manure, and work it into the soil to prepare the area for fall planting.

When bean plants finish bearing, pull them, add compost, phosphorus, and potassium to the soil, and replant with root crops for fall harvest.

Sometime when you get a spare moment, order seeds to plant in late summer and early fall. Anytime from midsummer on is time to start collecting materials for winter mulches. If you live in a rural area, a local farmer may be willing to give you hay that has been damaged by rain. You can also collect grass clippings, but spread them in inch-deep layers to dry out or they will rot.

Late summer is a good time to divide and transplant established clumps of chives and shallots. But if you don't have time now, division can wait until fall.

Summer Planting

In the northernmost parts of the country, gardeners are planting the last of the warm-weather crops in June. In these short-season areas, quick-maturing varieties of warm-weather fruiting crops are the best bets. Northern and high-altitude gardeners can also plant calendulas and carnations. Gardeners as far south as zone 6 can still plant succession crops of beets, carrots, beans, and corn in early summer. It's not too late to plant herbs, squash, kohlrabi, celeriac, mustard, and collard greens. And when spring-planted spinach bolts to seed, you can replace it with Swiss chard. There is also still time to direct-sow nasturtiums and giant sunflowers. The tenderest crops—lima beans and okra—cannot be planted until June in many places.

In zone 8 and south, where the frost-free growing season is long, some gardeners like to start new tomato plants in June to plant out in August to replace the tomatoes that have been producing all summer. The new plants will bear until the first frost, which probably won't come until early November.

Gardeners interested in extending the harvest season are not only gathering in crops and caring for established plants over the summer, we are also thinking ahead to future harvests and doing some planting.

Depending on your location, cool-weather crops can be planted from July to September. Many gardeners in zone 5 and north can plant in early July, zone 6 in late July, and zone 7 in August. In fact, many plants do better planted at this time of year than when planted in spring. Because the soil is warm, seeds germinate more readily and transplants get off to a faster start than they can in the colder environment of the spring garden. In addition, the vegetables mature in the cool weather of fall, which they love. These same crops are often trickier to grow in spring, when they mature as the weather is becoming hot. When hot weather arrives early the quality of the harvest declines.

Many crops can be planted for fall harvest. Many root vegetables and leafy greens make good fall crops, as do members of the cabbage family. Direct-sow beets, carrots, radishes, turnips, leaf lettuce, spinach, mustard, Oriental greens, arugula, cress, sorrel, and kale. To save garden space, start indoors in early summer and transplant out in mid to late summer cabbage, cauliflower, broccoli, brussels sprouts, Florence fennel, endive, escarole, kohlrabi, and collard greens. If you have the space and autumn weather in your area tends to be warm, you might want to try planting a late crop of fast-maturing snap beans or summer squash. It's risky, because an early frost will wipe out the crop, but most rewarding when the gamble pays off. Warm-climate gardeners can sow pansy seed for winter flowers. Sow broccoli in midsummer three months before the first expected hard fall frost. Gardeners in mild climates can sow Romanesco broccoli in late summer for fall and winter harvest.

When calculating planting dates for crops that will mature in fall, it is wise to add an extra week or two to the maturity time. The cooler temperatures and shorter days slow the growth rate of plants. Warm-climate gardeners must not sow any fall crops directly in the garden until after the middle of August, or temperatures will be too hot for the young plants.

At the end of summer, sow seeds in pots for plants that you will grow indoors in winter. See Chapters Five and Six for information on edibles to grow indoors in winter. Follow the directions for sowing seeds indoors in Chapter Two.

Do your summer planting late in the day, when it is cooler and water will not evaporate right away. Be sure to water newly planted seeds and seedlings thoroughly after planting. Pay special attention to young seedlings in the summer garden. Make sure they get plenty of water. Seedlings started indoors should be gradually exposed to outdoor conditions in the same way seedlings are gradually hardened-off in spring. Summer seedlings need time to become accustomed to the intense sun and heat of the outdoor garden. New plants, especially leaf crops, appreciate a bit of shade in the summer garden.

Planting in blocks instead of rows at this time of year will help conserve precious moisture. Your watering activities will be concentrated in a smaller area, and plant leaves will shade the soil and keep it cooler, thus slowing evaporation.

Late summer is a good time to take cuttings of mints, lavender, scented geraniums, oregano, rosemary, sage, and thyme to plant in pots for winter plants indoors. Take tip cuttings about 4 inches long, strip off the lower leaves, and stand the cuttings in a container of moist perlite or vermiculite. Keep the medium evenly moist, but not soggy, until the cuttings root. Then plant them in pots. The cuttings should be taken, at the latest, a month before you expect the first fall frost.

This is also the time to start seeds of herbs for indoor growing. Basil, dill, and parsley can all be grown indoors from seeds. Follow the directions in Chapter Two for starting seeds indoors and growing herbs indoors.

FIVE

The Autumn Garden

AUTUMN IS a gentle season, at least in its early days. The sun rides lower in the sky, suffusing the landscape with a soft, golden light. The intense heat of summer is past; although the days are still warm, the air is soft and nights are cooler. Although the garden is still flourishing, we sense the subtle cues that tell us the outdoor season will soon be slowing down. Slowing down but not ending, for there is still much to do in the garden—food to harvest, maintenance chores to perform, and planting to be done, as well. It's good that there's still so much to do, because autumn is a delightful time to be outdoors.

For those of us who do not live in warm climates, fall and winter are largely neglected as gardening seasons. But autumn has a richness of its own. Some summer crops keep producing well into fall, until the weather gets cold enough to stop them. You can still pick tomatoes, summer squash, eggplant, and peppers. The timely use of cold frames, hot caps, and other protective devices can extend the harvest past the first frost, so you can take advantage of the several weeks of warm, frost-free Indian summer weather that often follow the first frost. Some plants that need a long growing season to mature their crops—celeriac and winter squash, for example—are finally ready to harvest in fall.

Quite a few herbs and edible flowers continue into fall, as well.

But the real highlights of fall are cool-season crops that come into their own in these cooler temperatures and shorter days. They make up the bulk of the fall harvest. Many of these plants can also be grown in spring —salad greens, root crops, and some members of the cabbage family. But in fact, quite a few crops are easier to grow when planted in summer for fall harvest than during their traditional planting time in spring. Lettuce, spinach, and cole crops are more reliable and need less care when they mature their crops in fall; they taste better, have a finer texture, and are less likely to bolt to seed than when growing in late spring and summer.

Here's another point to consider: the leafy and root vegetables that grow so well in autumn need less care than the fruiting plants that are such a delectable part of the summer garden. What's more, many of them are highly nutritious foods, rich in vitamins and minerals.

Gardening in general is easier in fall than in spring. The soil is warm, so seeds germinate readily; and the garden has already been dug and worked for previous crops. There are fewer weeds in later autumn, and not as many bugs. Best of all, until late in the season, autumn's mild weather is ideal for plants. They suffer less from searing heat and drought, and temperatures drop at night without reaching dangerously low levels. Gardeners who live where frosts come early can cover their tender plants at night and still take advantage of the warm days.

A special treat in autumn, and perhaps the quintessential expression of the sweetness of the season, is found in a few particular vegetables that develop their best flavor after they have been exposed to some frost. These favored few—brussels sprouts, kale, and parsnips—are not exactly considered gourmet delights; in fact, lots of people detest them. And it is true that when harvested without the benefit of frost their flavors are less than thrilling. But if you have never tasted brussels sprouts, kale, or parsnips that came out of the garden after having withstood a few frosts, you really ought to try them again, the right way.

Cold weather improves the flavors of these vegetables because it changes the plants' metabolism. The chemical processes within the plants occur differently, allowing sugars to accumulate in the tissues. We experience these changes as a sweeter flavor, and when interestingly prepared, these vegetables are quite delicious.

You can prepare a few very hardy crops to stay in the garden all winter to harvest as

needed. Others can go into simple outdoor storage spaces that save room indoors.

Autumn, of course, is not only a season of harvest. It is also a time to do garden chores in preparation for next year: soil building, composting, and preparing the soil for early spring planting. It is also the time to clean up the residue of the summer blitzkrieg—pull up plants that are finished producing; put away stakes and supports that are no longer needed.

Finally, autumn is a season for planting, too. In warm climates, gardening begins again as the intense heat of summer softens and starts to recede. Farther north, gardening will continue in winter in cold frames and hot beds, and indoors under lights and on sunny windowsills.

THE AUTUMN HARVEST

Good planning can extend the harvest throughout fall and into winter, even in cool climates. It is a real treat to have garden-fresh vegetables in fall and winter, when the local farm stands are closed for the season. Imagine going out and picking vegetables from your garden for Thanksgiving dinner!

Here is a rundown of some of the highlights of the fall harvest. First, fall is the time to harvest slow-to-mature vegetables that have been in the ground since spring. Celeriac, or celery root, has a flavor similar to celery but milder. The gnarled roots are difficult to peel, but worth the effort: they have a fine, delicate texture. Celeriac is delicious when braised in broth, added to soups, or mashed together with potatoes. If sown in spring it will be ready to harvest in early fall.

Radicchio, whose bitter-flavored leaves have become such an important component of mixed salads, is another crop that matures in fall after a long season in the garden. In gardens where winter temperatures can be

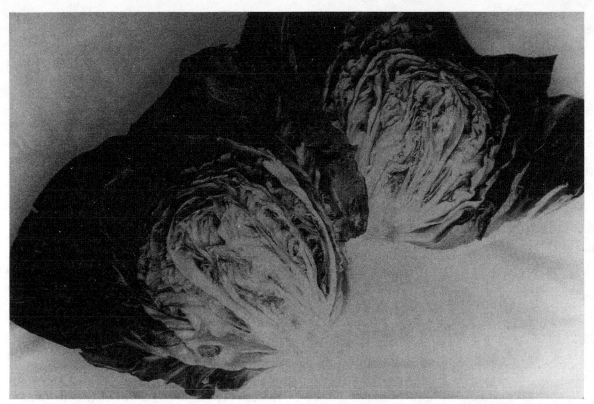

expected to drop below 10°F (zone 7 and north) radicchio is planted in late spring or early summer and allowed to grow through the warm months. At the end of summer or beginning of fall the plants are cut back, and by October or November will have formed the tight little heads that are harvested for salads.

Leeks, potatoes, winter squash, and Florence or sweet fennel are other slow-growing additions to the fall harvest. Leeks can be dug when they mature or left in the ground all winter (see Preparing Root Crops for Winter Harvest, later in this section). Winter squash should be picked in early fall, before the first hard frost (never mind poetic observations about the frost on the pumpkin if you are planning on long-term storage of the harvest). When you cannot dent the rind by pressing it with your fingernail the squash is ready. Leave 2 inches

The bitter-flavored red-and-white leaves of radicchio nicely complement mild-tasting greens such as lettuce and corn salad.

of stem attached when you cut it, and store indoors at about 60°F (winter squash will spoil indoors if the temperature is too cold).

Fast-growing cool-weather vegetables make up the preponderance of the autumn harvest. Most of them are easy to grow, especially at this time of year, when conditions are so hospitable.

The fall garden can provide lots of ingredients for the salad bowl. Lettuce can be had in abundance, especially fast-growing leafy types. Some cultivars are specially bred for the fall and winter garden (see the table, Vegetable Varieties for Fall, and Chapter Seven for suggestions). For different flavors, consider cress, sorrel, chicory,

The Autumn Garden 95

COURTESY JOHNNY'S SELECTED SEEDS

Red-leaf lettuces like the ones shown here are colorful in the autumn garden, and their tender texture and mild flavor are a welcome addition to salads and sandwiches.

young for ready-made salads. Mache, or corn salad, can be planted in fall, too. Rounding out the salad garden are endive and its broad-leaved relative, escarole. These bitter-tasting greens are sown in midsummer in northern gardens (up to New England) and harvested before the first hard frost.

Autumn offers other leafy crops besides salad greens. Swiss chard, a real workhorse, has been in the garden since spring and keeps right on producing in fall. Its red or white stalks add color, too. Some varieties of spinach are perfect for fall, and will not bolt like they do in hot summer weather. Kale is a star of the autumn garden; its flavor is improved by frost, so wait until you have had a few frosts to start picking the frilly leaves. Ornamental kales color up beautifully in fall—they are pretty but not terrifically tasty, and are best used as a garnish in the kitchen. Mustard greens (including Oriental mustards) are other good leaf crops for fall; so are collards.

To extend the harvest of leafy fall crops as long as possible, protect the plants from morning sun. When a cold night is followed by a bright, sunny morning, temperatures within plants can rise too quickly, and plant tissues will be damaged by the sudden fluctuations. To protect the plants, put up a screen of burlap or cloth supported by stakes or a wire frame, on the southeast side of the plants.

The cabbage family can contribute vegetables other than the leafy kales and mustards to the autumn cornucopia. Some members of the clan are decidedly easier to grow for fall harvest than at their usual spring planting time. If you are new to gardening, or if you just want to make your gardening easier, plant some of these in summer to harvest in fall.

and arugula. Cutting chicories that were planted in summer are ready to harvest in fall. The always-dependable arugula is even better to grow in fall than in spring, because it holds its flavor well with no sharpness and does not bolt to flower. In 1990, a year that saw a mild autumn on Long Island, I harvested arugula until nearly Christmas. You can also plant mesclun for fall; it is a mixture of salad greens that are sown together and picked while

*Raised beds like these are a good solution for gardens with poorly drained or compacted soil.
Plant lettuce and other salad greens in spring, or in late summer for fall harvest.*

Red and green varieties of romaine lettuce make a handsome combination in the spring or fall garden.

Take advantage of the many shades of green available in leafy crops when planning your autumn garden. Here, the bright yellowish green of leaf lettuce shimmers against the deep blue green of kale.

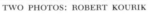

TWO PHOTOS: ROBERT KOURIK

Beets are a good addition to the fall garden. Pull them when they're still small, for the sweetest flavor and tender, juicy texture.

COURTESY OF NATIONAL GARDEN BUREAU

ROBERT KOURIK

COURTESY JOHNNY'S SELECTED SEEDS

Floating row covers protect plants from light frost and damage from birds and pests, while allowing in light, air, and water.

Corn salad, or mache, is an excellent crop for a fall salad garden. It grows fast and likes cool weather.

ROBERT KOURIK

Fast-maturing radishes are easy to grow and do best in cool weather. The variety shown here, Easter Egg, produces roots in shades of pink, red, lavender, and white.

Opposite, flowering kale, seen in the center of this autumn garden, comes into its own when the weather turns cool, and can withstand quite a bit of frost.

Brussels sprouts taste sweeter after they have been exposed to frost, so don't harvest them until you've had a few light frosts in fall.

Cabbage is outstanding in the autumn garden. The variety shown here is Perfect Ball.

THREE PHOTOS: COURTESY JOHNNY'S SELECTED SEEDS

A winter salad garden in a large pot—dwarf lettuce, chives, and baby beets. Try this in a light garden.

Curly parsley will grow indoors in winter under lights or on a sunny windowsill.

Round-rooted carrots like the variety shown here, Parmex, are ideal for container growing. Adventurous gardeners can try growing them indoors in a winter light garden, along with salad greens and herbs.

Oriental greens are among the best crops to grow in an insulated cold frame in winter. Their flavors are surprisingly diverse, ranging from mild and sweet to pungent and peppery.

COURTESY JOHNNY'S SELECTED SEEDS

ROBERT KOURIK

ROBERT KOURIK

Swiss chard and other crops get off to an early start in a cold frame.

VEGETABLE VARIETIES FOR FALL

The following varieties are recommended for harvesting and in some cases for planting in fall. It is by no means an exhaustive list; additional cultivars are also suitable for the fall garden.

BEETS

Detroit Dark Red
Early Wonder
Little Ball
Long Season
Ruby Queen

BROCCOLI

Bonanza Hybrid
Calabrese
Emperor
Purple Sprouting
Romanesco
White Sprouting

CABBAGE

Apex
Danish Roundhead
Perfect Ball
Safekeeper
Savory Ace
Superior Danish

CARROTS

Baby Spike
Minicor
Orbit
Parmex
Spartan Bonus

CELERY CABBAGE

Pak Choi
Lei Choi

CHICORY

Grumolo
Spadona

CHINESE CABBAGE

Blues
Michihli
Salad King
Two Seasons Hybrid
Wintertime
Wong Bok

COLLARDS

Georgia Blue Stem
Vates

CORN SALAD (MACHE)

Verte de Cambrai

ENDIVE AND ESCAROLE

Cornet D'Anjou (escarole)
Fine Curled
Full Heart Batavian
Nuvol (escarole)
President
Salad King
Sugarloaf

KALE

Blue Surf
Dwarf Blue-Curled Scotch
Vates
Winterbor

LETTUCE

Arctic King
Black-Seeded Simpson
Merveille des Quatres Saisons
Red Montpelier
Red Sails
Red Salad Bowl
Salad Bowl
Sangria
Winter Density
Winter Marvel

VEGETABLE VARIETIES FOR FALL

MUSTARD

Burpee's Fordhook Fancy
Green Wave
Karashina
Mizuna
Tatsoi
Tendergreen

SPINACH

Avon
Giant Nobel
Giant Winter
Melody Hybrid
Sputnik
Tyee
Virginia Blight Resistant

RADICCHIO

Angusto
Early Treviso
Medusa
Red Verona

RADISHES

Champion
Cherry Belle
Early Scarlet Globe
Easter Egg
Round Black Spanish (winter)
Saxa
Sora
Sparkler
Tokinashi (daikon)
White Icicle

TURNIPS

Amber Globe
Gilfeather
Hybrid Tokyo Cross
Purple Top White Globe
White Egg

Some broccoli cultivars—traditional types as well as uncommon ones—succeed beautifully in fall. The handsome Romanesco broccoli is one possibility; in mild climates it is best sown in late summer for harvest in fall and winter. Purple and white sprouting broccoli are also ideal. They will produce lots of small side shoots for fall harvest instead of a large central head; cut when the shoots are about 4 inches long. For recommendations of traditional broccoli cultivars that work especially well in fall, see the table, Vegetable Varieties for Fall, and Chapter Seven. If sown in midsummer, ninety days before the first expected fall frost, heading broccoli will mature in the cool weather it prefers. After the central head is cut most varieties will send out smaller side shoots for a second harvest a couple of weeks later.

A number of cabbage varieties are suited for fall cropping, along with savoy and Chinese cabbages. Cauliflower can be direct-sown in midsummer for fall harvest in areas where autumn tends to be mild; cauliflower tolerates less cold than other cole crops. Kohlrabi, both purple and white varieties, also grows well in fall, as does broccoli raab, which is actually a turnip grown for its flower stalks.

Probably the most misunderstood, least appreciated member of the cabbage family is brussels sprouts. Its reputation as an awful-tasting vegetable whose consumption is more punishment than reward is really undeserved. With the right preparation brussels sprouts can be delicious, especially if harvested after frost, when the cabbagey flavor becomes sweeter and sort of nutty. Don't harvest brussels sprouts until after you have had a few frosts, but do get them out of the garden before the mercury dips to 20°F.

You can plant a number of root crops to harvest in fall or, in some cases, to mulch and leave right in the garden all winter to dig when you are ready to cook them. Some, like potatoes, parsnips, and the previously mentioned leeks, have been growing all summer and mature in fall. Beets planted in midsummer and carrots planted in late summer will be ready for harvest in fall. Small salad radishes grow quickly to harvest size, and the slower-growing, larger-rooted winter radishes also mature in fall. Turnips can be planted for fall harvest, and so can green onions. Bulbing onions and garlic mature from late summer to early fall, depending on when they were planted. If you planted parsnips, do not dig them until after frost, when they taste sweeter. A really unusual root crop for fall harvest is salsify, also called oyster plant, which is said to have a flavor like its namesake. Salsify can be left in the ground all winter and dug in early spring when the ground thaws.

Some root crops can stay in the ground all winter under a thick layer of mulch, to be harvested as needed. Some can be dug and placed in outdoor storage areas along with a few other suitable vegetables. See Natural Storage, later in this chapter, for information on outdoor storage techniques.

PREPARING ROOT CROPS
FOR WINTER HARVEST

Some gardeners find it convenient to leave cold-tolerant root crops right in their garden beds or rows over the winter, protected by a thick layer of mulch. Really a form of outdoor storage, leaving the crops in place saves valuable storage space indoors, and also allows the vegetables to remain in good condition longer than they would if stored indoors in the refrigerator.

Carrots, leeks, parsnips, and turnips can be left in the ground all winter in most gardens, and where winters are not too severe the method also works for beets, celeriac, and winter radishes. In-ground storage offers some advantages over other natural storage methods. The vegetables stay firm because they draw moisture from the soil, and you don't have to handle them twice— all you do is dig them when you need them. Late autumn is the time to prepare them.

When the soil develops a frozen crust on top, mulch the vegetables with a 1- to 2-foot layer of shredded dry leaves, salt hay, or straw. Pull the mulch close around the stems of the plants. Lay pine boughs or boards on top to hold the mulch in place. If you think mice will be a problem, put hardware cloth over the mulch to keep them out. An alternative—and rather messy—method is to mulch with newspapers covered with chicken wire weighted down around the edges with rocks.

Mark the rows or beds with tall stakes so you can easily find the stored vegetables under snow.

The purpose of the mulch is to keep the ground from freezing solid to any appreciable depth, making it possible to dig the roots at any time. In northern New England and other very cold climates, the roots may not be harvestable much past Thanksgiving; farther south you should be able to dig them all winter. Northerners can either dig the vegetables before the soil freezes solid, or let it freeze; make sure the mulch stays in place all winter to prevent soil heaving, and dig the roots in spring when the ground thaws.

EXTENDING THE HARVEST
OF SUMMER CROPS

A number of fruit-bearing summer crops —indeterminate varieties of tomatoes, eggplant, peppers, and summer squash, in particular—often continue bearing in autumn until cold weather stops them. If you protect these sensitive plants through the first couple of light frosts, you can prolong

their harvest for several weeks. The techniques are described under Frost Protection, in the section Autumn Maintenance, later in this chapter.

Gardeners in warm climates can continue harvesting summer vegetables well into fall without worrying about frost (except in unusually cool years). When the last tomatoes and eggplants are picked, gardeners in the warmest zones can replace them with lettuce, carrots, beets, cabbage, and other cool-weather crops for harvest in late fall or early winter.

Vegetables are not the only summer holdovers in the autumn garden. A number of herbs and edible flowers also keep producing into fall. Parsley, chives, chervil, and fennel all hold up well. In mild seasons, basil, thyme, marjoram, oregano, and rosemary can be harvested early in the season, at least until the weather turns cold. In my 1990 garden I had beautiful basil in the middle of October, the chives, thyme, and rosemary were still in good shape at Thanksgiving, and the parsley held up until close to Christmas, when my garden finally got its first really hard freeze.

If you want to extend the herbal harvest further, fall is the time to dig and pot up some herbs to bring indoors for winter. For information see the section Autumn Planting, later in this chapter.

Several edible flowers tolerate cool weather and are still available in fall. Calendulas love the coolness and will flower until the first frost. Nasturtiums still bloom in early fall, along with marigolds. Canary creeper, a vining relative of the nasturtium, continues to produce its fringed yellow flowers through several light frosts before calling it quits for the year.

Turnips can be planted in spring and again in summer for a fall harvest. The variety shown here, Tokyo Cross, is a good choice for autumn growing.

HARVESTING AND STORING HERBS

You can pick most herbs as needed all summer long (never taking more than one-third of the plant at any one time), but in early fall it is time to harvest the herbs you will want to store. Some herbs are harvested earlier—seeds of dill and other plants have to be gathered whenever they mature—but the majority of herbs are harvested early in autumn.

The classic way to store herbs is in dried form, but they can also be frozen, or used to flavor oils and vinegars.

The best time to harvest herbs is on a sunny, cool day, after the dew has dried from the plants but before the hottest part of the day. Most herbs get their flavor and aroma from volatile oils. If you harvest in late morning, right before noon, the oils will be at maximum concentration in the leaves; the heat of the afternoon sun will draw some of the oils out of the leaves. Some of the oils are also washed away by rain, so it's best to wait two or three days after a rainstorm before harvesting, to give the aromatic oils a chance to collect in the leaves again.

Harvest only healthy plants for storage. You wouldn't want to eat diseased plants, and they wouldn't store well, anyway. If you garden organically you will not have to worry that herb leaves and flowers contain pesticide residues.

Snip the stems of nonwoody plants with a sharp knife or scissors. For rosemary, basil, and other plants with tough or woody stems use pruning shears. Do not pick individual leaves from stems—cut whole branches. If you are harvesting seeds, cut the seed heads with at least 6 inches of stem attached for easier handling. Cut when the seeds are ripe (most turn brown), but before the seed heads shatter. If you want the plants to self-sow, leave some seed heads on the plants.

COLD TOLERANCE OF VEGETABLES

These vegetables can all tolerate some frost and cold temperatures, and are the most cold hardy:

beets
brussels sprouts
cabbage
collards
kale
kohlrabi
parsnips
spinach
turnips

This group likes cool weather, but can be damaged by freezing; cover them when you expect *heavy* frost:

broccoli
carrots
cauliflower
lettuce
peas
potatoes

Onions and relatives like relatively warm temperatures in the range of 55 to 75°F, but can stand some frost:

onions
garlic
leeks
shallots

These plants will not tolerate any frost:

beans
corn
cucumbers
melons
some kinds of peppers
squash
tomatoes

These plants really thrive only when temperatures stay above 70°F; if exposed to 32°F for even a few hours they will suffer:

eggplant
okra
some pepper varieties
watermelon

Dried herbs are convenient to store and easy to use in the kitchen, and herbs that have been properly dried retain much of their color and scent. If you have never dried your own herbs before, you will probably be surprised to see how much greener they are than the dried herbs you buy in the supermarket. But the flavors of most herbs are altered in drying—dried herbs just don't taste the same as fresh ones. The change is not just a matter of the intensity of the flavor; the same herb when dried can impart a very different quality to foods than when it is used in fresh form. Take tarragon, for instance. Fresh tarragon has a strong note of licorice in its complex flavor, but dried tarragon has a sweeter, more mellow taste that to my palate is completely different. I love fresh tarragon, but in some recipes—béarnaise sauce, for instance—I definitely prefer the dried form.

Make sure herb leaves are clean before you dry them. Wash them only if it is necessary; washing may take away some of the oils and thus, the flavor. If you must wash the leaves, rinse them quickly in cold water and pat dry with paper towels. Let the herbs sit on dry paper towels for a couple of hours to allow any remaining moisture to evaporate.

Most herbs dry best in an evenly warm environment, where the temperature is from 95 to 100°F and there is plenty of air circulation. Keep them out of direct sun, as well. A well-ventilated attic is one good place to dry herbs. The classic way to dry herbs is to gather the stems into bunches and fasten them tightly with string or rubber bands (the stems shrink as they dry), then hang the bunches upside down from the rafters or ceiling, or on a drying rack. Hanging upside down lets the maximum amount of volatile oil collect in the leaves.

Instead of hanging the herbs in bunches, you can spread them in a single layer on paper towels, cookie sheets, or a screen. To make a simple rack for flat drying, staple some window screening to a rectangular wood frame and set the frame on something to elevate it so air can circulate underneath.

When flat-drying herbs, turn the stems once a day so the leaves dry evenly on all sides. You can also use a fan to increase air circulation, but don't aim it directly at the herbs; the idea is simply to keep air moving in the room.

You can also dry herbs in a conventional or microwave oven. Spread them in a single layer on cookie sheets and place them in a gas oven with just the pilot light on, or in an electric oven turned on to the lowest setting. In a gas oven the herbs will dry in a

Here are three easy ways to dry herbs. To dry leaves, you can hang the herbs in bunches on a drying rack, or strip the leaves from the stems and spread them on a screen rack. To dry seeds, such as those of dill and caraway, hang the bunches in paper bags, seed heads down, and the seeds will drop to the bottom of the bag as they dry.

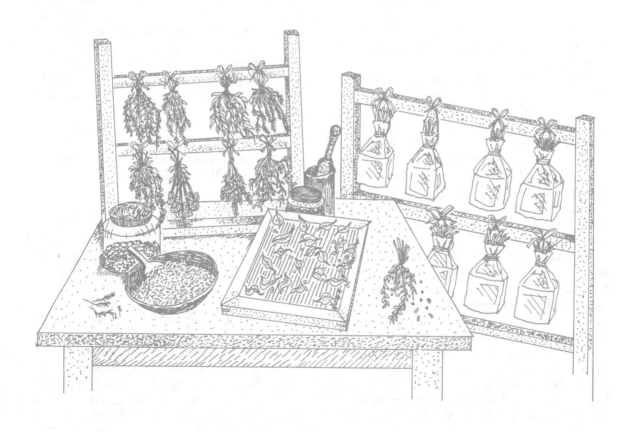

few days; turn them once a day. In an electric oven they will dry in just hours; the drying time depends on the size and moisture content of the leaves.

To dry herbs in the microwave, strip the leaves from the stems and spread them evenly on a double layer of paper towels. Microwave on high for two minutes, then stir the leaves. Microwave for two minutes more and stir again. If the leaves are not yet dry, microwave them for another two minutes.

When correctly dried, the leaves should be brittle enough to break easily, but not so dry that they crumble into powder when you touch them.

Herb flowers are more delicate than leaves, and more difficult to dry. If the temperature gets too hot or too cold they will discolor. You can tie flowers in bunches and hang them upside down, or dry them in the microwave. Snip the flowers from their stems and lay them on paper towels as for leaves. Microwave them for two-minute intervals until they are evenly dry. Like leaves, the flowers should be dry but not crumbly.

To dry seeds of dill, fennel, caraway, and other herbs, place the stems in a paper bag with the seed heads toward the bottom of the bag. Tie the top of the bag tightly around the bunch of stems, and hang upside down by the stems. When the seeds are dry they will fall to the bottom of the bag, where you can easily collect them.

Store your dried herbs in tightly capped glass jars, and keep the jars in a cool, dry, dark place. Plastic containers may allow air and moisture to enter, decreasing the storage life and quality of the herbs, so always use glass.

Some herbs—chives especially—are better frozen than dried, and are more like fresh herbs than dried ones. Spread snipped leaves of chives on cookie sheets to freeze them, and transfer to freezer containers when stiff. Other herbs freeze best when blanched in boiling water for one minute. After blanching, plunge the herbs immediately into ice water, dry them, and freeze them in a single layer. Pack the herbs in containers when frozen. Or you can puree the leaves with water and freeze the liquid in ice-cube trays. When frozen, store the herb cubes in plastic freezer bags (don't forget to label them). These cubes are great for adding flavor to soups and stews.

NATURAL STORAGE

Natural storage methods—quite simple, most of them—offer a way to provide fresh vegetables from the garden through all or part of the winter, without having to can, freeze, or dry them. These techniques seem quaint and old-fashioned today, but they are still perfectly feasible for gardeners who grow more food than they can eat right from the garden. The basic principle involved is that of the traditional root cellar: you create a cold storage area, indoors or outdoors, where vegetables can be held until needed in the kitchen. Not many people build root cellars these days, and unless you are so serious about gardening that you grow most of the vegetables your family consumes, you probably will not want the bother and expense of building one. But there are simpler ways to store garden produce and in effect extend the harvest.

STORAGE CONDITIONS

Root crops and most other storage vegetables need a very humid atmosphere (80 to 95 percent relative humidity) to keep well without shrivelling. As with all rules, there are exceptions to this one, and they include onions, garlic, and winter squash, which will rot if the humidity is higher than 70 percent.

Good air circulation is essential for long-term storage; without it the vegetables are likely to develop mold. Brussels sprouts, cabbage, cauliflower, endive, garlic, onions, leeks, and squash in particular need lots of air. They are best stored indoors in open boxes, wooden fruit crates (the kind made from wood slats), garlic or onions in mesh bags hung from the ceiling, or in single layers on shelves lined with newspaper.

Vegetables in storage need darkness, too. Light can cause onions and some other vegetables to sprout.

Whatever storage method you choose, be sure the stored vegetables (except for onions or garlic) do not touch one another.

Harvest vegetables for storage when they are mature, but before the first killing frost in fall. Store only the most perfect specimens; damaged vegetables won't keep as well. Make sure the vegetables you put in storage have no nicks, cuts, bruises, holes, insect damage, or signs of disease.

Wait for a day when the weather is cool and dry to pick vegetables for storage; the crops should be in peak condition then, and neither wet nor stressed by heat. Brush off all the loose dirt from the surface of the vegetables, but do not scrub them or you run the risk of damaging the skins and shortening the storage life.

Some vegetables, such as garlic, shallots, onions, and winter squash, need to be cured before they are put into storage. See Chapter Seven for directions where necessary.

OUTDOOR STORAGE

A range of vegetables can be stored in a window well or outdoor stairwell (like an outdoor entrance to a basement). To prepare the area for storage, first line the bottom with hardware cloth to keep out rodents. Lay down a layer of straw or hay, then a layer of vegetables, and be sure the vegetables do not touch. Follow with another layer of straw, then a layer of vegetables, repeating the layers until the well is full or you have used all the vegetables. Always end with a layer of straw or hay. Put a board over the top, cover with a waterproof tarpaulin or sheet of heavy plastic to keep out water, and weight down the edges with stones.

If the window can be opened from inside the basement you will have easy access to the hoard without having to go outdoors in the cold to retrieve the food. Otherwise,

WINDOW WELL STORAGE

The vegetables listed here are all candidates for storage in a window well. The storage times are all approximate, and will vary with environmental conditions and the quality of the crops.

Beets—2 to 5 months
Broccoli—2 months
Brussels sprouts—3 to 4 weeks
Cabbage—all winter (5 to 6 months), but cabbage develops an odor in storage
Carrots—all winter, up to 5 months
Cauliflower—3 to 4 weeks
Celeriac—all winter, up to 5 months

Chinese cabbage—1 to 4 months
Kohlrabi—all winter, up to 5 months
Leeks—2 to 3 months
Parsnips—all winter, 5 to 6 months
Winter radishes—2 to 4 months
Acorn squash—4 to 6 weeks. Other kinds of winter squash should be stored indoors.

when you want to remove some of the vegetables, remove the coverings, take out what you want, and replace the coverings. Although they are outdoors the vegetables should not freeze because they are next to the house.

When packing the window well, put in the vegetables with the longest storage life first. Alternating layers of different vegetables will bring more variety to your menus.

See the table, Window Well Storage, for vegetables appropriate for this kind of storage, and the approximate length of time you can expect them to last.

OTHER OUTDOOR STORAGE METHODS

There are a couple of other ways to create storage conditions similar to those of a window well and suitable for most of the same vegetables.

If you don't have a window well and you feel industrious, you can dig a pit or trench 2 to 3 feet deep. Put a layer of stones in the bottom, then a layer of leaves or straw. Put vegetables in boxes or, if you dug a pit, in barrels or metal garbage cans. Layer the vegetables in the containers with straw or leaves, moist peat moss, or wood chips, as for window well storage. Put the containers in the pit or trench, and pack straw, hay, or salt hay all around them. Make sure you put at least a 6-inch layer of the packing material on top of the storage containers. Cover

---

To store root vegetables in a window well, layer the vegetables with hay or straw, lay a heavy board on top, then cover with a sturdy tarpaulin to keep out water.

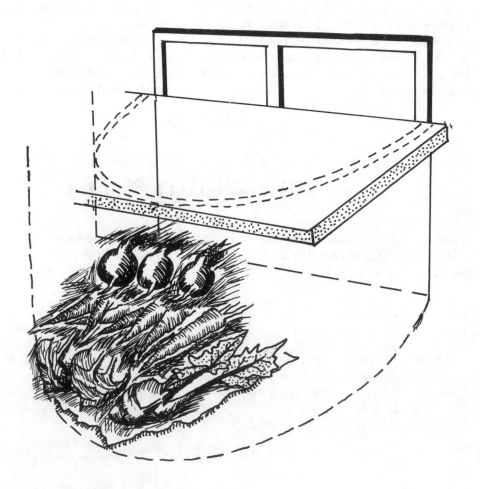

the pit or trench with boards, anchored with stones.

A cold frame (if you are not using it for fall and winter gardening) offers another potential storage location. You can layer vegetables with packing material in the cold frame, ending with a 6-inch layer of the packing material, and cover the lid of the frame with a heavy tarp or some boards to keep out light.

Or you can store carrots or some other crops in boxes of moist (not wet) builder's sand. Set the carrots vertically, like they grew in the garden. Do not let them touch one another. The same method will work for brussels sprouts, Chinese cabbage, or leeks, but you must dig these plants along with their roots and actually replant them in the sand. The roots will not grow, but they will draw moisture from the sand and keep the vegetables crisp and fresh. Water occasionally to keep the sand from drying out. If your cold frame is in use, try putting the box in an unheated basement. Carrots stored this way should stay in good shape all winter; the other crops should keep about as long as they would in a window well.

INDOOR STORAGE

Some vegetables keep best in less humid conditions than those afforded by outdoor storage, and some need warmer temperatures, as well. Garlic, onions, shallots, and dried beans need cool temperatures of 32 to 40°F, and a humidity level between 60 and 70 percent. An unheated spare room or attic can provide these conditions, but be careful not to let the temperature drop below freezing or pipes may freeze. Most winter squashes, except for acorn, have the longest storage life where temperatures are in the 50 to 60°F range, again with 60 to 70 percent humidity. A basement that receives some warmth from a furnace is one possible location. If you have electric heat that can be regulated from room to room, turning down the thermostat in a seldom-used room may provide the right conditions. Green tomatoes that are fully mature (the green color is beginning to lighten) will ripen in this sort of environment, too. Wrap them individually in newspaper before storing them.

AUTUMN PLANTING

The idea of planting food in autumn is not one that most of us northerners are used to. We routinely set out hardy bulbs, shrubs, and some perennials at this time of year, but the food garden has traditionally been cleaned up and closed down after the autumn harvest is complete. However, there are some edibles to plant outdoors in fall, even in the North. The cold frame becomes invaluable in autumn. And the indoor gardening season gets underway as well. Southerners can plant late crops of a number of their favorite vegetables. In fact, in the far South and desert Southwest, autumn is a much better gardening season than summer, which is too hot for both plants and gardeners.

Gardeners in cool climates can plant some crops in fall to produce an early harvest next spring. Some kinds of cutting chicory (which, unlike the Witloof type described later, are grown for their leaves and tender stems) are planted in fall for harvest the following spring. As soon as seedlings of chicory and other fall-planted spring crops come up, mulch them with evergreen boughs or other coarse material. Uncover the plants in early spring and they will start to grow again when the ground thaws. Some lettuce cultivars have also been bred especially to tolerate short days and cold, wet weather. In northern gardens they are planted in early fall and harvested in late fall or early spring. Farther south these lettuces are grown in winter. Some cultivars, such as Red Montpelier, can be grown in a cold frame in winter.

Gardeners in zone 7 and north can also plant late turnips and parsley to harvest in spring. Plant earlier in September the farther north you live. Northerners can also set out winter cabbages in mid to late fall.

If you live in a temperate climate, why not dare the elements and plant beets, carrots, kale, leaf lettuce, and turnips in early September to harvest in late fall? If temperatures stay mild and you protect the plants from early frosts, you should be able to harvest in November. Remember to plant the fastest-maturing varieties of these vegetables at this time of year. As the days grow cooler and shorter, the time to maturity grows longer, maybe as much as 50 percent longer than for the same vegetables planted in spring.

Seeds of hardy flowers can also be sown outdoors in fall. Pansies, garden pinks (*dianthus*), and calendulas can all be seeded directly in the garden where you want the plants to grow. They will bloom earlier next spring if given this head start.

A whole host of salad crops can get going in the cold frame in fall. You can plant lettuce, arugula, cress, sorrel, mache or corn salad, and mustard. Beets, spinach, parsley, broccoli, cabbage, and turnips are also good cold frame crops. If autumn weather turns cold early where you live, start seeds indoors of *dianthus* and calendulas, and move the young plants out to the cold frame after they have developed their second set of true leaves. The plants like cool weather, but the seeds need warmth to germinate.

If you like, you can transplant your cool-season crops into a cold frame after the first frost to make it easier to continue harvesting them. If you install a soil heating cable in your cold frame, you can grow hardy crops through much of the winter, depending on the severity of the weather.

Farther south, fall is a good time to plant peas, kohlrabi, mustard, radishes, squash, and other vegetables. Lucky southerners can even plant snap beans in September to pick for Thanksgiving dinner. Do *not* try and plant a late crop of okra, corn, or melons —they will not be able to stand the cooler temperatures.

Cool-weather vegetables can also be planted along the West Coast and in the Northwest. Southwesterners can continue to set out transplants of the cabbage family, and sow peas, parsley, and chives. In warm climates, pansies and calendulas planted in fall will bloom in winter.

If you live where winter temperatures do not drop below 10°F (zone 8, or even zone 7 in a mild year) plant radicchio in fall to harvest next spring. You can also plant endive and escarole in fall.

In the few parts of the country that are frost-free all winter, gardeners can plant eggplant and tomatoes in fall. This is also the time to prepare a bed for planting asparagus crowns in December. Double-dig the soil in the asparagus bed, and work in lots of compost and rock powders.

Warm-climate gardeners may find it helpful to cover newly planted seedbeds with burlap to help keep the soil moist until the seeds germinate. Remove the cover as soon as the first sprouts poke through the soil. Be sure to water the garden when necessary, especially during hot, dry weather.

Fall is also the time to prepare for winter harvests indoors. One specialty crop to consider for winter is the forcing of the delicate small heads of chicory known as Belgian endive. To grow Belgian endive you must first grow a crop of Witloof chicory for its roots. The chicory is planted in spring, allowed to grow all summer, and the roots are dug in fall. Trim the roots and plant them in boxes as described in Chapter Seven, and put them in the basement to force the growth of small, creamy white heads called chicons. Water starts the forcing process, which usually takes about three to four weeks.

Early fall is also the time to sow seeds of herbs that cannot be transplanted from the garden for indoor growing. Parsley and basil, in particular, can be started now. Parsley must be started fresh for a winter crop because, as a biennial, it needs a winter dormant period; plants that were growing in the garden all summer will peter out over the winter if brought indoors. Also, sow basil in pots outdoors and bring in the young plants before the first frost. By fall, garden basil plants will be large, and the tough stems almost woody. Start new plants from seed (you probably won't find young plants at the garden center at this time of year) to have winter plants indoors.

BRINGING GARDEN HERBS INDOORS

Some herb plants can be potted up and brought indoors to spend the winter on a sunny windowsill or in a light garden. If the plants themselves are too big, you can propagate cuttings of most of them. Some of the herbs to bring indoors are tender perennials that will not survive winter outdoors except in the warmest climates. Bay, marjoram, oregano, lemon verbena, rosemary, and scented geraniums must all be moved indoors for winter in most of the United States. You can also pot up some hardier herbs for the indoor garden; chives, mints, lavender, thyme, and winter savory are some examples. If you just want to winter over these plants, and don't need them to grow actively, you can put the pots in an unheated sun porch.

Herbs to be moved indoors will need time to become accustomed to the confines of their pots, and also to the lower light levels indoors, so start the transition process well before the onset of cold weather. Dig the plants before the first frost, taking care to damage the roots as little as possible. Carefully plant them in pots slightly larger than the diameter of the rootball, in one of the soil mixtures recommended for herbs in Chapter Two under Starting Seeds Indoors. Try to preserve as much of the original soil around the roots as possible, to minimize disturbance to the roots.

If you have clumps of chives and garlic chives that have become crowded, dig and divide them, and pot up some of the divisions to bring indoors. Chives and garlic chives are handled somewhat differently from the other herbs described here, and their treatment is discussed below and in Chapter Seven.

Water the rest of the newly potted herbs, and set them in a shady place for about a week. This period will give them a chance to adjust to having their roots bound in a pot and to receiving less light. Check the plants carefully for signs of pests before you bring them indoors. It is a good idea, when you move them inside, to keep them away from the rest of your houseplants for a couple of weeks, just to make sure no bugs came sneaking in with them.

Chives and garlic chives need a cold dormant period before you bring them indoors, the way hardy bulbs must be chilled before you force them into early bloom indoors. In fact, growing chives indoors in winter is a forcing procedure like that used for bulbs. After potting up the chives and garlic chives you want to bring indoors (which can be done after the weather turns cold), set the pots in a cold frame or other cold but protected place, such as a garage. Leave the pots in place for about eight weeks (longer if the weather is mild—chives need eight weeks of cold weather before they will grow again). After the dormant period, cut back the leaves to 1 to 2 inches above the soil, bring the pots indoors to a sunny windowsill or light garden, and water.

AUTUMN MAINTENANCE

Fall is a good time to test your soil. Take samples and send them to your local County Extension office for analysis. Contact them in advance for instructions. You will find them listed in the phone book under U.S. Government, Department of Agriculture. Or you can use one of the do-it-yourself soil test kits available in garden centers. After getting the test results, apply lime, rock powders, and other phosphorus fertilizers as needed. Also add organic matter.

If you plan to mulch your garden over the winter, to protect root crops still in the ground, to keep perennials from heaving, or just to add organic matter to the soil as the mulch breaks down, collect whatever materials you will use for mulch before the weather turns cold. Use whatever is readily available to you—hay, seaweed, fallen leaves.

Autumn leaves, in fact, are a real bonus for gardeners. We can use them for mulch, add them to a compost pile, or compost them by themselves to make rich leaf mold. Leaf mold is the spongy black humus found on the forest floor. To make leaf mold, rake up the leaves and put them in pens made of chicken wire or hardware cloth. Shredding them first will make them decompose faster. Keep the leaves moist but not wet. Adding some soil or manure will add microorganisms to help the decomposition process. Or you might try a compost maker by Ringer (see Appendix) that is intended for use with brown leaves, and also helps along the decaying process. If you don't want to be bothered composting leaves, dig shallow trenches in the garden and bury the leaves —they will break down eventually.

In warm climates where gardens are still in high gear, mulch lightly to conserve moisture. When new seedlings are several inches high, or right after setting new transplants in the garden, lay down a mulch of straw, shredded leaves, or grass clippings to conserve moisture and help keep down weeds and soil temperatures. Be sure to water during hot, dry weather—or whenever plants need it—all through fall. Make sure both seeds and plants get enough moisture. Some regions tend to have dry weather in autumn and others tend to be rainy; water your garden according to its needs.

As fall progresses and the weather cools down, weeds will be less of a problem than they were in spring and summer. But early in fall you will still need to weed and cultivate often. It is still important to keep the garden free of weeds, especially when seedlings are just starting to grow. The tougher weeds will take moisture and nutrients the crops need to grow well. If weeds do get a start in your garden, at least pull them before they go to seed or you will be overrun next year!

If your kitchen garden contains perennials, mature plantings will need attention in fall. In addition to chives, which we've discussed earlier, crowded clumps of daylilies (whose buds are a delicacy known as golden needles in China) can be dug and divided in fall. If you have more of the tuberous roots than space in which to replant them, you may be interested to know that they, too, are edible. You can slice and fry them like potatoes, or substitute them for water chestnuts in stir-fry dishes. They are said to have a rather nutty flavor.

Check the other perennials in your garden for signs of disease. Pull up and dispose of any sick plants so they do not infect others nearby. Do *not* put diseased plant material on the compost pile. Even if you make hot compost, the temperatures may not be high enough to kill pathogens. Seal diseased plant parts in plastic bags and put them out with the trash.

In cool and temperate climates, if you have perennials like asparagus or biennials such as parsley, watch for the ground to freeze as fall edges into winter. When the soil freezes solid, lay down a loose mulch of leaves or evergreen boughs. The purpose of this winter mulch is to keep the ground frozen so perennials are not subjected to soil heaving from alternate freezes and thaws that can damage crowns and rootstocks.

FROST PROTECTION

As temperatures drop in autumn, make sure frost protection devices are in place for summer crops that are still producing. Frost usually strikes on clear, still nights, when the lack of cloud cover allows temperatures to fall quickly after the sun goes down. If you do not know when to expect the first frost, call your local County Extension office; they can tell you the average date of the first frost in your area. Remember, the date they give you will be only an average. The onset of frost varies with weather conditions from year to year, and the microclimate in your garden.

When you expect frost, cover late beans and eggplant, pepper, and tomato plants with hay, straw, or floating row covers (these are made of spun-bonded polypropylene and come in several different sizes; for more information on row covers and other frost protectors, see Chapter Two).

Depending on the layout of your garden, you could instead protect plants with a temporary cold frame. Pile bales of hay around a group of plants and cover with an old storm window.

Cloches, row covers, plastic tunnels, and even burlap or old tablecloths can protect plants overnight. Protect individual plants with hot caps, peach baskets, or boxes.

Floating row covers admit light, air, and moisture, and you can leave them in place as long as the plants stay in the garden. Other coverings should be removed in the morning, so plants can get light and moisture, and to provide necessary air circulation and prevent the buildup of too much humidity.

If you are growing plants in a permanent cold frame, open the lid during the day, and close it only when you expect frost at night.

Gardeners who have the time and inclination can set up various other structures to keep their tender plants warm in fall. You might take advantage of passive solar techniques and mulch around the base of the plants with stones or bricks. The mulch will absorb and store heat from the sun during the day and release it slowly at night. Jugs of water placed next to plants, especially if dark-colored, will do the same thing. Remove the lower leaves of the plants so the sun will shine directly on the stones or jugs. To hold the heat around the plants, sur-

EARTHWORMS AND WINTER MULCH

Earthworms are very good for garden soil— they aerate it, help break down organic matter, and leave behind nutrient-rich castings. In fact, lots of worms are a sign of healthy soil; they thrive in soils with lots of organic matter and are seldom found in depleted, chemical-laden soils. Earthworms cannot survive frost, and in fall when soil temperatures start to drop, they burrow deep into the soil to hibernate for the winter. A thick layer of winter mulch keeps the soil surface from alternately freezing and thawing in winter (important in perennial beds), but

also keeps the soil from freezing as deeply as it might if left unprotected. The thicker the mulch in the garden, the higher the frost line will be.

If you want worms to tunnel deeply into your garden soil—and they can go down as deep as 6 feet—to aerate the subsoil, lay down just a thin layer of mulch for winter. A thick layer of mulch will allow the worms to hibernate closer to the soil surface. In spring when the soil warms, the worms will become active again.

round each plant, along with its mulch or water jug, with a cylinder of hardware cloth that is wrapped in heavy plastic. Or make a cylinder from plastic that has wire grid fencing embedded in it.

Or you can make a sort of miniature greenhouse for the plants. Hammer a pole or tall stake into the ground at each end of the row you want to cover. Stretch a piece of rope or clothesline between the poles. Drape a sheet of heavy translucent plastic over the line, and pull out the sides to make a tent. Weight down the edges with stones or bricks, or peg them down. This structure should protect tomatoes, peppers, and eggplant through the first few light frosts.

Commercial growers in areas where frost does not often threaten crops protect their plants in emergencies with overhead sprinklers. The water being sprayed on the plants is warmer than the ambient air temperature, and as it cools it releases heat. This heat warms the leaf surfaces of the plants and keeps the tissues from freezing. You could try this technique at home as a last resort. Or try putting containers of warm water among plants under cloches or tunnel covers, or in the cold frame; if you are lucky the water will freeze and the plants won't.

If plants do freeze partially you may still be able to save them, but you'll have to get up with the chickens to do it. Water the plants with a fine spray or mist of *cool* water early in the morning, before the sun's heat thaws them. The mist will allow the plant tissues to thaw more slowly, and perhaps suffer less damage in the process.

These watering techniques may save the plants, but they will not save the fruit. Harvest any frost-damaged vegetables right away. If the damage is not too severe and the vegetables are ripe, cook and eat them; they will not store well. Otherwise, throw the damaged produce on the compost pile.

A temporary cold frame can save tomatoes, eggplant, and other tender crops from an early frost. Stack bales of hay around the plants and cover with one or more old storm windows.

A plastic tent can protect a group of peppers or other tender plants from several light frosts to extend the harvest by a few weeks.

SOIL PREPARATION

If your soil tends to be cold and wet in spring, fall is the time to prepare the garden for early spring planting. In cool climates especially, gardeners should prepare the garden now for next year's peas and onions. Along the West Coast, late fall weather is dry in many places, making this a good time for soil building. In any location, to be effective carry out soil improvement activities before the ground freezes.

Spread a layer of manure, compost, and other soil conditioners as needed, and till these materials into the soil. Dig the soil to a depth of at least a foot. The nutrients are released slowly from organic soil conditioners and will be available for plants by planting time next spring. Cover the surface with a layer of loose straw or hay over winter. When the ground starts to thaw in spring,

pull aside the mulch and plant early crops as soon as the soil becomes workable.

If your soil is very heavy and poorly drained, or if you have severely compacted subsoil, additional labor may be needed. You may have to double-dig as described in Chapter Three under Preparing for Planting Outdoors. If the drainage is very poor, remove the soil to a depth of 2 feet. Lay drainage tiles or a layer of gravel, then replace the soil.

In parts of the garden where you will not be planting in early spring, and where you do not have root vegetables in storage, or perennials in place, you may wish to leave the soil surface rough and unmulched over winter. Soil heaving that occurs during alternating freezes and thaws can be beneficial for soil—it brings up nutrients from the subsoil (stones, too, which you will have to remove in spring).

If your garden is very large, you can plant a winter cover crop such as rye grass or clover in areas where you will not plant again until spring. The potato farmers in my area on Long Island do this after they harvest in early fall. Till under your cover crops in early spring with a rotary tiller, to add organic matter and nutrients to the soil. Till at least a month before planting.

GARDEN CLEANUP

Fall is cleanup time! As you finish up the harvest, clean up the area, whether you will be replanting immediately or waiting until spring. Remove all plant debris and, as long as there are no signs of disease, put it on the compost pile. Pull up dead plants and pick up dead plant leaves from the ground. Leaving such debris to rot in the garden may seem like a good idea, but it could lead to pest and disease problems next year. Dead plants provide great hiding places for pests to winter over.

Rake up fallen leaves that have blown into the garden, and put them in the compost bin as well. Plant material and leaves will all break down more quickly if you shred them first. For composting procedures, see Chapter Two. Before winter really settles in, cover the compost pile with a tarp or sheet of heavy plastic to protect it from heavy rain and snow.

If you gardened in containers, clean out all the pots, tubs, and window boxes that held summer plants whose time is past. Remove the soil mix (dump it in the garden, unless the plants had disease problems). Scrub out the containers with warm, clear (not soapy) water, then soak them in a solution of one part liquid chlorine bleach to nine parts water for an hour. If the containers are too big to soak, at least rinse them with this disinfectant solution. Let the pots dry completely, then store them in the basement, garage, or garden shed until you need them next spring.

In permanently mounted window boxes and other big planters that cannot be moved, take out the plants, scoop out at least half the soil mix, and add fresh potting mix and sieved compost to refill the containers.

Cut back all perennials to within a few inches of the ground after the first frost, to eliminate winter hiding places for pests. Do not cut all the way back to ground level or you might damage plant crowns.

Put away stakes, tomato cages, and any other temporary plant supports that you will not need again until next year.

SIX

The Winter Garden

Winter has traditionally been a time of rest and contemplation for gardeners. With the garden retired for the year, there is time to reflect on the successes and failures of last season's garden, and to make plans for next season's plantings. The flurry of seed and nursery catalogs that begins before Christmas in January becomes a blizzard. Their lush photographs and florid prose entice gardeners with promises of bigger harvests and delectable new flowers from an ever-broadening array of plants.

As the cold winds howl outside our doors, we gardeners sit in our armchairs, our laps full of catalogs, daydreaming of spring. We dog-ear pages, thinking about trying this new eggplant or that new radicchio. We make lists of all the new plants we want to add to our gardens, and all the old favorites we couldn't possibly do without. Caught up in our desire, we forget that we have only so much space in the garden. We forget that we have jobs to go to and families to care for, that our time to garden is limited. We forget, too, how the knees ache and the back stiffens after a couple of hours of weeding and hoeing in the hot sun.

At some point, some measure of reality sets in (with luck, *before* we order all those seeds), and we set about trimming our wish lists to better reflect the amount of space and time we have for the garden. Most of us order too much anyway, but somehow there's always room to squeeze in a few more plants. And the fantasy gardens we plant in our winter dreams are marvellous creations indeed.

Winter will always be the season of renewal and planning for gardeners, at least for those of us outside of the tropics. But winter need not bring the cessation of all gardening activities. We can harvest food throughout the winter—a surprisingly diverse selection of food—we can putter in our indoor gardens, and we can also plant. As the days begin to lengthen and spring draws nearer, we begin preparing for the start of the new outdoor gardening season.

It is time to start seeds indoors for plants to move outdoors when the weather warms and settles sufficiently.

If you exercise some creativity and foresight, winter can be far more active than you might expect.

HOW SNOW AFFECTS THE GARDEN

We define a cold-hardy plant as one that can tolerate winter conditions in the location where it is being cultivated. Hardy plants are able to withstand varying degrees of freezing because their cells are structurally different from those of plants that are tender. The cells of hardy plants have a water-permeable membrane. When temperatures fall, as long as they do not drop too quickly, water is forced out of the cells through these membranes and into the spaces between the cells. When the water freezes the cells themselves are not damaged.

The hardiness of plants in a given location is determined not only by the degree and duration of cold temperatures in the garden over the course of the winter, but also by how deep the frost line goes. The depth of the frost line is in turn affected by the presence or absence of snow cover.

Snow is a big help to the garden in winter, and gardeners wish for it as devoutly as skiers do. A more or less dependable snow cover in winter is one of the benefits of living in the far North, or in a mountainous area, where growing conditions are otherwise rather harsh.

It is not easy to predict how much snow any given winter will bring. One old truism states that a wet summer will be followed by a snowy winter, and a dry summer is succeeded by a winter with little snow. According to another tradition, the weather over the course of a year balances out: a harsh winter follows a hot summer; a dry winter follows a wet summer. Weather conditions in the continental United States are determined by the path of the jet stream, which carries weather from west to east across the continent. The path of the jet stream shifts in response to ocean currents and other factors.

Whether or not you can predict how much snow you are likely to get, understanding how snow affects the garden will make it easier to cope with its presence or absence.

When soil freezes hard, water cannot reach plant roots in the frozen area. Plants whose roots cannot tolerate such conditions will die. A blanket of snow insulates the ground, and supplies moisture when it melts. If you get a good snow cover early in winter, before the ground freezes solid, and if the snow remains on the ground all winter, there may be enough moisture in the soil to keep alive plants that would not be hardy that far north without the blanket of snow. When the soil remains unfrozen under the snow, with temperatures above 32°F, the bottom layer of snow melts gradually during the winter, and the water soaks down into the soil.

If the soil does freeze on top, and is then covered by a light snowfall, the sun can penetrate the snow and reach the dark-colored soil underneath it. The sun warms the soil slightly, and again the snow melts from the bottom.

On the other hand, snow that accumulates after the ground has frozen solid is of little benefit to plants of marginal hardiness that would be helped by additional moisture. There are, of course, cases in which it is good to allow the soil to freeze; where perennials are present, for example, and when heaving could bring up nutrients from the subsoil to enrich a poor topsoil. But gardeners with root crops stored in the garden, and gardeners living in certain locations need to keep the soil from freezing deeply. In parts of the upper Midwest and the Mississippi Valley, the ground usually freezes early, then is covered by deep snow.

When the snow melts in spring the soil is still frozen, and there is no place for the water to go. It runs off and causes flooding. It is obviously to gardeners' benefit if they can prevent such flooding in their gardens.

Keeping the soil in gardens in these areas warm in winter can thus help prevent spring flooding. As described in Chapter Five, a 2-foot layer of loose mulch, laid down in autumn when the soil surface starts to freeze, will insulate the soil. The loose surface of the mulch will trap and hold snow—an added benefit.

The kinds of trees growing in the vicinity can also affect the amount of snow falling on the garden. Conifers trap snow in their branches and keep it from reaching the ground. But deciduous trees have lost their leaves in winter, and snow sifts through their branches and onto the ground. If you have a lot of closely planted evergreens on your property, the ground beneath them will tend to freeze early and deeply.

The Winter Harvest

Gardeners willing to bestir themselves from their winter lethargy will be able to enjoy fresh garden produce consistently throughout the season. The harvest will not be huge, but it will be most welcome, as will the chance to engage in the activities of gardening. Even northerners can garden—and harvest—all winter.

You will be able to dig carrots, leeks, parsnips, and turnips that are waiting in the garden under mulch or stashed in a window well or other outdoor storage cache. Winter carrots may come as a surprise; their flavor gets better, sweeter, after frost. They will stand up to quite severe freezes if mulched as directed in Chapter Five. Just be sure before laying the mulch that the tops (shoulders) of all the roots are covered with soil; frost can damage exposed roots, even under

mulch. Adventurous souls who grew salsify can dig those roots all winter, too.

If winter weather is not too severe, beets sown in midsummer can also be dug all winter. Plant a storage variety, and make sure the harvest is well protected when cold weather sets in.

In the early part of winter, outdoor storage caches can also yield cabbage, brussels sprouts, acorn squash, celeriac, kohlrabi, and winter radishes in addition to the other root crops. From indoor storage facilities you can take garlic, onions, winter squashes, and dried beans.

Salad crops sown in the cold frame in early to mid-fall will be ready to harvest in December.

An insulated cold frame (modified as described below) or hotbed can supply Oriental greens, kale, mustard, and salad greens even farther into winter, in all but the coldest climates. In milder climates, a conventional cold frame will provide lettuce, spinach, endive, and other greens through December. Insulate the frame on cold nights as described later under Maintenance in the Outdoor Garden.

The indoor garden offers Belgian endive and other forced roots, mushrooms, sprouts, and herbs and salad greens from windowsill or light gardens.

Modify a Cold Frame for Winter Growing

Cold frames are invaluable for extending the growing season in spring and fall. But in winter, problems develop. A standard cold frame tends to get not only too cold in winter, but also too wet and humid. Plants either succumb to the low temperatures or fall prey to molds and fungi. But there are some things you can do to insulate the frame and make it warmer. And understanding how to manage the cold-frame environment in winter improves the chances that you will be able to continue harvesting throughout the season.

First, pay attention to the structure itself. Locating the frame next to the south-facing wall of the house will afford protection from the cold north wind. Make the back of the frame higher than the front so the lid will be angled toward the south, to catch the maximum amount of sun. Make the walls thick, especially in the direction of the prevailing winds. If the cold frame is not located next to the house, it would be prudent to make the east, west, and north walls of the structure extra thick. Caulk all the joints —the frame must be airtight to hold warmth absorbed through the glazing during the day.

Line the inside of all four walls with polystyrene foam insulation 2 inches thick. The white foam will reflect light and heat onto plants in addition to insulating the structure. You can also, if you wish, place insulation underneath the frame to keep the wood out of contact with the ground. You do not have to excavate to do this. Just put down 2 inches of insulation before you put the frame in place. The frame should in this case have a bottom, and it will have to be deep enough to accommodate the root systems of the plants you want to grow. Luckily, leafy plants tend to have relatively shallow root systems. The soil level in the frame will be somewhat higher than that of the surrounding soil, but that should not be a problem. The foam both insulates and extends the life of the frame by preventing the wood from rotting from contact with the soil.

Insulate the lid of the cold frame as well. Use two layers of plastic or wire-reinforced plastic as glazing on the lid. The double glazing will trap air between the layers for an additional insulating effect. Staple the plastic to a wood frame to make the lid. Seal the joints as you did on the frame. For convenience, mount the lid so that you can open it just a few inches or nice and wide. When closed the lid should fit tightly.

Start plants for the winter cold frame in early fall. You can either sow directly in the cold frame, which is still open at that time of year, or you can start plants in the garden and transplant them into the cold frame when the weather turns cool. Transplant only the sturdiest, healthiest plants—disease problems would spread quickly and wipe out the crop. The toughest plants have the best chance of holding up under the adverse conditions to come.

The soil in the cold frame should be well drained, and rich in organic matter. Work in plenty of compost or leaf mold and composted manure before planting.

Cut back on watering as the weather turns colder. You will water seldom if at all during the winter when the cold frame is closed most of the time.

When temperatures fall below freezing and stay there, close up the frame for the winter. But whenever daytime temperatures go above freezing, open the lid of the cold frame a few inches to let in fresh air. Ventilation is extremely important. The tight construction of the frame prevents the water vapor transpired by the plants from escaping. The inside of the frame gets very humid.

When the frame stays closed during prolonged cold spells, watch out for aphids. If you see any when you open the frame, spray the plants with insecticidal soap.

With a bit of luck you should be able to harvest from your insulated cold frame all winter long. Pick the outer leaves of the plants, taking just a few from each plant at a time. The plants will continue growing— although very slowly—throughout the winter.

A variety of greens should grow in the winter cold frame, but Oriental brassicas are some of the best bets. Nonheading varieties generally produce the best results. Many Oriental greens can tolerate the broad temperature swings that can occur in the cold frame on clear, sunny winter days. They are able to produce better than other greens under such conditions. Most develop a mild flavor and tender texture, and they can be ready to harvest in as little as a month after transplanting into the cold frame.

Look for Oriental brassicas in the catalogs of companies specializing in Chinese or Japanese vegetables, or those of Comstock, Ferre & Co., Nichols Garden Nursery, or J. L. Hudson, Seedsman, which are listed in the Appendix. Below is a list of vegetables to try in an insulated cold frame or hotbed in winter.

Celery cabbage, mustard cabbage, or bok choy

Chinese cabbage: Hukucho, Siew Choi, Tah Tsai

Kale: Dwarf Blue-Curled Vates

Lettuce: Arctic King, Brune d'Hiver, North Pole, Red Montpelier, Salad Bowl, Winter Density

Mustard: Fordhook

Oriental greens: Green in Snow Mustard, Joi Choi, South China Earliest

Spinach: Winter Bloomsdale

Gardeners in the warmest parts of the country can grow in the outdoor garden through most of the winter the cool-season crops that the rest of us planted for fall. For most gardeners, though, the winter garden outdoors is limited to the insulated cold frame or hotbed, and vegetables kept in storage.

MAINTENANCE IN THE OUTDOOR GARDEN

If you live up north where winter comes early, and you haven't got anything growing in a cold frame, winter maintenance is a pretty simple affair. About all you need to do is check mulched areas regularly to make sure the mulch over perennials and stored root vegetables remains where it belongs. If some of the mulch blows away, replace it and lay chicken wire or boards over the top to hold it in place.

Gardeners in more moderate climates will be watching for the soil to freeze on top and then laying down their mulches.

Where the weather permits, finish any garden cleanup chores you didn't get to complete in fall. Keep checking perennials for frost heaving. If any roots are exposed, push them gently back into the ground and cover with soil. Mulch with evergreen boughs, straw, or other loose material.

If you have plants in a cold frame, remember to ventilate it when the temperature gets above freezing. Water if necessary while the frame is open. Check to make sure the plants are not too crowded. Air circulation is important to prevent disease. The leaves of neighboring plants should not touch. Maintaining adequate air circulation is problematic in winter when it is too cold to open the cold frame often; just do the best you can.

If you have installed a heating cable in the cold frame to make a hotbed, it is important to check periodically to see if the cables are still working properly. Check the temperature of the soil to see if it closely matches the cable setting. Check the air temperature inside the frame as well, to gauge the effectiveness of the cables.

If there is no snow cover, it is important to insulate the outside of the frame in cold weather to try and moderate the temperatures inside. Rapid temperature swings inside the frame hinder plant growth and encourage fungus disease. Even hotbeds will need insulation during extremely cold weather. Pile leaves against the sides of the frame. Stuff more leaves into burlap or cloth sacks and lay them on top of the lid at night. Cover the bags with a tarp or blanket and weight down the edges.

Gardeners in warm climates have more to do in winter. There are still plants in the outdoor garden to be weeded and watered when necessary. Cover tender plants with hot caps or other frost protectors if you expect freezing weather. It is better *not* to use winter mulch in warm climates to protect plants from frost; it could actually help cause the plants to freeze by trapping cold air around them after the cold snap has passed and the weather has moderated. If you live in a very warm climate, cut back winter-flowering annuals to encourage them to continue blooming.

As winter draws to a close, start watching for the ground to thaw. When the soil becomes workable, prepare a bed for asparagus to be planted in spring. Dig the soil deeply, and work in lots of organic matter and rock powders. Turn under cover crops as soon as the ground thaws. If the weather in your area tends to be dry in early spring, you can mulch until planting time to conserve soil moisture. Otherwise leave the soil uncovered. Turn compost piles made last fall as soon as they thaw.

FORCING ROOTS FOR WINTER HARVESTS

There are several ways to grow food indoors in winter, where the weather is much more amenable to the gardener than outdoor conditions.

The first indoor gardening method requires no special conditions—not even light. You can dig the roots of certain plants and bring them indoors to force from them winter crops of leaves or stalks. Asparagus, beets, dandelion, witloof chicory, and rhubarb can all be forced, according to the methods described here.

As noted in Chapter Five, the forcing process actually begins in fall, before the soil freezes solid, when you dig up the roots in the garden. The basic procedure is as follows. Replant the roots in a tub or wooden box at least 8 inches deep. Put a 3- to 4-inch layer of soil or builder's sand in the bottom of the tub or box. Set the roots in the soil with their tips pointing downward, the way they grow in the garden. You can set the roots closer together than they were in the outdoor garden because the roots themselves will not grow during forcing. Setting the roots close together will let you get the most possible production from the limited space in the container. Cover the roots with sand or soil, and water until the growing medium is evenly moist but not soggy. Put the box in a dark place where the temperature is around 50 to 60°F—your basement will probably be ideal. Check periodically to make sure the medium is moist; add water when necessary.

In three to four weeks the shoots and leaves should be large enough for harvesting to begin. You will find that forced shoots and leaves will be paler in color, more succulent and tender in texture, and milder flavored than the same plants grown outdoors in the garden.

Asparagus and rhubarb need a cold period before you can force new growth from them. When the roots are planted in the tubs or boxes, set them in a garage, shed, or other unheated but protected place for six weeks before moving them indoors. If the weather is unseasonably warm, you will have to leave the containers in the cold location longer than six weeks, so that they get the necessary amount of chilling. Do not water the roots until you bring the containers indoors to the basement. Thereafter, water as needed. Following are some tips on forcing individual roots.

Asparagus: roots for forcing should be three years old. You may be able to buy roots grown especially for forcing; otherwise, dig them from the garden. Unfortunately, you must throw out the roots after forcing; the process exhausts the roots to the point where it is useless to replant them in the outdoor garden. The forced spears will be tender, pale green, and rather slender. Break or cut them off at soil level when they reach the desired size.

Beets: when replanting beets in the forcing containers, be sure to set them deep enough so they are completely covered with soil or sand. The roots will produce several pickings of tender leaves to use in salads.

Dandelion: dig the roots carefully; dandelion develops a long taproot. The first leaves should be ready to harvest five weeks after replanting indoors. They will be tender, and without the very bitter flavor they develop when grown outdoors in sunlight.

Rhubarb: force two- or three-year-old roots. Dig the roots, cut off all the top-growth, and replant. The new, light pink stalks should be ready to cut in about six weeks. Use them for pies or sauces, or stew them with sugar and serve over custard.

Witloof chicory: Belgian endive, the small, creamy colored heads (called chicons) forced from the roots of this type of chicory, are expensive in supermarkets and specialty shops. To grow your own you will need a deep container in order to blanch

---

If you have no snow cover, you can pile bags of dry leaves around the sides and on top of the cold frame to insulate it during very cold weather.

The Winter Garden 121

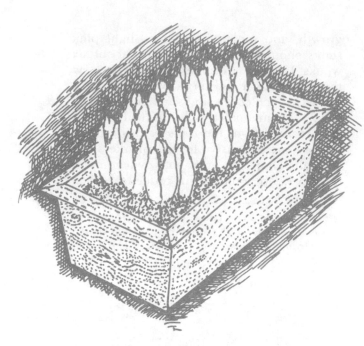

Creamy-colored Belgian endive is easy to force in the basement in winter, provided you grew Witloof chicory outdoors in summer to produce roots for forcing. The forced chicons have a mild, slightly bitter flavor and are delicious cooked in broth.

the endives. After digging the plants from the garden, cut back the leaves to 1 inch. Bury the roots in 10 inches of moist soil, then put a 4- to 6-inch layer of sand on top of the soil. In about three weeks, when the tips of the chicons poke through the sand, the Belgian endive is ready to harvest. Scoop out the sand to uncover the heads, and cut them off at the base. Serve Belgian endive braised or in salads.

Growing Your Own Mushrooms

One of the easiest and most interesting winter gardening projects to try is growing your own mushrooms. Raising mushrooms can be a very complex and demanding process involving culturing spores in a sterile medium in laboratorylike conditions and inoculating a special growing medium with the resulting spawn. But a number of seed companies and specialty suppliers sell kits preinoculated with spawn for home gardeners. All you do is water them to grow your crop. It's something of a novelty item, but the kits are fun, and offer an easy way to get fresh exotic mushrooms that can be difficult to find and expensive in the market.

You can grow the mushrooms in the basement—they need no light and most are adaptable to a range of indoor temperatures between 50 and 75°F. Mushrooms do need humidity, however, at a level of 80 to 85 percent, and the basement is the most humid part of most homes during the winter when the heat is on upstairs. Most companies ship mushroom kits only in fall and winter. The kits do not produce large harvests—don't expect to make a big batch of cream of mushroom soup—but you will get enough mushrooms to use in other kinds of dishes.

A number of kits are currently on the market. You can buy a kit for the familiar white button mushrooms, which is basically a box of special compost inoculated with the necessary spawn. These kits usually produce several flushes of mushrooms over a period of several weeks. When the harvest is complete, dump the spent compost in the garden—it's an excellent soil conditioner.

As American tastes have become more adventurous and sophisticated in recent years, kits have become available for some more exotic mushrooms. You can now purchase shiitake, golden oyster, pearl oyster, lion's mane, enokitake, and white trumpet mushroom kits for indoor growing.

Shiitake mushrooms take four weeks or perhaps a bit longer to reach harvestable size. Gardener's Supply Company (see Appendix) sells a kit that is a bag full of growing medium inoculated with spawn. You open the bag, place it out of direct sunlight, cover it with the plastic "humidity tent" included in the kit, and mist the medium according to the directions. The kit is said to produce up to 2 pounds of mushrooms.

Kits for oyster mushrooms, shiitakes, and several other kinds can be ordered from a company called Fungi Perfecti in Washington (see Appendix). Oyster mushrooms grow in about two weeks.

A company called Agristar markets kits for trumpet mushrooms by mail and in some supermarkets in New York and New Jersey. The medium is a synthetic log made of compressed cereal cellulose inoculated with spawn. You place the log in a plastic compartment and give it some water every day. The first harvest should be ready in about a week, and the log should give you a few more harvests, for a total production of about a pound.

If you find yourself taken with gourmet mushrooms, Gardener's Supply and Fungi Perfecti sell kits for other kinds of exotic mushrooms to grow outdoors in warm weather. You can try your hand at morels, King Stropharia, lion's mane, chicken-of-the-woods, and cauliflower mushrooms. If you decide you want to become a serious grower, Fungi Perfecti also supplies equipment for collecting spores, preparing and inoculating your own medium, and growing your own mushrooms "from scratch."

A CROP OF SPROUTS

Sprouts used to be thought of as strictly health food, eaten only by purists and dieters. But these days you can find them in salad bars all over the country. They're also good in pita sandwiches, stirred into soups, and of course, an essential part of Oriental stir-fry dishes. Sprouts are nutritious, tasty, and incredibly easy to grow. They are especially good to grow in winter, another modest but welcome addition to the selection of fresh, homegrown food available at this time of year.

The most commonly sprouted seeds are mung beans and alfalfa, both of which are available in natural food stores. But you can

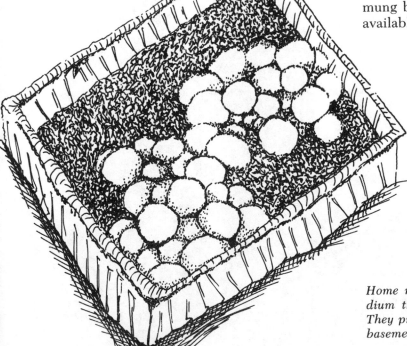

Home mushroom kits come with growing medium that is already inoculated with spawn. They provide a fun winter crop to grow in the basement.

also sprout radishes, lentils, soybeans, mustard, garden cress, and other seeds. It is best to purchase seeds intended for sprouting, rather than garden seeds. If you do use garden seeds, you must make absolutely sure that they have not been treated with fungicides or other substances that would be toxic to consume. Ask the supplier before you buy them.

The sprouting procedure is simple. Put a heaping tablespoonful of seeds in the bottom of a quart-size glass jar (a canning jar with a screw top is ideal). Cover the seeds with 1 inch of lukewarm water and let stand overnight. In place of the flat metal lid you would use to seal the jar if you were canning food, cover the opening with a piece of plastic mesh or a few thickness of nylon net. Hold the material in place with the screw-on band. The permeable covering makes it easy to rinse the seeds while you wait for the sprouts to grow.

Drain off the water from the sprouts and rinse them with lukewarm water. Rinse them two or three times each day. Set the jar upside down on paper towels after rinsing to allow all the water to drain out. Then set the jar on its side, so air can get in. Keep the jar in a dark spot, out of direct sun or bright light, with normal household temperatures. Underneath the kitchen sink has always been my favorite sprout farm.

Your sprouts should be ready to eat in about a week, depending on how quickly the seeds germinate.

Sprouts are easy to grow in a jar, and the quality is superior to that of sprouts you buy in a supermarket. The homegrown kind are fresh and crunchy, and will keep for several days in the refrigerator.

An Indoor Salad Garden

A variety of salad greens can add to the diversity of the winter harvest. Besides the satisfaction of having fresh, homegrown food in winter, there are other arguments to be made in favor of growing edibles indoors at this time of year. For one thing, you will be in such close contact with the plants that you may learn things about their behavior that will be useful in the outdoor garden, too. At least you will gain a renewed appreciation for their form. Many edible plants are good to look at as well as good to eat. Pots of leafy greens and herbs can be attractive in their own right, and offer a decided change from the usual ferns, philodendrons, and African violets.

Bear in mind that indoors is not the natural habitat of these—or any other—plants. Growing conditions are vastly different from the outdoor garden environment. However lovingly you care for your indoor crops, you cannot expect to get as big a harvest as you would from the same plants grown outdoors. But you can get a harvest, even if it is a modest one.

To improve the odds I would not recommend planting fruit-bearing crops like tomatoes and eggplant. Some talented gardeners have managed to produce a harvest from such plants indoors, without the benefit of a greenhouse, and you can certainly give it a try if you are looking for a challenge. But you will have to pollinate the flowers yourself, with a brush, and the vegetables, if you are lucky enough to get any, just won't taste like the ones you had in the outdoor garden in August. Your indoor farming efforts are better aimed in other directions.

The best vegetables for an indoor winter garden are those that can tolerate some shade and cool conditions outdoors—leafy greens. Because your space is limited, concentrate on growing nonheading plants of compact habit.

You will be able to grow the greatest quantity and variety of plants in a light garden. Chapter Two contains instructions for setting up a simple light garden. To grow salad greens, keep the lights anywhere from 5 to 10 inches above the tops of the plants (young seedlings will need the greatest concentration of light). Leave the lights on for twelve to sixteen hours a day. Keep in mind that the lower light intensity indoors means the plants will grow more slowly indoors than out.

Some edibles to try in a winter light garden are arugula, corn salad, garden cress, endive, leaf lettuce, mustard, small radishes, spinach, calendulas, and nasturtiums. You may find that the stronger-flavored greens such as endive taste milder when you grow them indoors under lights than when grown outdoors in sunlight.

If you sowed leaf lettuce in the outdoor garden in early fall, you can try digging up a few of the plants (leave as much of the original soil around the roots as you can), planting them in pots, and moving them into the light garden in late fall.

If you don't have a light garden, experiment with small salad greens on your brightest windowsills. The plants will need six hours of bright light a day, but all the light need not be direct sunlight. It is especially important at this time of year to give the windowsill plants the maximum possible amount of light. Use an unobstructed south, east, or west window; avoid a northern exposure, for there will simply not be enough light. Try to provide white or foil-covered surfaces under, beside, and behind the plants to reflect incoming light back onto them.

Some seed catalogs are now carrying a device called The Lighthouse, which is a collapsible, foil-lined box with an adjustable top designed to maximize the light received by windowsill plants. According to the manufacturer, the box was invented by a gardener frustrated by the difficulty he habitually encountered when trying to start seeds on a windowsill. The seedlings would develop weak, spindly stems that stretched toward the window—symptoms of insufficient light that came from one direction. The box comes in two sizes and is manufactured by Packaging Un-Limited, Floral Products Division, 1121 W. Kentucky St., Louisville, KY 40210.

Two particularly good bets for windowsill crops are mustard and cress seedlings, which you can pick when young and use to jazz up winter salads. Or put them in a sandwich, British fashion.

Pots with a diameter of 6 to 8 inches will accommodate most indoor edibles, whether you are growing them in a light garden or on a windowsill. Grow the plants in a light, well-drained soil mix, such as a blend of equal parts of peat moss, horticultural grade vermiculite, and potting soil, or equal parts

of peat, builder's sand, and soil. You can also add one part of crumbled compost if you wish; to minimize the threat of disease pathogens, you can pasteurize the compost before you put it in the potting mix.

Sow seeds slightly more shallow than their normal outdoor planting depth.

A cool location is best indoors (remember, these are cool-weather plants), and good air circulation is an important factor in preventing disease. Use common sense in regard to fresh air—icy blasts from an open window near the plants will be worse for them than no fresh air at all. A better course is to simply leave the door of the garden room open to the hall or adjoining room.

Use your light garden to grow salad greens and herbs indoors in winter.

You can occasionally open a window a crack in the next room. Or set up a small fan in the garden room to circulate the air.

Make sure the plants never dry out completely, but do not let the pots sit in standing water or the soil will become waterlogged. The potting mix must drain well between waterings to allow oxygen into the pores between soil particles—roots need air as well as water to grow. Stick your finger into the soil every few days; when the soil feels dry an inch or so below the surface it is time to water.

Give the plants plenty of space in the indoor garden; crowding hinders growth and promotes the spread of disease.

When seedlings are a few inches high, you can begin to fertilize them every two weeks with a liquid, all-purpose fertilizer diluted to one-half the strength recommended on the label. Seaweed concentrate and fish emulsion both work well, but be warned that the smell of fish emulsion may be less than welcome in the house. Liquid fertilizers are easier to apply to a lot of plants in separate pots than granular or powdered fertilizers that have to be scratched into the soil. You can water liquid fertilizers into the soil or use them as foliar feeds, spraying them (after diluting) directly onto the leaves.

Mustard and cress seedlings are easy to grow on a bright windowsill. Use them in sandwiches or to add zip to salads and soups.

GROWING HERBS INDOORS

A surprising number of herbs will grow well indoors, especially under lights. The flavor of herbs grown indoors will be less pronounced than when they are grown in the outdoor garden, and the leaves will be limper in texture and a bit smaller, but they will still be most welcome in the kitchen. There's nothing like the quality fresh herbs impart to dishes, particularly in winter when the outdoor herb patch in most gardens lies dormant. Basil, chives, parsley,

marjoram, oregano, rosemary, bay, mints, thyme, and lavender can all be grown indoors. So can tarragon, if you can give it enough humidity. See Chapter Seven for more information on individual herbs.

Be sure you plant enough herbs in your indoor garden; one parsley or basil plant indoors will not give you enough leaves to supply all your culinary needs. Plant several pots of the herbs you use frequently in the kitchen.

Grow your herbs in a window facing south or west, or under lights. Most herbs need five hours of sun a day on a windowsill, and pots must be turned every couple of days to keep stems growing straight. In a light garden, keep the lights 5 or 6 inches above the tops of the plants, and keep them lit fourteen hours a day.

A 6-inch-diameter pot will be fine for most herbs. Herbs with creeping rhizomes, such as mints, will probably do best in a wide, shallow bulb pan, and those having a long taproot, like parsley, will appreciate a deep container.

Most herbs need a richer soil when grown indoors than when growing out in the garden. One good growing medium for herbs is a mixture of equal parts of sand, peat moss, and potting soil. Or you might try a mix of two parts soil, one part leaf mold or compost, and one part sand, with a tablespoon of bonemeal added for each quart of the mixture. Or use a blend of equal parts soil and vermiculite, or equal parts of crumbled compost, sand, and perlite.

If you are starting herbs from seed, when the seedlings have their second set of true leaves, transplant them into individual 4-inch pots. When they outgrow these pots, transplant them once more into 6-inch pots. Feed your herbs with a mild liquid fertilizer once every three or four weeks while they are actively growing. They need enough fertilizer to grow steadily, but overfeeding causes too rapid, leggy growth and weaker flavor. Herbs in the outdoor garden go dormant in winter. If you dug up plants from your garden in fall and brought them indoors in pots, you may not need to feed them until early spring. But if you took cuttings in fall and planted them, it is a good idea to begin a fertilization program when the cuttings have rooted.

Most herbs will thrive in temperatures of 65 to 68°F; if you can give them temperatures in the low 60s at night, it's even better. They need lots of humidity indoors, along with good air circulation; leaves of adjoining plants should not touch. A basement light garden can be a good place for indoor herbs, because basements are generally more humid than the rest of the house. Try some of the humidity-boosting techniques recommended in Chapter Two.

Water most herbs thoroughly when the soil feels dry below the surface. Never let the pots stand in water; pour off any water still remaining in drainage saucers ten minutes after watering. Check Chapter Seven for watering needs of individual herbs—some like constant, even moisture and some like to dry out more thoroughly between waterings.

If you are growing your herbs on a windowsill, move the plants away from the windowpane during very cold weather.

Harvest your indoor herbs by snipping off a few leaves as needed.

MAINTAINING INDOOR GARDENS

When indoor plants are actively growing, fertilize them every two weeks with a half-strength all-purpose liquid fertilizer.

If you are growing sprouts, remember to rinse them every day until they are ready to eat.

Keep the leaves of plants on windowsills from touching the glass. On extremely cold nights, slide a piece of cardboard between the glass and the plants for protection. Move the tenderest plants off of windowsills on the coldest nights.

Be careful not to overwater indoor plants, and make sure they remain well spaced to get better air circulation. Too much water and too little air encourages fungus disease. Also keep a constant watch for aphids. The relatively soft, succulent growth of indoor plants is a favorite target for these sap-sucking insects. If you spot any, spray the plants with insecticidal soap. Isolate any plants exhibiting symptoms of pests or disease to prevent problems from spreading to the rest of your plants.

WINTER PLANTING

In the early part of the new calendar year, it's time to think again about planting crops that will mature outdoors. Gardeners in warm climates will be planting the earliest crops—asparagus, peas, onions—outdoors in the garden. If you are adventurous and your garden is far enough south, you can start some tomato seeds outdoors under hot caps or cloches.

Farther north, it is time to start some seeds indoors. The first step is to perform a germination test on any seeds you have saved since last year. See Some Tips for Starting Vegetables Under Lights, under Light Gardens, in Chapter Two for directions on testing stored seeds for germination. Starting seeds indoors is among the most rewarding activities of the gardening year. It is always amazing to find that from those dry, tiny packages in their myriad shapes comes new life. The tiny black beads of arugula, wrinkly peas like half deflated volleyballs, the little asteroids that are the compound seeds of beets—all hold the pattern and material for the next generation, ready to burst into growth when given water, warmth, and later on, light.

After testing for germination, discard any seeds that germinate poorly and order replacements. Calculate planting dates for starting seeds indoors, and for direct-seeding or transplanting to the garden, based on when you expect the last spring frost. The entries in Chapter Seven give planting dates for spring crops relative to the date of the average last frost. You can assign calendar dates for your garden.

Slow-growing, warm-season vegetables like tomatoes can be seeded indoors as early as late January. In February start seeds of the cabbage family, parsley, peppers, eggplant, endive, onions, and leeks. You can also start sunflowers to transplant outdoors after the last frost.

Late in February, before the soil in the garden is ready to work, you can give some plants a head start and sow seeds in a hotbed. Lettuce, beets, leeks, and brussels sprouts are some plants to sow in the hotbed. Transplant to the garden in early spring when conditions are amenable.

As soon as the soil in the outdoor garden is workable, plant onion sets, peas, asparagus and rhubarb crowns, corn salad, garlic, pansies, calendulas, spinach, and early cabbage and head lettuce plants. Around the same time you can sow carrots, cauliflower, Swiss chard, chervil, chives, collards, garden cress, kale, mustard, parsley, and turnips in the cold frame. These early plantings come as winter is fading into spring.

PLANNING THE NEW GARDEN

Now the process has come full circle and it is time to begin a new cycle in the garden. See the guidelines in Chapter One on planning the garden. Make a new garden plan and prepare seed and nursery orders. It's a good idea to order early to be sure of getting everything you want, and to make sure you get the seeds in time to start indoors those that need it.

Be conservative in terms of how much you order—we gardeners always order too many seeds, and buy too many plants. But be bold in your choices. Diversity is what keeps gardening fun. Try something new each year, even if it's just a new variety of bean. Try plants on the borderline of hardiness for your area, push the seasons, dare the impossible—such efforts may succeed or fail, but the successes are so rewarding that a bit of gambling is worth it.

Catalogs can make us forget all the wonderful plants we already have in our gardens, and make us want what we haven't got. They can make us want to live someplace else so we can grow what we can't grow now. Before you order seeds, take a little time to step back and think about what you grew this year. Pat yourself on the back for your accomplishments, appreciate your successes. Review the garden year.

Which crops did well last season? Which performed better than you expected? Which did not do so well? How did weather conditions compare with other years? Did you have any unusual pest or disease problems?

If you don't already keep a garden notebook, start one now. Making notes on plant performance, weather, pests, and other events throughout the gardening year is extremely useful in letting you compare your garden's success from year to year. You can keep track of the life cycles of woody and wild plants in your home landscape as well, and perhaps find some plants that make reliable indicators of the last frost and other climactic events. After several years you will have in your notebooks a solid base of information about the growing conditions in your own garden. It is also fun to look back on special moments from years past—the earliest tomato you ever picked, a bumper crop of autumn lettuce, or the year that song sparrows built a nest near the garden.

After flipping through the new crop of seed catalogs, go back through and start to make lists of what you might want to grow. Plan to rotate crops, especially the cabbage family (see Chapter Two for details). Think about good companions in the garden, for pest control, nutrient needs, and also for form and color. Maybe this is the year to grow eggplant in front of a screen of climbing purple beans, and brighten the scene with a frilly lime green leaf lettuce in front of the eggplant, and maybe some little lemon yellow marigolds in front of the lettuce. Or you might want to try setting your salad plants in squares or diamond patterns instead of rows.

On those long winter nights dream about the perfect garden. Use your imagination. Play with the possibilities. Plot out your dream garden in your head and in your garden notebook. If you decide in the end you don't like it, you can wipe it out and start again in the twinkling of an eye.

After the seed orders are mailed off it's time to start looking for the first sign of spring. The first sign of spring (if you don't count the arrival of the first seed catalog) comes just when it seems like winter will never loosen its chilly grip on us. February 2 has become associated with the groundhog, especially a particular groundhog in Punxsutawney, Pennsylvania, who may or may not see his shadow. Thinking of February 2 only as Groundhog Day is *not* a sure sign of spring; if the animal sees his shadow we are to expect six more weeks of winter. There is a much more optimistic meaning to attach to this date if we are willing to rummage around in the past a bit. In pre-Christian Europe February 2 was known as Candlemas, one of the great pagan festival days of the year. On Candlemas, candles were lit to welcome the sun back from its winter sojourn in the southern hemisphere, and to speed its journey back to our part of the world. Although people at that time didn't understand the motions of the earth and the sun, they did know that in winter the days were short and cold, and the world seemed dark. They needed the sun to keep them warm and to grow their crops. Candlemas was a time to anticipate the coming spring, and to let the sun know its light and warmth were appreciated.

We can light our own candles on February 2, to honor the return of the sun. Or at least we can notice how the days are lengthening; night doesn't fall as early as it did in December, and spring is definitely on the way, travelling northward with the sun across the face of the earth.

SEVEN

Plants for Kitchen Gardens

In THIS CHAPTER you will find specific information on vegetables, herbs, and edible flowers to consider including in your kitchen garden. For each plant there is a description of the plant and its edible parts, suggestions for how to use it in the garden and the kitchen, and information on how to grow it. I have also included, where relevant and feasible, information on different types and varieties in the hope of making your choices easier and better informed.

Please note that general cultural techniques such as seed starting, watering, and pest control are covered in Chapter Two and are not repeated here. This chapter will tell you which methods are needed for each plant, such as whether you need to start seeds indoors; for instruction on how to start seeds indoors you can refer to Chapter Two. I have not included information on pH needs for the majority of plants in this chapter either because they prefer the mildly acid range preferred by so many plants or because they adapt to a wide range

of pH. In the cases of plants for which pH is an important factor in their success I have noted their requirements.

I wish I'd had space to include many more plants in this chapter than I did. You will not find entries for corn or potatoes, two space-hungry crops for which there are really no compact varieties, or for celery, which is very difficult to grow. But you will find here some unusual choices in addition to the old favorites, and I hope you will be inspired to experiment on your own, as well. Remember, try something new in your garden each year to expand your horizons and keep gardening fun.

Arugula

This savory salad plant was seldom seen in American gardens until relatively recently. But now that Americans have discovered gourmet salads, we have also discovered how easy it is to grow some of the leafy plants that add so many interesting flavors to salad bowls.

Arugula, *Eruca vesicaria* subsp. *sativa*, also known as rocket, roquette, rugola, Mediterranean rocket salad, and by various other names, is widely used in Greece, Italy, and France. The plant has dark green, deeply lobed leaves that grow in a loose cluster. The strong flavor of arugula is difficult to describe—at once nutty and peppery and spicy—but undeniably distinctive. You will either love arugula or detest it, but by all means try it.

Arugula is extremely easy to grow. A hardy annual, it grows best in cool weather and can be planted in both spring and fall. Because it grows so quickly and is compact in habit, it's good for interplanting.

Sow early crops as soon as the soil can be worked in spring, as much as eight weeks before you expect your last frost. Sow seeds ½ inch deep, as little as 1 inch apart. Cut young plants when a few inches tall to thin the rows or beds, eventually leaving plants 6 inches apart to develop more fully. Plants can be set in rows 18 to 20 inches apart, or 6 inches apart in all directions in intensively planted beds. Make a new sowing every two or three weeks for a continuous harvest throughout the spring.

You can continue planting all summer, but the plants bolt when summer is at its height, so you will have to harvest when they are still fairly young. Shade cloth and extra moisture will help prolong the harvest, but it's easier to stop planting in late spring and wait until it's time to plant a fall crop.

Pick leaves when they are 4 to 6 inches long for best quality. They will reach this size about five or six weeks after planting. Use young leaves to add flavor to tossed salads, or eat them by themselves with a tangy vinaigrette dressing. The older leaves develop a sharper taste and coarser texture, but you can cook them along with other leafy greens. The plants bolt in midsummer, and when they do the leaves become very hot—too strong flavored for many pal-

ates. The flower stalks, though, are edible. A neighbor from Greece told me that people in her hometown use the flowers and stems of arugula as a cooked vegetable. You can also toss a few of the flowers into a salad.

For fall harvest, direct-sow at the end of summer, about six weeks before you expect the first fall frost. In most gardens, arugula planted in fall will survive the winter. The plants go dormant in subfreezing weather, but they will start growing again when the temperatures moderate. Protect arugula with cloches or hot caps in winter, or grow it in a cold frame, to keep the leaves tender. Uncover the plants in early spring and they will resume growing, producing early harvests.

Arugula is not a hybrid, so you can let a few plants bloom and set seeds, then collect and save the seeds for future planting.

You can also grow arugula as a seedling crop—a growing method that is widely known in England and the Continent but far less common here. To plant a seedling crop, sow the seeds thickly in a flat (or in the garden) and harvest the plants when they are only a couple of inches tall. Just snip off the plants at ground level with scissors. Use the tender seedlings in salads. Try growing a seedling crop of arugula indoors in winter, on a windowsill or in the light garden.

Asparagus

Asparagus (*Asparagus officinalis*) is one of the greatest treats of the spring garden. It belongs to the lily family, and a comparison of asparagus spears with the flower stems of lilies shows the similarity. You don't need a whole lot of space to grow asparagus, but consider the pros and cons before ordering any. Asparagus is harvested for just several weeks out of the year, but it stays in place year-round so you cannot plant succession crops to make efficient use of the same space. And you must wait two or three years after planting before you can harvest. On the other hand, once established, asparagus needs little maintenance. And the feathery foliage the plants produce after the harvest ends is really quite handsome—a nice backdrop for other plants.

The plants are perennial, and an established bed may keep producing for as long as twenty-five years. Asparagus roots grow deep into the soil, so the plants can survive quite cold winters. In fact, they need a winter dormant period and cannot survive in very warm climates.

Asparagus grows best in full sun, although it will also grow in partial shade. The ideal soil is a well-drained, sandy loam that is fertile and rich in organic matter and that is loose to at least 18 inches deep. But asparagus will adapt to a range of soils, as long as the soil is well drained; soggy soil will rot the roots. If your soil is dense and clayey, lighten it by working in coarse builder's sand.

Because the plants will be in place for a long time, it is worthwhile to prepare the soil well before planting. If you can, prepare the soil the autumn before you plan to plant. Asparagus is best planted in a trench that is about 1 foot wide by 1½ feet deep. When you dig the trench, reserve the topsoil and get rid of the subsoil. Put a good layer of compost, leaf mold, composted manure, or peat humus in the bottom of the trench, and work it into the soil with a spading fork. Sprinkle in some rock phosphate or bonemeal for phosphorus, and some greensand or granite dust to add potassium. Or add an all-purpose organic fertilizer right before you plant. Work the material into the soil.

Asparagus is easiest to grow from dormant, one-year-old crowns, which are available at garden centers and from many mail-order seed and nursery companies. Plant crowns as soon as the soil can be worked in spring, two to four weeks before the last spring frost. Most nurseries try to ship close to the proper planting date for your area.

You can also grow asparagus from seed, and seed-grown plants have the advantage of greater disease resistance and heavier production. Sow seeds ½ inch deep, twelve to fourteen weeks before setting out plants. Do not set out seedlings until a month after your last frost; the plants should be a foot tall. Soak the seeds for twenty-four hours before planting to improve germination. Soak crowns in lukewarm water for an hour before planting to soften them.

Plant asparagus 1½ to 2 feet apart, in trenches 3 to 4 feet apart. Plant about 6 inches deep, 8 inches deep in very light soils. Planting a bit deeper (10 inches deep) will give you larger, somewhat later, spears.

At planting time, make a mound of soil every 1½ to 2 feet along the bottom of the trench. Set a crown on top of each mound, with the eyes facing up. Spread the roots down and over the sides of the mound. If you are setting out seedlings, set one on top of each mound. Cover crowns with 2 inches of soil (or pack the soil around the base of each seedling); use your fingers to work the soil into the spaces around the roots. Water to eliminate air pockets and settle the crowns. If necessary, add more soil to fill the holes.

Add a couple of inches of soil to the trench from time to time as the plants are growing. The trench should be full by halfway through the growing season. When the soil in the trench is even with the surrounding soil, mulch with shredded leaves, grass clippings, or compost.

For the first two years asparagus is in the ground, you should not harvest, so the plants can establish themselves. Some catalogs recommend cutting a few spears the year after planting, but it is better for the long-term productivity of the bed to refrain from taking even a light harvest too early on. The first harvest season will be the third year after planting, when you can harvest for two weeks. The following year, pick spears for four weeks. In subsequent years the harvest period can last six to eight weeks.

Harvest spears when they are 8 to 10 inches tall and less than an inch in circum-

Basil can be an ornamental—as well as flavorful —addition to the garden. The variety shown here, Purple Ruffles, has deep purple leaves with frilly edges.

COURTESY ALL-AMERICA SELECTIONS

ference, while the leaf bracts at the tips of the spears are still tightly closed. Snap off the spears at ground level instead of cutting them, to avoid damaging the crown.

Keep the bed weeded all summer; water deeply during spells of very dry weather. If you have seed-grown plants in their first year, before the root system is too extensive, pull up plants that produce berries; they are female and produce thinner, weaker spears than male plants because they put their energy into producing berries (which contain seeds).

In early autumn topdress with 6 to 8 inches of compost to enrich the soil and serve as a protective winter mulch.

Rust is the biggest problem with asparagus; fusarium wilt, crown and root rot, and asparagus beetles can also cause trouble. By all means plant a rust-resistant variety. Mary Washington, Jersey Giant, and Waltham are all time-tested, rust-resistant varieties. Connover's Colossal is good to grow from seed. Syn-456 has grown well in the Northeast, Midwest, and Mid-Atlantic areas. UC 157 does well in the warm climates of the South and West Coast. Jersey Giant, Syn-456, and UC 157 produce mostly male plants and are thus higher yielding than other varieties.

Basil

Basil is a paragon of the herb garden. If your sole acquaintance with *Ocimum basilicum* is a jar full of little bits of dry brownish leaves that go into spaghetti sauce, you owe it to yourself to get to know this herb better. It has been known since ancient times, and regarded quite differently in different places. The medieval Europeans believed that basil bred scorpions in the brain, but in India it was sacred to some of the Hindu gods.

The rich flavor of fresh basil is spicy and pungent, with a hint of licorice and mint, and there are cinnamon-, clove-, lemon-, and licorice- or anise-scented varieties, too. There are large- and small-leaved basils in a range of heights, and some with leaves of deep purple. The foliage of some basils has frilly, ruffled edges.

Basil contributes to so many luscious dishes. For example, a handful of chopped fresh leaves blended with garlic, chopped tomatoes, and extra virgin olive oil makes a light sauce for pasta that captures the very essence of summer. It is also tasty with grilled baby eggplant. One of the classic preparations for fresh basil is pesto sauce, in which the leaves are ground with olive oil, garlic, pine nuts, parsley, and Parmesan cheese to make a rich, spicy pasta sauce. The scented basils are an interesting addition to salads and pastas.

In the garden, standard-sized basil, which grows 1 to 2 feet tall, belongs in the front to middle of the garden, depending on the sizes of the other plants being grown. The small-leaved miniature cultivars, some of which form low, globular mounds, work best in the front of the garden, as edgers, or in pots. All basils will grow happily in a pot or a generous-sized window box. The rich green or deep purple foliage of basil combines nicely with flowers. Try green-leaved varieties with calendulas or nasturtiums, or purple basil with pink dianthus, or with chives and garlic chives. Basil is a traditional companion plant for tomatoes.

The plants produce small spikes of white flowers in midsummer (or pale pinkish purple flowers in the purple varieties). The flowers don't add much to the visual content of the garden and are best picked off to retain the best leaf quality. The flowers are edible, though, so if some of them open before you get a chance to pick them you can use them in the kitchen.

The plants are branching annuals that need to be pinched back to grow into a bushier form. Pinch back the tips of the stems every few weeks to promote branching.

Basil loves sunshine and warmth. Give it a spot in full sun, in crumbly, loose-textured, moist but well-drained soil that is rich in organic matter and well supplied with nitrogen. The soil should be reasonably fertile but not too rich, or the leaves will have less flavor.

Start seeds indoors, planting ¼ inch deep, three to four weeks before you expect the last frost. Cover the containers with plastic to maintain high humidity until sprouts appear.

Plants can go out to the garden one or two weeks after the last frost, when the soil temperature is at least 50°F. This is also the time to direct-sow, or to plant nursery transplants. Do not be in a hurry to plant out—basil needs warm soil, and seeds may rot in soil that is cold and soggy. Thin plants to stand 10 to 12 inches apart in rows 1½ to 2 feet apart, or 1 foot apart in all directions in a bed.

Like most other members of the mint family, basil does not like to be dry. Mulch is a good idea, but wait to apply it until the soil is good and warm. Water whenever the soil becomes dry an inch or two below the surface. It is best to water at ground level—the leaves may develop spots if hit with cold water.

You can harvest individual leaves as needed, or cut back the stem tips to harvest and prune at the same time. Cut back to right above another pair of leaves to avoid leaving a length of bare stem on the plant, and to encourage the plant to branch and grow bushier. Handle carefully during harvest—the leaves turn black if you bruise them.

Basil will store well for several days in the refrigerator, but leaves will start to go limp. You can dry the leaves for long-term storage, although they will lose a great deal of their flavor. To preserve more of the fresh quality, grind the leaves with olive oil in a blender or food processor and freeze the resulting paste.

Basil in its common species form is among my favorite garden herbs, and the cultivars are interesting as well. Purple Ruffles has purple, ruffled, frilled leaves and grows to 2 feet tall; Dark Opal is a smaller purple-leaved variety. Green Ruffled has frilly leaves and a rich, spicy flavor, as does the Italian variety Genovese. Small-leaved varieties include Spicy Globe, Green Bouquet, Greek Miniature basil, Dwarf Italian, and Fino Verde Compatto. Lettuce Leaf has very large leaves. Napoletano has large, crinkly, light green leaves and a mellow flavor. Indian basil or holy basil, also called Tulsi, has green leaves, purple flowers, and a touch of clove in its taste. Several seed and nursery companies also carry one or more of the scented basils, as do mail-order herb suppliers.

Snap Beans

These beans *(Phaseolus vulgaris)* are picked while the seeds inside them are small and immature, and eaten pods and all. Green beans are American natives. We used to call them string beans, but since most varieties these days are stringless, we now call them snap beans instead, because the crisp pods snap when you break them into pieces. There are climbing pole varieties and shorter bush varieties, yellow-podded "wax" varieties and green-podded varieties. There are also a few varieties with deep purple pods that turn green when you cook them. There are broad-podded Italian or romano beans, and slender French filet beans, or *haricots verts* (green beans in French), which are picked young and eaten whole.

Although snap beans are easy to find in supermarkets and produce stands, the only way to get really top quality is to grow them yourself. Snap beans lose their crunchy texture during shipping, storage, and time spent in produce bins, and the beans sold in stores are usually limp and tough by the time you buy them.

If you have a sunny spot, snap beans are well worth your while to grow. There are so many kinds from which to choose—some of them quite ornamental as well as tasty—and as a bonus the plants help improve soil quality. Like all legumes, bean roots have nodules containing bacteria that fix nitrogen in the soil. Dusting the seeds with a legume inoculant powder before planting

French filet beans are picked while they are young and slender, and eaten whole. The variety shown here, Triumph de Farcy, is an heirloom.

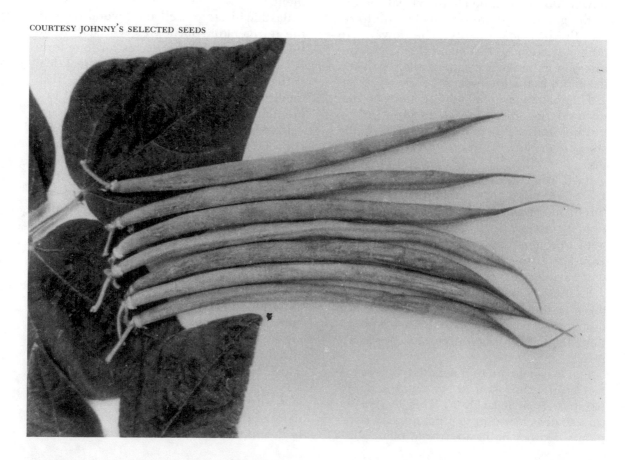

improves the plants' nitrogen-fixing ability and also enhances their growth. Legume inoculant is available from garden centers and mail-order seed companies.

Sow snap beans directly where they are to grow, after all danger of frost is past in spring and the soil temperature is at least 60°F. If you live where the frost-free growing season is very short, you may have to start your beans indoors two weeks before your last frost date and set them out four weeks later. Start the seeds in individual peat pots to minimize root disturbance during transplanting.

Snap beans grow best in well-drained soil with a near-neutral pH, but they will tolerate a pH range of 6.0 to 7.5. Sow them 1 inch deep in most soils, but 1½ to 2 inches deep in very light, sandy soils in summer. Sow 2 to 3 inches apart, then thin to leave the strongest plants 4 inches apart for bush varieties, 6 inches apart for pole beans.

Most snap beans are ready to pick in about two to two-and-a-half months. Pole beans mature later than bush beans, but they bear heavier crops over a longer period, so you only need to make one planting. For a larger harvest of bush beans, make succession plantings three weeks apart through midsummer. Rotate beans on a three-year cycle to avoid disease problems.

If your soil is very sandy, your beans will appreciate a mid-season potassium boost. For best production keep the soil evenly moist from the time the flowers open until the pods are set.

Never, ever harvest or work around beans when the plants are wet, or you can spread rust and other diseases by brushing against the plants. If your plants are attacked by Mexican bean beetles, spray or dust with rotenone or pyrethrum.

Some gardeners swear pole beans have the best flavor. They grow on vines up to 8 feet tall and the plants will need support. Put the supports in place when the plants have two leaves. Grow netting, strings, trellises, towers, and tripods are all good supports for pole beans.

Harvest snap beans just whens the pods begin to swell. Filet beans must be harvested when very young, as described below. Pick beans often to keep the plants producing. Freeze any excess for long-term storage. Bean blossoms, too, are edible.

French filet beans, or *haricots verts*, are bred to have slender pods. You must pick them young—when they are not even ⅛ inch thick—and eat them whole. These beans get fibrous and tough if you let them get as big as regular snap beans. Filet beans are usually about 4 to 6 inches long at harvest time, but it is the thickness, not the length, that determines when they are ready to pick. The best-known filet variety among American gardeners is the heirloom Triumph de Farcy. Other good varieties are Camile, Finaud, Marbel, and Morgane.

Green beans are the classic snap beans, and myriad varieties are available—far too many to describe or even list here. Some reliable bush green beans are Bountiful, Bush Blue Lake, Derby, Early Contender, Greencrop, Greensleeves, Lancer, Landreth's Stringless, Provider, Tendercrop, Tendergreen, Topcrop, and Venture. Good pole beans include Blue Lake, Emerite, Fortex, Kentucky Blue, the classic Kentucky Wonder, Kentucky North, and Northeaster.

Yellow, or wax, beans have a less "beany" flavor and are not quite as crunchy-textured as green beans. Bush varieties include Brittle Wax, Buerre de Rocquenfort, Cherokee Wax, Goldencrop, Improved Golden, Pencil Pod Black, and the exotic-looking Dragon Tongue, whose light yellow pods are streaked with red purple. Some good pole varieties are Burpee Golden, Kentucky Wonder Wax, and Yellow Annelino.

Many snap bean fanciers prefer Italian green beans—usually called romano beans—for flavor. Romano beans produce broad, flat pods with a superb nutty, beany taste. Try Bush Romano, Roma II, or Jumbo Bush. For pole beans consider Frima, Garrafal de Encarnada, Green Annelino, and Romano.

Purple-podded beans are quite ornamental in the garden, with their pale purple blossoms and deep purple pods. Pole varieties make an attractive screen or backdrop for lower plants. The beans turn green when you cook them. They freeze well, too, and when they turn green you know they've been blanched just long enough. Bush varieties of purple beans include Royal Burgundy, Royalty Purple Pod, and Sequoia (a purple bean with a flavor like a romano bean). Pole varieties include Purple Peacock and the lovely Trionfo Violetto, which, in addition to light purple flowers and dark purple pods, boasts deep green leaves with purple veins.

Runner beans, while a different species from snap beans (*Phaseolus coccineus*), are used the same way, and can be used to great ornamental effect in the garden. Runner beans have brilliant red, white, or bicolored flowers, and are quite tasty if you pick them while they are small. The pole varieties make handsome screens. Painted Lady has red and white flowers, Scarlet Runner and Scarlet Emperor have rich red flowers contrasted against deep green foliage, and Butter, Desiree, and White Dutch Runner have creamy white blossoms.

Lima and Shell Beans

Lima beans (*Phaseolus limensis*) are the most widely grown shell beans, and like many other shell beans, you can use them as either green shell beans or dried beans, depending on the variety. Limas have a multiplicity of uses, as a fresh vegetable or dried in soups and for baking. Most other shell beans are also used for baking and in soup, and some have become closely associated with the cuisines of particular countries, such as the pinto bean, which is such an essential part of Mexican cooking. Dried beans are extremely nutritious, high in protein, fiber, and complex carbohydrates, and low in fat. They are also quite delicious when prepared with a little flair. Green

shell beans are a very pleasant experience —they are delicious and many are easier to grow than limas, especially in cool climates. They are hard to find in supermarkets, so you may never have tried them, but by all means do so. The French know green shell beans as *flageolets*, and love to serve them with lamb.

Bush shell beans other than limas are grown like bush snap beans, but take longer to mature. Limas have slightly different requirements.

Lima beans are among the tenderest of all our garden vegetables in terms of their temperature needs, and cannot go into the garden until the soil temperature is at least 65°F. Do not under any circumstances plant them in cold soil. Direct-sow limas at least two weeks after your last frost. If you live where frost stays late in spring and comes early in fall, choose a bush variety of lima— they mature a few weeks earlier than pole beans. If your frost-free growing season is less than about sixty-five days long, you may have to start your lima beans indoors in peat pots, a month before your last expected frost.

Space bush limas 3 to 6 inches apart in rows 2 to 2½ feet apart, or 8 inches apart in all directions in intensive beds. Pole limas need more space, but produce more beans per square foot of garden space. Support them on tripods, sturdy trellises, or bean towers. Space pole limas 7 to 10 inches apart in rows 2½ to 3 feet apart.

Space other shell beans 3 to 4 inches apart in rows 1½ to 2 feet apart. They can go into the ground anytime after the last frost, when the soil temperature is 60°F or more.

Plant limas and other shell beans in full sun, in well-drained soil that contains lots of organic matter and sufficient phosphorus and potassium to support the plants. The soil's nitrogen content is less important because the plants fix their own. Plant 1 inch deep in soils that are heavy and dense, 1½ inches deep in light, sandy soils. Beans growing in sandy soil will benefit from a mid-season application of a seaweed fertilizer or other source of trace elements, along with an all-purpose fertilizer or one rich in phosphorus and potassium. Water deeply when the weather is dry, and keep the growing area well weeded.

It is important to stay out of the garden when bean plants are wet, to avoid spreading diseases among them. Lima beans, in particular, are at risk of bacterial spot and downy mildew. Practicing a three-year rotation will also help minimize the threat of disease.

Bush limas mature, on the average, in sixty-five to ninety days, while pole varieties need eighty to ninety days. The time to maturity of other shell beans can be anywhere from sixty-five to over a hundred days, depending on the variety.

Fresh limas and other green shell beans are ready to pick when the beans have grown to full size inside the pods, but the pods are still firm and fresh. Lima beans will still be rather flat, and the ends of the pods will feel rather spongy, but other shell beans will be plump. If you are in doubt, pick and shell a sample bean or two to see if it is time to harvest. The beans will be just starting to separate from the sides of the pod.

If you plan to dry the beans, do not harvest until the plants have dropped most of their leaves and the pods are wrinkled and papery dry; the beans will rattle in the pods. You can pick the dry pods individually or simply pull up the whole plant. Hang the plants in a dry, airy place for a couple of weeks to let them finish drying. If the weather turns cold or wet before the pods are dry, pull the plants and bring them in early. Hang them in a warm, airy place until the pods are dry.

There are a number of ways to get the dried beans out of the pods. If you feel the need to vent some pent-up aggression, spread the plants on a thick layer of newspapers, put an old beach towel over the top, and beat with a stick. The cushioning is necessary so you don't bruise the beans. Or

put the plants in a bag and walk on it. If you just want some busy work to do while you listen to music or watch your favorite TV show, you can open the pods one at a time, the way you shell fresh beans.

Whether you are shelling fresh or dry beans, the easiest way to open the pods is to press with your thumbs along the seam—the pods will usually pop open.

After all your dried beans are shelled, test to see if they are completely dry. Bite down on a bean; if your tooth leaves a dent, the beans need further drying. Spread them on screens, drying racks, or an old tablecloth in a warm, dry, well-ventilated place for a few weeks. Keep drying until you can no longer dent them by biting.

Before storing the beans, put them in the freezer for several hours to kill any weevils that might be present. Then store them in airtight containers in a cool, dry place.

Some outstanding bush lima beans are Henderson Bush, an early, productive, heat-tolerant variety good for northern gardens; Fordhook 242, for high yields of large beans that freeze and can well; Baby Fordhook; Baby Thorogreen; and Burpee's Improved Bush Lima.

If you are interested in pole limas, try Christmas, with its large, buttery tasting, red-speckled beans; King of the Garden, which produces early and well; Cliff Dweller, which bears purple-spotted baby beans; Burpee's Best, for large beans that freeze well; and Prizetaker, with large beans.

Black Turtle produces small, black beans ready to harvest for green shell beans in about a hundred days, or for dried beans a couple of weeks later. Midnight Black Turtle, an improved strain, matures a little quicker.

Early Chevrier is a classic French *flageolet* to use as green shell beans or dried. Try them cooked with garlic, thyme, and tomatoes to accompany a leg of lamb.

Dwarf Horticultural has beige pods and beans splotched with red, with a delicious, nutty flavor. It matures quickly, in a little over two months, and with its compact plants is a good choice for small gardens. Wonderful as a green shell bean (try them with a garlic cream sauce), it can also be frozen, canned, or dried.

Great Northern is a traditional white baking and soup bean that matures in about sixty-five days for green shell or eighty-five days for dried beans. The high-yielding plants are a good choice for northern gardens.

Jacob's Cattle, also known as Trout bean, is an heirloom well known in Maine that matures in about eighty-five days. Use it as a fresh shell bean or dried.

Pinto is the favorite for Mexican refried beans. The sprawling plants need a bit more space than the other shell beans described here, although Agate Pinto is more compact. Pinto beans are ready to dry in approximately three months.

Soldier, another heirloom variety, got its name because the reddish brown eye on each white bean was thought to look like a little soldier. This variety tolerates drought better than the others, and matures in about three months.

Vermont Cranberry, also an heirloom, produces its red beans in about eighty-five days.

Beebalm

Beebalm (*Monarda didyma*) is at home with both herbs and perennials, and is an asset to any garden of edibles. It has a fresh, citrusy scent and a tangy flavor that is rather like a blend of orange and lemon. Because of its flavor, some people call the plant bergamot, although it is not the source of the bergamot oil used to scent perfumes and cleaning products; the commercial oil comes from the rind of a citrus fruit. Beebalm is not a citrus; it is a member of the mint family.

The tubular flowers are gathered into clusters at the tops of the 3- to 4-foot stems, creating a graceful, feathery look. The flow-

ers can be brilliant scarlet, deep crimson, purple, pink, salmon, or creamy white, depending upon the variety. They attract bees and the scarlet ones draw hummingbirds to the garden. The toothed, deep green leaves are quite fragrant.

Beebalm blooms in mid to late summer. Toss the flowers into salads, float them in a bowl of chilled soup, or scatter them on top of a fruit salad. Both leaves and flowers can be dried and added to potpourris. The dried leaves make a pleasant tea, too.

Plant beebalm in either full sun or partial shade; in southern climates some shade is necessary. The ideal soil is fertile, moist, and rich in organic matter. Seeds are very slow to germinate, sometimes taking as long as three weeks, so it is easiest to grow beebalm from nursery plants. If you do decide to use seeds, sow them indoors four to six weeks before the last frost, or outdoors anytime from early spring to midsummer. Young plants will benefit from a mulch to help them get through their first winter. Set out plants in either spring or fall.

Space plants a foot apart in the garden. Don't crowd them; good air circulation is important for the plants to avoid the mildew and rust to which they are susceptible.

Like many members of the mint family, beebalm spreads by means of underground runners, and plantings will become crowded. Divide the clumps of beebalm every two or three years to keep the plants healthy and blooming heavily.

If you cut back the plants when they finish blooming, they may flower again in fall.

Beets

One of the more nutritious offerings of the garden, beets (*Beta vulgaris*)—both the roots and the greens—are rich in iron and vitamins. Rather unfairly criticized by people who have eaten only tough, old roots overcooked and poorly seasoned, beets that are grown properly and pulled in their prime are crisp, sweet, and truly delicious. The plants are attractive, too, with their red-stemmed, red-veined, crumply, deep green leaves. Their compact size makes beets ideal for small gardens, and baby varieties make good container plants. Grow them behind yellow nasturtiums, marigolds, or other annual flowers.

Beets are best when they grow quickly in more or less constant, cool conditions. Long hot spells and extreme fluctuations in soil moisture and temperature toughen the roots and create discolored, pale rings in the flesh instead of an even, deep red purple color.

Give your beets full sun and a fertile but light and sandy loam, moist but well drained, with a pH above 6.0. Working in plenty of organic matter will help guard against scab, to which beets, like potatoes, are susceptible. In cool and temperate climates, sow them directly in the garden in early spring, two to four weeks before you expect the last frost, or start seeds indoors or in a cold frame five or six weeks before the planting-out date. If your summer weather is not usually intensely hot, make succession plantings every three weeks until midsummer, for an extended harvest. For a fall crop, plant in midsummer, about ten weeks before you can expect to get a heavy freeze. In the very warmest climates, plant beets in fall for a winter crop.

Sow ½ inch deep, thinning to 3 to 4 inches apart, in rows 10 to 12 inches apart. Or plant 6 inches apart in all directions in a bed. Seeds are slow to germinate; soaking for several hours before planting may help. Beets have compound seeds that are actually dried fruits, each of which produces several seedlings, so you will have to thin them. Wait until the plants are a few inches tall and use the tender thinnings in salads.

Most beets mature in fifty to sixty days. Pulling them when just mature or a bit young will give you the tenderest beets.

You can pull smaller-rooted varieties when they are just a couple of inches in diameter, for baby beets to cook and serve whole. Good varieties for baby beets include Little Ball, Dwergina, Spinel, and Burpee's Red Ball.

For winter storage, Long Season and Lutz Winter Keeper are especially recommended. If you can keep them from freezing you can harvest these two all winter.

Several beets have been bred to an elongated shape to facilitate slicing. Cylindra and Formanova have these long roots, and are good for canning and freezing as well as fresh use.

If beet greens are your goal, plant Early Wonder or Early Wonder Tall Top.

Golden beets (Golden and Burpee's Golden) are a deep yellow color and do not bleed like red beets when you cook them.

Crosby's Egyptian and Early Wonder are early varieties that are great for spring, while Little Ball produces especially well in fall.

If you are seeking the sweetest beets, you might want to plant a variety that has a sugar beet in its genealogy, such as Sweetheart or Big Red.

Finally, here are some excellent all-purpose beets, to use fresh, freeze, or can, in spring or fall: Detroit Dark Red, a classic, and Improved Detroit Dark Red; Big Red; Red Ace; MacGregor's Favorite, an old Scottish variety; Chioggia, which has concentric rings of pinkish red and white; and Ruby Queen.

Borage

The celestial blossoms of this rather unassuming plant (*Borago officinalis*) are star-shaped and sky blue in color, and appear in midsummer. The bushy plants grow 2 to 3 feet tall, and their deep green leaves and stems are covered with bristly white hairs.

Borage was favored in several ancient cultures. It was used to flavor wine, and Dioscorides wrote that it gladdened the heart. The Romans and Celts believed that borage brought courage to their soldiers during battles. The medieval herbalist John Gerard echoed the sentiments of the Greeks in his famous herbal. The plant still has a variety of uses today. Both leaves and flowers possess a refreshing flavor that resembles cucumber more than anything else. Chop the young leaves and toss the flowers into salads. Or float the lovely blossoms in glasses of iced tea or a bowl of punch, or use them to garnish warm or chilled potato, cucumber, or cream of carrot soup. The flowers can also be candied (see Feasting on Flowers in Chapter Four). Borage is best used fresh from the garden; it does not freeze or dry well.

Plant borage in full sun, in light, loose, moist but well-drained soil that is rich in organic matter and reasonably fertile. It will be at home in the middle ground of the garden, or in a large container indoors or outdoors. It is easy to grow from seed, but does not transplant well.

Direct-sow as soon as the danger of frost is past in spring, later thinning plants to stand 2 feet apart. The plants will self-sow, and you will probably only have to plant borage once.

Borage is an annual, but sometimes it behaves like a biennial and does not bloom until its second year in the garden. If your borage fails to bloom, leave the plants in place to winter over, and they should flower next year.

If you practice companion planting you will be interested to know that borage is considered a good companion for many different plants. The flowers attract bees, too.

Broccoli

As President Bush has made rather unforgettably clear, not everyone likes the taste of cooked broccoli. And some people have trouble digesting it. But someone should tell the President that many people who can't eat cooked broccoli find that they like it raw, especially with a dip as part of a platter of crudités. Broccoli (*Brassica oleracea*, Botrytis Group) is highly nutritious—rich in vitamins A and C, and offering substantial amounts of B vitamins, iron, and calcium— and serving it raw keeps its nutritional value at a maximum. Broccoli freezes well, too.

Most broccoli varieties produce central "heads" that are actually large, flat-topped clusters of tightly closed blue green flower buds. Botanically, broccoli is really an edible flower. There are also purple and creamy white sprouting broccolis, and the pretty, light yellow green Romanesco.

Broccoli grows best in cool weather, with temperatures between 40 and 65°F, and large plants can tolerate light frost. Young seedlings, however, are often damaged by frost, and if seedlings experience temperatures below 40°F the plants may fail to head up later on. The key to a good crop of broccoli is for plants to grow at a fast, steady pace, which in turn depends on fertile soil, plenty of moisture, and cool weather.

Plant broccoli in full sun, in rich, moist but well-drained soil that contains lots of organic matter and has a pH that is in the neutral range or slightly acid. The pH is more important for broccoli than for many other vegetables; in acid soils clubroot can be a problem, so add lime if your soil pH is below 6.7. The cabbage family is subject to a number of soilborne diseases, and broccoli is no exception. It is vital to rotate these crops to help avoid problems; don't grow cabbage-family members in the same place more than once every three years.

Gardeners in cool and temperate climates can plant broccoli in either spring or fall. If summers are hot where you live, concentrate on autumn planting. Warm-climate gardeners can plant for harvest in late fall or early winter. Start plants in spring indoors, about twelve weeks before your last frost date, and set out plants five to six weeks later, or direct-sow four to six weeks before the last frost. Sow broccoli for fall harvest ten to twelve weeks before you expect the first fall frost. Sow ¼ to ½ inch deep.

Thin when plants are just an inch or two tall, pinching them off at the soil line to avoid disturbing nearby roots. Plants should stand 2 feet apart in all directions in beds, or 1½ to 2 feet apart in rows 2½ to 3 feet apart. If cutworms are a problem in your garden, place a cutworm collar around each plant. Where root maggots are a problem, cover new transplants with floating row covers to keep the flies that produce the root maggots from laying their eggs.

Broccoli needs lots of space to grow well; do not crowd the plants. The plants take quite a while to reach full size, and while they are young you can interplant radishes, cress, arugula, or leaf lettuce between them. The smaller crops will be ready to harvest by the time the broccoli needs the space.

Because it has shallow roots, broccoli needs water on a regular basis. Water deeply at least once a week during dry weather. A mulch will help keep the root zone cool and moist. If you prefer not to lay down a mulch, be sure to keep the area well weeded, or the weeds will compete with

Delicious raw or cooked, broccoli is rich in nutritional value. The variety in this photo, Green Comet, can be planted in spring or for fall harvest.

COURTESY ALL-AMERICA SELECTIONS

your broccoli for moisture and nutrients. A mid-season feeding with fish emulsion or a good all-purpose organic fertilizer will help keep the nutrient-hungry plants in peak condition.

Most broccoli matures in about fifty-five to sixty-five days from the time you set out transplants. Cut the main head when it has reached full size but the flower buds are still tightly closed. If you notice the buds starting to lighten in color and loosen, cut the head right away. If a spell of very hot weather pushes the little yellow flowers into bloom, save at least some of them to toss into salads.

Leave the plants standing when you cut the main heads and most of them will produce additional harvests of smaller side shoots a couple of weeks later. Look for these shoots to develop in the leaf axils of secondary stems. Cut the shoots often to keep them coming for a few more weeks.

Many broccoli varieties grow well in either spring or fall. Some of the best are Premium Crop, a popular market variety; Emperor; Emerald City, which does best in cool climates; DeCicco, a nonhybrid heirloom variety with excellent flavor; Bonanza; Green Comet; and Packman.

Varieties that perform especially well in spring are Calabrese, Green Goliath, and Spartan Early.

Saga tolerates heat better than other varieties, and is a good choice where late spring or early fall weather tends to be quite warm.

Some especially good candidates for fall are Green Valiant, which is tolerant of both frost and heat, and Waltham 29.

Old-fashioned sprouting broccolis produce lots of tender shoots instead of a central head. Before World War II, they were practically the only kind of broccoli grown. You can plant White Sprouting or Purple Sprouting for a fall crop or plant in fall in a cold frame to winter over and produce the crop in early spring.

Romanesco is probably the most unusual-looking broccoli, producing light green heads that are clusters of little cones of buds arranged in spiral patterns. Romanesco's tender texture and good flavor make it especially nice for crudités. It needs more time to mature than other varieties but is worth the wait. A smaller Romanesco variety called Minaret is recommended for small gardens.

A small variety of conventional broccoli is Green Dwarf, with 5-inch heads on compact, 8-inch plants that fit happily into containers or small gardens.

Brussels Sprouts

Brussels sprouts are kind of weird-looking in the garden. The plants develop a straight, thick stem as much as 3 feet tall, with leaves on longish petioles at intervals along the main stalk. The top is crowned with a rosette of cabbagey leaves. The sprouts develop along the main stem, and by fall the stalk is covered with what look like tiny cabbages an inch or two across, clinging like little alien creatures.

Brussels sprouts (*Brassica oleracea*, Gemmifera Group) will occupy their space all season, from spring to fall, but the plants do produce a sizable crop. Because the plants grow slowly, when they are small you can interplant with leaf lettuce, cress, arugula, or radishes. Like other members of the clan, brussels sprouts are very nutritious. The plants are hardier than other members of the cabbage family, and can tolerate more frost.

This crop must have cool weather to mature; it does not perform well in intense heat. In warmer climates, where the long summers are hot and dry, grow the sprouts to mature in late fall or winter. It may be difficult to nurse the young plants through the summer, because they grow best when temperatures are 60 to 65°F. But shade cloth and extra water can help. Hot weather makes developing sprouts grow loose and leafy; in a cooler climate the sprouts may become tighter and firmer again when the weather cools off.

Plant brussels sprouts in full sun, in fertile, moist but well-drained soil rich in organic matter. Prepare the growing area in fall for planting next spring. Spread a thick layer of compost and work it in. Sprinkle with greensand, granite dust, or wood ashes for potassium, and rock phosphate or bonemeal for phosphorus.

Direct-sow or set out transplants in summer, then to twelve weeks before you expect the first heavy frost. Start transplants indoors five to six weeks before you set them out. It is best to start brussels sprouts from seed because they are hard to find in garden centers in summer, the best planting time. Garden centers sell plants in spring; if planted then, however, the crop will mature too early, before frost can sweeten the sprouts.

Sow seeds ½ inch deep. Set out transplants when they are about 6 inches tall. Plant the transplants deeper than they were growing in their containers; bury the plants almost up to their lowest leaves. Firm the soil around the roots and water to eliminate air pockets; if the soil is too loose the sprouts will also be loose, instead of firm and tight as they should be. Space plants 1½ feet apart in rows 2½ to 3 feet apart.

Cutworms love brussels sprouts, so give each new transplant a cutworm collar. Cover the plants with shade cloth for their first few weeks in the garden to help them adjust to the heat. The plants do best when they receive even moisture throughout the growing season; mulch can help. Keep the plants well weeded, too, but be careful you don't damage their shallow roots while cultivating.

The leaves of the plants turn yellow as the sprouts form. As the leaves yellow, remove them but leave a couple of inches of each petiole (leaf stem) attached to the main stalk. Trimming the leaves opens up more space for the sprouts to develop, and also seems to encourage their growth.

The sprouts mature from the bottom of the plant up, and can be harvested over a period of about four weeks. Cut them with a sharp knife when they are 1 to 1½ inches in diameter. It is best to wait to harvest until the plants have been exposed to a few frosts. Frost decidedly improves the flavor of brussels sprouts; they become mellower and sweeter, quite different from the brussels sprouts you may be used to from the supermarket.

If the temperature drops below 30°F and stays there, and you haven't had a chance to harvest all the sprouts, pull or dig the plants before the ground freezes and bring them into your basement. Plant them in tubs of soil or damp sand, packing it around the roots so they don't dry out. The sprouts should remain in good condition for about a month. You can also store freshly picked sprouts in a window well or outdoor storage cache as described in Chapter Five. Brussels sprouts freeze well, too.

When you prepare sprouts, cook them until just tender; overcooking ruins the flavor.

Dependable varieties include Jade Cross, and the improved Jade Cross E, Catskill, and Long Island Improved. Oliver, Green Marvel, and Early Half Tall are all fast maturing. Widgeon and Silverstar are from England, where more brussels sprouts are consumed than anyplace else in the world. The most unusual variety is Rubine, sometimes listed as Rubine Red, a European introduction with a deep purplish red color like that of red cabbage; the sprouts retain their color during cooking.

Cabbage

Cabbage (*Brassica oleracea*, Capitata Group) is not the pedestrian vegetable so many people think it is; it is really quite versatile. Besides shredding it into coleslaw, pickling it for sauerkraut, or boiling it with corned beef on St. Patrick's Day, you can stir-fry or steam it, put it in soups and casseroles, braise it, or serve it with a sauce. Homegrown cabbage tastes better than the supermarket kind—it's juicier and sweeter. However you prepare cabbage, it is impor-tant not to overcook it; the characteristic clinging cabbage odor that can be objectionable comes from long cooking.

There are many cabbage varieties to consider for the garden. You will choose among early, mid-season, and late-maturing varieties. There are the savoys, with their puckered, crinkled leaves, varieties with round, conical, or flattened heads of smooth green leaves, and handsome heads of red violet leaves. Some varieties are good for long-term storage in winter, others make great coleslaw, still others are ideal for sauerkraut. There are even ornamental varieties that are less desirable in the kitchen but highly decorative in the garden in autumn and winter.

Plant cabbage in full sun to partial shade, in fertile, moist but well-drained soil rich in organic matter and with a pH of at least 6.0; very acid soil encourages clubroot, which will ruin the crop. If you have had problems with clubroot in the past, add enough lime to raise the soil pH to neutral or slightly above. Cabbage will grow in sandy or clayey soil, as long as it has plenty of moisture and nutrients, and drains well. Prepare the soil a season ahead of planting, if you can. Work in lots of compost, composted manure, rock phosphate, and greensand or granite dust.

Like its relatives, cabbage grows best in cool weather. In cool and temperate climates it is planted in spring or for fall harvest; in warm climates cabbage is grown as a fall or winter crop. It can tolerate some light frost.

Sow early varieties indoors in late winter or very early spring, four to six weeks before you want to plant it outdoors. The goal is to have the cabbage harvested before the hottest part of summer. Sow indoors, ½ inch deep, six to eight weeks before you expect the last frost, and move the plants to the garden two weeks before your last frost date. The best soil temperature for germination is around 75°F, but as soon as the plants are up move them to a cooler place, with plenty of air circulation and ambient temperatures around 60°F. The seedlings should be about 5 inches tall when you transplant them out to the garden. In warm climates plant early cabbage in fall for a winter harvest.

Mid-season varieties are started the same time as early cabbage, but the plants are somewhat larger and later to mature. They are bred to mature in warm weather, but they must be well established in the garden before the weather turns hot.

Late cabbage is started in early summer for harvest in fall. Sow it directly in the garden, or in a nursery bed to transplant to the main garden later on, ten to twelve weeks before you expect the first fall frost. Plant in early winter for early spring harvest in warm climates.

Transplant all cabbage varieties deeper than they were growing previously; bury the plants just about to the lowest leaves. Space compact and early varieties 1 to 1½ feet apart in rows 2 to 2½ feet apart, larger and mid-season varieties 1½ to 2 feet apart in rows 2½ to 3 feet apart. In intensive beds, grow compact varieties and place the plants 14 to 15 inches apart in all directions.

Put floating row covers over new transplants to keep off root-maggot flies and flea beetles. Later on in the season, *Bacillus thuringiensis* (BT) will take care of cabbage loopers if they attack.

To decrease the risk of the diseases to which cabbage is susceptible, rotate on a three-year cycle, keep the garden clean, and start seeds in a sterile medium.

Water regularly in dry weather; cabbage's shallow roots need even moisture. Mulch will help conserve moisture in the soil. When you water, water the plants at the base rather than from above; getting the heads wet at the expense of the roots will not help the plants and could lead to disease problems. Moisture can also help the plants to hold up during spells of hot weather. It is important to maintain the moisture at as constant a level as possible. Giving the plants lots of water after a dry spell can cause the heads to split. Splitting

can also happen when the heads become overmature.

Cabbage is a heavy feeder and needs a good supply of nutrients throughout the growing season. If you notice the leaves turning yellow, give the plants a nitrogen boost from a quickly available source such as fish emulsion. A mid-season feeding with a good all-purpose fertilizer is also beneficial.

Harvest cabbage when the heads are well developed and feel firm and solid when you squeeze them. They should feel heavy for their size. Cut off the heads at the base with a sharp knife. Discard the outermost leaves. If you will be putting the cabbage into long-term storage, inspect the heads for signs of insects. Storage varieties of cabbage will keep for several months in a window well or other outdoor storage area. Another way to store cabbage, for up to two months, is to pull plants when the heads are mature and hang them upside down by the roots in a dry place. See Chapter Five for additional information on storage.

If you want to delay the harvest without the heads splitting, give each head a sharp quarter turn to break some of the roots and halt growth—this is an old gardener's trick.

Many early varieties of cabbage make superb coleslaw. There are lots to choose from, and the following are just some of the reliable ones available to gardeners. Early Jersey Wakefield, a nonhybrid heirloom that has been grown since the late nineteenth century, has small, conical heads and is resistant to yellows disease; Greyhound is similar but matures earlier. Golden Acre is another nonhybrid, of which Primax is an improved strain. Dakri and Golden Cross both mature very early. Stonehead Hybrid and Salarite are compact and good for small gardens. Perfect Action resists yellows disease and splitting; Primo tolerates a range of soils.

Some excellent mid-season varieties are Atlas, which resists black rot; Green Cup, which can handle a soil that is not as highly fertile as the soil usually required for cabbage; and the well-known Copenhagen Market, a classic nonhybrid variety.

Late cabbages grown for fall harvest and for storage have big, solid heads. They are outstanding when cooked, and make good sauerkraut. Danish Roundhead or Danish Ballhead is perhaps the best known, with round heads that store quite well; Superior Danish matures a bit faster. Late Flat Dutch produces huge, flat-sided heads that store well. Apex is a fall variety with good frost resistance but a shorter storage life than the others.

Savoy cabbages are very hardy, tolerating more frost and shade than many other cabbages. Savoy King can be grown in either spring or fall, Julius is a good early variety, and January King and Savoy Ace are two outstanding late savoys.

Red cabbages are crispy and sweet, and have that marvellous red violet color. A bit of red cabbage adds a grace note of color to a symphony of salad greens, along with a pleasant crunch. Sweet-and-sour red cabbage is a classic accompaniment to pork. Early red cabbages to try include Ruby Ball; Lasso, which is open-pollinated; Red Rookie, which stores well; and the compact Red Acre. Ruby Perfection is a recommended mid-season variety, and Mammoth Red Rock matures late.

Ornamental cabbages, like ornamental kales, which they closely resemble (they may in fact be the same vegetable), have beautifully colored leaves in combinations of deep green and creamy white, or blue green and rosy violet red. The plants can tolerate heavy frost, and maintain their beauty well into winter in many gardens. They are rather strong flavored, though, and are best used as ornamentals in most gardens.

Calendula

The daisylike flowers of calendula (*Calendula officinalis*) were known in England in days of old as marigold (a shortened form of Mary's gold, referring to the Virgin Mary). The name pot marigold, which is still used today, indicates calendula's use in the kitchen. The flowers come in several shades of yellow, but the classic color is rich, brilliant gold or striking orange. The leaves are oblong and dark green. Calendulas bloom all summer and well into fall.

The Elizabethans and Europeans of several centuries ago used calendulas quite a bit in cooking, particularly in soups. Today calendula makes a good, inexpensive substitute for costly saffron, which also comes from a flower, a species of crocus. Dry and grind calendula petals (which are actually individual ray flowers) and use them to color and season paella, curries, and other dishes that call for yellow coloring. Calendula also has medicinal applications, and herbalists use it in ointments to treat skin problems. The flowers dry well and are nice in arrangements.

Calendula is a hardy annual that grows about 1½ feet tall. Dwarf varieties reach a height of about 1 foot. Plant in full sun, in well-drained soil that is of average fertility. Direct-sow as soon as the soil can be worked in spring, or start seeds indoors five to six weeks before the average date of your last spring frost. In warm climates, sow in fall for winter flowers. The plants grow best in cool weather, tolerating temperatures to 25°F, but they can also stand quite a bit of heat. Where summers are hot, give the plants some shade in the afternoon.

Thin dwarf plants to stand 8 inches apart, standard varieties 10 to 12 inches apart.

Calendulas are easy to grow and need little in the way of maintenance. If crowded too closely together, or in very wet years, the plants may develop mildew. Slugs love them, too, so set up traps if slugs are a problem in your garden. Calendula self-sows in many gardens.

The flowers dry most quickly if you first pull off the petals. Spread the petals on a screen rack and dry them as described under Harvesting and Storing Herbs in Chapter Five. Store the petals in airtight containers; they will absorb moisture from the air and discolor if not kept in a sealed container.

Carrots

Carrots are easy to grow, and an important source of beta carotene, from which our bodies manufacture vitamin A. There is a carrot variety for any size garden—even containers—and almost any type of soil. Carrots (*Daucus carota* var. *sativus*) are delicious raw or cooked, and can be grown for winter storage, freezing, or canning. Baby carrots are quite a hit these days, cooked and served whole; they're delicious with just a bit of butter or a light glaze. And young carrot tops can be used as soup greens. The plants tolerate both light frost and summer heat. In cool and temperate climates, grow them in spring, summer, and fall; in warm climates, grow them in fall, winter, and spring.

The perfect soil for carrots is loose to a depth of 1½ to 2 feet, a sandy loam rich in nutrients and the organic matter that allows it to retain moisture and still drain well. In such a crumbly, fertile soil, carrots can easily grow long, straight, and smooth. Such soil is important if you want to grow the long-rooted Imperator types, but other kinds of carrots perform quite well in denser, shallower soils. Any good garden soil can produce a decent crop of carrots if you choose the right variety.

Carrots do need a growing bed free of stones; if the roots encounter stones they split and warp. And plenty of moisture is important to promote the fast growth that creates the tenderest, sweetest roots. The nutrients in the soil should be well balanced, if anything, heavier on phosphorus and potassium. Too much nitrogen causes the roots to grow forked and hairy; for this reason, never use fresh manure in a carrot bed.

Raised beds, in which you can blend your own soil mix, can produce superior crops of carrots. A raised bed filled with a crumbly mixture of soil, compost or leaf mold, and sand offers an ideal place to grow even the long-rooted carrot varieties.

Carrots grow best in full sun, but will also produce a harvest in partial shade. Sow directly in the garden in early spring, two to four weeks before you expect your last frost. The seeds are tiny and hard to handle. To attain more even distribution when planting, either pour some seeds into a folded piece of paper and tap them out gently with your finger, or mix the seeds with an equal volume of sand before you sow them. Sow ¼ inch deep, and make successive plantings every two weeks until midsummer for a continuous harvest. To harvest in fall, for fresh use or winter storage, sow twelve weeks before the average date of the first fall frost in your area.

Carrot seeds germinate slowly, often taking two weeks or more. Soak the seeds in water several hours or overnight before sowing to speed up the process. Keep the soil evenly moist until the seeds sprout. The delicate little shoots may have difficulty breaking through the soil surface. To keep a crust from forming on top of the soil, cover the seeds with moist sand, vermiculite, or peat moss instead of soil when you plant.

When the plants are a couple of inches tall, thin them to stand 2 to 3 inches apart in rows 1 to 1½ feet apart, or 3 inches apart in all directions in beds. Snip off the unwanted plants with a manicure scissors instead of pulling them up, to avoid damaging nearby plants. You may need to thin once more, if plants become crowded later in the growing season. Pull extra plants carefully, to avoid disturbing their neighbors, and use these late thinnings as baby carrots.

Water your carrots deeply when the weather is dry, before the soil dries out and growth slows down. A lot of water following a drought can cause roots close to maturity to split. Keep the area weeded, but be careful when cultivating with a hoe or other tool so you don't injure the roots. Make sure the shoulders (tops of the roots) remain covered with soil throughout the growing season or they will turn green. If they become exposed, draw more soil over them.

Fertile soil will help your carrots avoid problems from wireworms and carrot-rust flies. If you have problems with any of the blight diseases carrots are prone to, rotate carrots through the garden on a three-year cycle.

Carrots are ready to harvest anytime after they develop a bright orange color. The peak harvest period for most carrots usually lasts about three weeks, longer in cool weather.

To harvest carrots in light soil, take hold of the stems at the base and pull gently. Twist or rock gently to loosen them. In heavier soil, loosen the soil with a spade or spading fork (carefully!) before pulling the carrots.

If you grew late carrots to store over winter, you can cover them with a thick layer of mulch and dig them as needed all winter in mild climates where temperatures seldom dip below 20°F, or until at least Christmas in the North. The foliage will keep growing in fall until the weather turns quite cold. When growth stops, make sure the carrot shoulders are covered with soil—frost can damage them.

You can, if you prefer, dig the carrots after the first few light frosts, but before the ground freezes solid. Break off the tops, pack the roots in damp sand, soil, or peat moss, and store in cold, humid conditions such as a window well or outdoor storage cache, as described in Chapter Five. If you have never tasted late carrots that have been touched by frost, you will be surprised by their sweetness.

Small, round-rooted carrots, collectively known as Paris Market carrots, are perfect for containers or heavy soil. These carrots are globe-shaped, and ready to harvest when they're 1 to 1½ inches in diameter. Parmex, Planet, Parisier, and Kundulus are all round-rooted varieties.

Little, finger-shaped roots that are ideal for delectable, tender baby carrots include Minicor, Little Finger (also known as Early Scarlet Horn), Baby Spike, and Lady Finger. These are all known as Amsterdam-type carrots.

Chantenay carrots are short and fat with tapered roots. They grow well in somewhat dense soils, and are good for a late crop. These varieties will winter over where winters are not too severe. Red-Cored Chantenay has smooth skin and freezes well; Tokita's Scarlet is an improved form, and Burpee's Goldinhart is a patented version. Kinko is an early variety, and Royal Chantenay is another good performer, well suited to northern gardens with a short growing season.

Danvers Half Long is thinner and longer than Chantenay types. The blunt, reddish orange roots are 6 to 8 inches long, and similar to Nantes carrots.

Nantes varieties produce cylindrical roots of medium length. Touchon is an heirloom widely admired for its sweet, delicious taste; traditional Nantes has very crisp roots; and Clarion and Napoli both mature early. Toudo Hybrid can be harvested for baby carrots, when full sized, or at any stage in between. Other good Nantes varieties include Ingot, Rondino, and Rumba.

Imperator and similar varieties produce the largest, longest roots of all. They need loose, deep soil to develop properly. These carrots are well suited to storage and overwintering. Imperator is the classic of this type, with slender roots up to 9 inches long when grown in home gardens. Gold Pak is another good performer. A Plus and Savory are both especially rich in carotene.

Cauliflower

Cauliflower (*Brassica oleracea*, Botrytis Group) has a milder flavor than most of the other vegetables in the cabbage family. Except for the purple varieties, cauliflower is not a nutritional powerhouse, but it is delicious when not overcooked, and when consumed raw most of its vitamin content remains intact. Purple cauliflower is rela-

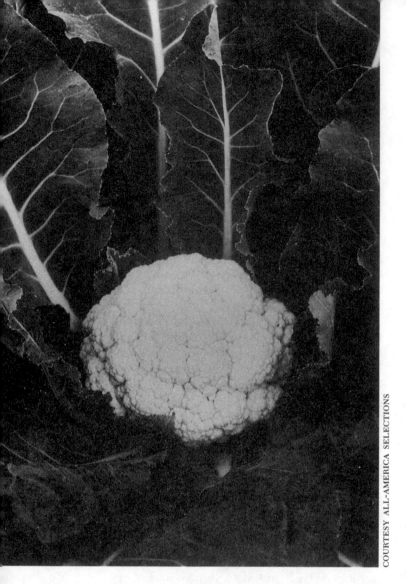

COURTESY ALL-AMERICA SELECTIONS

For the best crop of cauliflower, plant in fertile soil and make sure the plants receive even, abundant moisture throughout the growing season.

tively easy to grow, and an entirely different gustatory experience from traditional white cauliflower. The deep purple heads actually resemble broccoli more than cauliflower, and like broccoli, the plants may produce side shoots after the main heads are cut. Purple cauliflower has a milder flavor than either broccoli or cauliflower, and a delicate, tender texture. It freezes well, turns green when cooked, and is not usually troubled by insects.

Cauliflower has a reputation for being difficult to grow, which despite improved varieties is not entirely undeserved. The plants suffer in both hot and cold weather, preferring an average temperature of 60 to 65°F. In many areas it is better to plant it as a fall crop than to risk losing a spring-planted crop to an early summer heat wave. In warm climates plant in fall for a winter crop.

Cauliflower demands rich, fertile soil and constant, abundant moisture. Providing these conditions can be a tall order, but if you can give cauliflower what it needs your efforts will be amply rewarded.

Cauliflower is grown much like cabbage. Plant it in full sun, in moist, fertile, well-drained soil rich in organic matter, with a pH between 6.4 and 7.4. In more acid soils clubroot can be a problem; in more alkaline soils boron, a trace element that is essential for cauliflower, may be unavailable to the plants. In moist, nutrient-rich soil the plants can grow and develop their heads quickly, which is important for success.

Prepare the soil a season ahead of planting, if possible. Work in lots of compost, composted manure, and greensand or wood ashes. For phosphorus use rock phosphate, which will also add boron to the soil. Do not plant cauliflower where it or any other brassica has grown in the past two years.

If you want to try an early crop, sow seeds indoors, ½ inch deep, about six to eight weeks before you want to move the plants outdoors, which can happen two to four weeks before you expect the last spring frost. Seeds germinate best in warm soil (about 70°F), but when the shoots appear, move the seedlings to a cooler location with a temperature near 60°F.

The plants should have at least three true leaves when you set them out, and you should see a small bud in the center that will develop into the head. Transplant out as soon as the plants are ready; older plants will undergo greater shock during transplanting and may not produce good heads. Handle transplants carefully. Damage to leaves sometimes causes buttoning, a condition described below.

For a fall harvest, sow directly in the garden in midsummer, twelve weeks before you expect the first fall frost.

Thin direct-seeded plants or set out transplants 1½ feet apart in rows 3 feet apart, or 1½ to 2 feet apart in all directions in a bed. To make more efficient use of space you can interplant with arugula, cress, radishes, or leaf lettuce when the cauliflower is young.

Water deeply during dry weather, at least once a week, to keep the soil moist. Mulching will help conserve soil moisture. Hot, dry weather can cause buttoning, in which the head remains small and does not develop properly. Heat can also turn the curds ricey, a condition in which the curds start to separate into flowerets and the head takes on a grainy appearance. Cauliflower is still good to eat in the beginning stages of ricing, but if it goes on too long the flavor declines.

Traditionally, white cauliflower has had to be blanched before harvest to preserve the whiteness of the heads. Sunlight turns cauliflower brown and ruins the flavor. Start blanching when the head is big enough to be seen through the leaves. Tie the outer leaves together above the head with a rubber band or piece of string. Many varieties today are described as self-blanching; the outer leaves curve inward to cover the heads. But watch self-blanching plants closely—you may need to tie the leaves to insure that the heads are completely covered.

Heads may be ready to harvest in a week or less in warm weather, two weeks in cool weather. Check their progress often and don't let them pass their peak. When the heads are well developed and the curds are tight, it is time to harvest. If you are in doubt, it is better to harvest too early than too late. Cut the heads below the inner leaves with a sharp knife.

There are lots of cauliflower varieties on the market. Snow Crown is a good early cultivar, suitable for either spring or fall crops, and self-blanching. Early Snowball, an old favorite, produces well in mild climates and makes a good fall crop farther north. Milkyway and Early White Hybrid are two more early varieties. All the Year Round is a hardy European entry. Montano and Self Blanche are self-blanching; Dominant matures late and tolerates more dryness than other varieties. Andes is self-blanching, freezes well, and is an excellent performer, but needs the very richest of soils. Alverda forms an unusual, yellowish green head that does not need blanching.

Recommended varieties of purple cauliflower include Violet Queen, Purple Giant, Sicilian Purple, Purple Cape, and Purple Head.

Celeriac

Celeriac (*Apium graveolens* var. *rapaceum*), also called celery root or celery knob, tastes a lot like celery and is a close relative, but it is grown not for its stalks, but for its enlarged, turnip-shaped root crowns. With its thick, gnarled, knobby brown skin, celeriac looks anything but edible. But beneath that rough exterior is a most refined and delicate vegetable, whose smooth, creamy white flesh resembles an apple or turnip in texture. Its celerylike flavor is sweet and mild. Celeriac is delicious when braised, served au gratin, mashed with potatoes, added to soups, or even grated raw into salads. It deserves to be better known in this country.

Celeriac needs a long growing season—about 110 days—but it adapts to a range of climates and is easier to grow than celery. In cool and temperate climates plant in spring to harvest in fall; in warm climates plant in fall and harvest in winter.

The plants grow best in fertile, moist but well-drained soil rich in organic matter. Like most vegetables, it prefers a slightly acid pH. A pH below 6.0 will hinder growth.

Start seeds indoors eight to twelve weeks before you expect the last spring frost and transplant out to the garden when the danger of heavy frost is past. Plants can tolerate light frost. Gardeners in warm climates can sow directly in the garden. Seeds germinate slowly, so be patient.

In the garden space plants 6 to 8 inches apart in rows 1½ feet apart, or 1 foot apart in all directions in a bed.

The plants need abundant moisture when young, and regular water throughout the growing season. They have shallow feeder roots close to the soil surface, so weed and cultivate with care. Remove any lateral roots you see growing from the tops of the crowns to produce the biggest, smoothest knobs.

The crowns are ready to harvest anytime after they reach 2 inches in diameter; the usual harvest size is 3 to 5 inches. Celeriac can stay in the garden during several light frosts. After the first heavy frost, dig the rest of the crowns, or cover with a 1- to 2-foot layer of mulch and leave them in the garden all winter. Mature celery root can be stored in a window well or outdoor storage cache like other root crops.

Prague, or Giant Smooth Prague, is the classic variety, and has been in cultivation since the nineteenth century. Two newer varieties are Jose and Dolvi, which performs well in the garden and stores well but matures slowly, needing 150 days.

Chard

Alternately known as either chard or Swiss chard, this vegetable (*Beta vulgaris*, Cicla Group) is actually a type of beet that produces large leaves instead of a swollen root. Chard tastes a great deal like beets, and produces its big, crumpled leaves on broad, ribbed stalks. For my money this is one of the most outstanding vegetables in the garden. It produces from late spring all the way through summer and well into fall—longer than practically any other vegetable. It tolerates both summer heat and quite a bit of frost. It is very easy to grow, does just fine in partial shade, and adapts to a range of soils. It is nutritious, too, offering vitamin C, iron, calcium, and in the red-stemmed varieties, vitamin A, as well. The leaves are a good substitute for spinach.

Chard is also quite ornamental in the garden. Some varieties bear their bold, dark green leaves on white stems; in others the leaves have red veins and the stems are a brilliant pinkish red. Chard is handsome behind yellow marigolds or pansies, and with salad plants in their varied shades of green. Peas make a nice backdrop, or try scarlet runner or purple beans behind the white-stemmed varieties.

In mild climates chard can be brought through the winter with a mulch blanket to produce again in spring. Elsewhere grow it as an annual.

For the very best crop, plant chard in fertile, moist but well-drained soil that contains plenty of organic matter. It is easiest to sow chard directly in the garden, one to two weeks before the last frost, when the soil temperature is 50°F or more. Sow ½ inch deep. Gardeners in warm climates can also plant chard in late summer, about ten weeks before the first frost, for a fall and winter crop.

Like beets, chard has compound seeds that send up more than one plant—you will have to thin. Thin to 9 inches apart in all directions in a bed, or 7 to 8 inches apart in rows 1½ feet apart. If the thinnings are big enough, use them in salads.

Make sure the plants get plenty of moisture all season; if their roots get dry, they tend to bolt to seed. If your soil is sandy and drains fast, mulch to help hold in moisture. If your soil is not very rich, feed plants monthly with fish emulsion or another high-nitrogen fertilizer.

Harvest begins as early as forty days after planting, and the best-quality leaves are no more than 10 inches long. Cut outer leaves as needed. Chard is delicious stir-fried or steamed. Or try it chopped and sautéed with a bit of oil and soy sauce, chopped shallots, or onion. The stems need a minute or two more cooking than the leaves, so put them in the pan first.

White-stemmed chards include Giant Lu-cullus, Lucullus, and Lucullus Light Green, which have lighter green leaves than most; Fordhook Giant, which has very large leaves; Monstruoso, which has bigger-than-usual stems; and Large White Ribbed, with smoother leaves. Swiss Chard of Geneva is very hardy and will winter over farther north than other varieties. Argentata is an Italian heirloom, and Paros is a French variety with an especially mild flavor. Perpetual Spinach has fine-textured leaves that resemble spinach, and like other chards, produces over a long period.

Some red-stemmed chard varieties are Charlotte, Rhubarb, Ruby Red, and Vulcan.

Chervil

Chervil (*Anthriscus cerefolium*) is one of the French *fines herbes*. Its subtle, mild flavor has a touch of anise in the way that fresh tarragon does, as well as a suggestion of parsley, which it somewhat resembles. Chervil leaves are finely divided and look like a more delicate version of parsley; like parsley, there are both flat-leaved and curly types of chervil.

The unique taste of chervil is delicious in salad dressings, with vegetables or fish, and in omelets, butters, soups, and sauces. This herb is best used fresh from the garden; when the leaves are dried much of the flavor is lost.

Chervil is a 2-foot-tall hardy annual that is easy to grow from seed. The plants grow best in cool weather, and may bolt in summer heat. To extend the harvest make several plantings two to three weeks apart. Some catalogs list a European winter chervil that performs especially well in cool weather and short days; try this variety on a south or east windowsill in winter.

Plant chervil in either sun or shade; in many gardens it does best in partial shade. It prefers a moist but well-drained, reasonably fertile soil that is rich in organic matter. A neutral to slightly alkaline pH is best.

Direct-sow in spring, anytime after the danger of heavy frost is past. It is best to sow directly where you want plants to grow; chervil does not transplant well. The seeds need light to germinate; press them lightly into the soil but do not cover them. You can also plant in late summer to harvest in fall.

Thin plants to stand 6 inches apart. Chervil will also grow happily in containers.

Leaves are ready to harvest six to eight weeks after planting.

Chervil often self-sows if you let some of the plants flower and go to seed. Young plants may also winter over in a cold frame if sown there in autumn.

If you want to grow chervil indoors in winter, plant it in a moderately rich, well-drained potting mix.

Chicory

Chicory (*Cichorium intybus*) is a vegetable with a history; it's been found on plates for a long time. The ancient Romans ate chicory in salads and also as a cooked vegetable. The Italians still cultivate many kinds of chicory, probably more than anyone else in the world. The most distinctive are the red-leaved chicories that are better known as radicchio. Because most of us know them by that name, you will find them covered later in this chapter under a separate entry. Still, there is no shortage of chicories to consider here.

There are three basic types of chicories: those grown for leaves, others grown for their big roots, and varieties valued for their flower stalks. Cultivars have been bred to best fulfill the mission of each type.

All chicories are easy to grow, and all share to varying degrees a characteristic bitter flavor that is best when combined with milder, sweeter greens. A little chicory goes a long way.

As a group chicories are quite cold hardy, and quite a few of them will winter over when planted in fall, even in the North. In most climates chicory is best grown for

Catalogna or dandelion chicory has bitter leaves resembling those of wild dandelion. Plant in spring or fall, and harvest leaves young or let them grow to full size—about 1½ feet long.

spring and fall crops, for they prefer temperatures that average between 55 and 75°F. Witloof and other chicories grown for their roots must stay in the garden all summer, and may need extra care during spells of hot, dry weather.

Chicory tolerates a range of soils from sandy to clayey, but the ideal growing medium is a loose, crumbly loam containing lots of organic matter.

Most of the plants are perennials and will self-sow if allowed to bloom—in their second year they produce the familiar sky blue flowers seen in the chicory that grows wild along roadsides and in vacant lots in so many places in the United States. The flowers, if you have them, can be used in salads. The plants are self-pollinating and most

come true from seed, so you can let a few plants bloom, and save the seeds for future plantings. Some newer cultivars, such as Zoom and Toner, two improved witloof types, are F_1 hybrids and will not come true from seed. Most chicories are treated as annuals, because the leaf quality declines after the first year.

Whatever kind of chicory you plant, sow it directly in the garden where you want it to mature. The plants are more likely to bolt to seed early when they are transplanted. They are seldom bothered by pests and diseases.

Leaf Chicories

Sow leaf chicories in midsummer to mature in the cooler weather of fall. You can plant them in early spring, but the plants may bolt and the flavor become too intensely bitter in hot summer weather. Sow seeds ¼ inch deep, about eight weeks before you expect the first fall frost. Thin

COURTESY JOHNNY'S SELECTED SEEDS

plants to stand 8 to 10 inches apart in all directions in an intensive bed, or 8 to 10 inches apart in rows that are 2 feet apart. If you plan to harvest young, when leaves are 4 to 6 inches tall, space the plants 6 inches apart. Leaves should be ready to harvest anywhere from eight to fourteen weeks later, depending on the variety. Cut individual leaves when they are 4 to 6 inches tall. Snip off leaves with a scissors, or cut the entire plant at the crown. Generally, young plants are milder tasting than older ones, and inner leaves, because they receive less light, are less bitter than outer ones.

You can also use leaf chicories as seedling crops, as described for Arugula. A good variety for seedling and mesclun crops is Biondissima Trieste. If you grow it for mesclun, and harvest when the plants are no more than 6 inches high, you can get several cuttings from the plants. Give them plenty of moisture, fertilize with a liquid fertilizer after each cutting, and you should be able to harvest again in a few weeks.

If you decide to let leaf chicory reach full size, you should probably blanch the plants before harvesting to get the best flavor. Blanching starts about three weeks before harvest. Make sure the leaves are dry when you start the blanching process or the plants will rot. Do not start blanching right after a rainstorm. To blanch the plants you can either tie the outer leaves together or cover the plant with an upside-down flowerpot (cover the drainage hole).

To harvest the blanched heads, cut them off at the base. Chicory will usually keep for several weeks in the refrigerator.

A good variety for spring planting is Crystal Hat, which has elongated leaves and looks somewhat like romaine lettuce. The leaves are quite bitter, but rinsing in warm water should remove some of the bitterness and leave a milder, slightly sweeter flavor.

For late planting, try the cold-hardy Grumolo or Spadona. You can sow them in mid to late summer for harvest in late fall. Where winters are mild plant in fall for a winter crop. Or plant in fall and let plants winter over to produce a crop in early spring. If you harvest by cutting off the entire plant at the base you may get a second flush of leaves.

Perhaps the best-known leaf chicory in the United States is the classic Sugar Loaf. Unlike other chicories, this variety needs fertile, moist but well-drained soil to thrive. Sow anytime from spring to fall for a seedling crop, or if you want to let the plants mature, plant in midsummer for fall harvest. This is not the best variety to winter over—although it will, with protection—because the leaves tend to rot in cold, wet conditions. Keep an eye on it during the winter and promptly remove mushy leaves.

For information on Castelfranco, Red Treviso, Red Verona, and other red-leaved chicories, see Radicchio.

Asparagus Chicory

Chicories grown for their tender flower stalks are called asparagus chicory because that is how they are used. Sow them in early spring, as soon as the soil can be worked, or in midsummer, ½ inch deep, six to eight inches apart, in beds or rows 2 feet apart. You can cook the succulent stalks like asparagus or harvest leaves to use in salads or as a potherb.

Most of these varieties have leaves resembling those of dandelion, and can withstand a few light frosts. For leaves, plant anytime in spring or summer, and cut leaves as you need them. Catalogna is a good cutting variety. Another, more unusual one is Puntarella, which is planted in spring for its tender, twisting, curling stems. Plant it just as soon as you can work the soil, and it should be ready to harvest around the same time as asparagus.

Chicories for Roots and Forcing

Chicories grown for their roots are used, like witloof chicory, to force winter crops of Belgian endive, or the roots are dried, roasted, and ground and added to or substituted for coffee. Sometimes chicory roots are grated and added to salads, raw or cooked and chilled. The aim in growing root chicory is to keep the plants growing steadily all summer to produce the largest possible roots by late fall.

Root chicories need a loose, crumbly soil; dig to 2 feet deep and remove all sizable stones so the roots can easily penetrate straight down into the soil. Sow seeds in early summer—June in most places—¼ to ½ inch deep. Thin plants to stand 8 to 10 inches apart in rows 1½ to 2 feet apart. Wait until the plants have at least four true leaves before you thin, so you can easily pick out the biggest, healthiest plants. Leave the sturdiest plants in place and pull up the weaker, smaller seedlings.

Keep the plants evenly moist all summer; a mulch will help. Feed the plants once in midsummer (late summer in warm climates), sidedressing with compost or an all-purpose organic fertilizer.

Dig the roots after the first few light frosts; dig deep to avoid injuring the long taproot when digging. Do not dig roots of forcing varieties too soon—they need some cool weather before they will produce Belgian endives. The roots look rather like parsnips, and should be at least 1½ inches in diameter at the top in order to be forced. Trim the bottom tips of the roots to leave the roots 8 to 10 inches long.

The procedures for preparing roots for forcing and completing the forcing process are detailed in Chapters Five and Six. Basically, you "plant" the roots in containers of moist sand or peat, in a dark place with temperatures of 50 to 60°F and 95 percent humidity. Covering the roots with a layer of sand produces tightly closed chicons; covering with flowerpots produces looser heads.

Cut off the chicons right above the crowns and the roots should produce a second—or perhaps even a third—harvest. Keep the Belgian endives in the dark after harvest to preserve their creamy pale green color. Exposure to light will turn them green and unpleasantly bitter.

Toner and Mitado are two improved forms of witloof that are handled the same way. Zoom and Robin will produce their crops without covering with a layer of sand; Zoom produces tight, creamy yellow chicons, and Robin's are pale pink.

Large-Rooted Magdeburg can be grown to produce roots for coffee.

Chinese Cabbage and Other Oriental Greens

It can be difficult to figure out from catalog descriptions just what kind of plant you're going to get when you grow Chinese cabbage. The plants known to us as Chinese cabbage are actually more closely related to mustard than to cabbage, but they are grown more like cabbage and some of them resemble cabbage, so that's what we call them. They offer several advantages over conventional cabbage: Chinese cabbage matures faster, has a better flavor, is easier to digest, and makes an excellent crop for fall—a largely neglected season in too many gardens. Chinese cabbage matures in as little as five weeks, depending on the variety.

There are two main types of Chinese cabbage. The first group (*Brassica rapa*, Pekinensis Group) encompasses heading varieties called Chinese cabbage or celery cabbage. These plants form tight heads that are either tall and cylindrical, or squat and barrel-shaped. Their outer leaves are medium green, puckered, and crinkled, and the inner leaves are creamy, pale green. The leaves have a wide midrib. Most Chinese cabbage has a mild, sweet flavor with a bit of a zip to it. It is truly delectable when stir-fried in a little peanut oil, and is also tasty in salads and soups.

The name celery cabbage is also sometimes incorrectly applied to the other kind of Oriental cabbage, bok choy or mustard cabbage (*B. rapa*, Chinensis Group), which has nonheading plants with dark green leaves and broad, succulent, white stems. Bok choy is an indispensable ingredient in stir-fry dishes and delicious in soups, and its stems can be used instead of celery to add crunch to salads.

In addition to the "cabbages" there are some other Oriental greens, most of them brassicas, that are easy to grow and versatile in the kitchen. Some of them are described below.

Most of the Oriental greens are best grown for fall harvest. In warm climates plant in fall for winter harvest, or in winter for harvest in early spring. Some of these make good winter cold-frame crops. Most of the plants need cool temperatures (averaging 60 to 65°F) and a short daylength; when the days are long and the weather is hot they will bolt to seed. There are, however, some bolt-resistant varieties that can be grown in spring. If you want an early crop, choose one of these varieties. There is also an amaranth that makes a good spinach substitute in hot weather.

The key to success with Chinese cabbage is fertile soil and abundant, even moisture. Plenty of organic matter in the soil will help to hold moisture. A mildly acid to near-neutral pH is best. If you can provide these conditions, and time the planting to meet the daylength needs of the particular variety, you should have no trouble growing a good crop of Chinese cabbage. If you can grow cabbage you can grow Chinese cabbage.

For an early crop, sow indoors, ¼ to ½ inch deep, three to four weeks before you expect the last spring frost, and transplant to the garden a week or two after the last frost date. Do not move the plants outdoors too early. If young plants are exposed to frost or cold temperatures in spring they may bolt early when the weather turns warm. Seedlings should have at least six leaves before you transplant them out. Starting them in peat pots will minimize root disturbance during transplanting.

Direct-sow fall crops in midsummer, twelve weeks before you expect the first frost. Plant seeds ½ inch deep.

Thin direct-sown crops or space transplants 1 to 1½ feet apart in rows 1½ to 2 feet apart, or 1½ feet apart in all directions in a bed. Cover young plants with floating row covers to keep out cabbage-maggot flies and flea beetles. Mulch spring-planted crops. Water deeply during dry weather. Plants will benefit from a mid-season nitrogen boost—water with fish emulsion.

Nonheading varieties can mature fully for harvest, or you can use them as cut-and-come-again crops. To harvest heads, pull the plants and cut off the heads at the base. If you are harvesting in fall, you can trim the outer leaves and store in an outdoor storage cache or window well for about a month.

Chinese cabbage and Oriental greens will take quite a bit of frost in fall, and can withstand temperatures as low as 20°F. This cold tolerance, coupled with the early maturity of some varieties, makes them good plants to grow in a cold frame in winter. In cold climates, insulate the cold frame as described in Chapter Six.

Heading Chinese cabbages to plant in spring include Takii's Spring A-1 and Nerva. Two-Seasons Hybrid and Springtide are good for spring or fall. For late crops, try Dynasty Hybrid, Orient Express, Blues, Michihli, Wong Bok, or Treasure Island. Early Jade Pagoda is a good choice for northern gardens.

Bok choy varieties to plant in spring are Komatsuna, Lei Choi, and Shanghai Pak Choi. Joi Choi is an early variety that performs very well in fall and winter, and also tolerates heat. Mei Quing Choi is a compact variety that can be grown in spring as an interesting baby vegetable.

Several Oriental mustards are very cold tolerant and make outstanding fall and winter crops, among them Tatsoi, Karashina, Green in Snow Mustard, and Japanese White Celery Mustard.

Green Lance is a Chinese kale (gai lon) that is grown in spring or fall for its juicy flower stems. Harvest the stalks as soon as the buds form, and cook them along with their leaves. The flavor is somewhat similar to broccoli.

Hin Choy, sometimes called amaranth spinach, is ready to pick in as little as a month, and performs well in hot weather. You can use this mild-flavored green as a spinach substitute.

Shungiku, or chop suey greens (*Chrysanthemum coronarium*), is actually a type of chrysanthemum that is grown for its edible leaves. If allowed to bloom the plants produce small yellow mum flowers, which are also edible.

Chives

Chives are native to the Orient, and one kind, garlic chives, is sometimes called Chinese chives. Chives are a type of onion, but the plants are grown for their upright, grassy leaves rather than their clumps of tiny bulbs. Regular chives (*Allium schoenoprasum*) have tubular leaves with a mild onion flavor, and round flowerheads of purplish pink in early summer. The flowers also have a slight onion flavor and are delightful in salads. Garlic or Chinese chives (*A. tuberosum*) have flat leaves and starry white flowerheads with a mild garlic taste.

Chives can be dried but they are best preserved by freezing. Snip the leaves into short pieces and spread them on cookie sheets to freeze them. When frozen store the chives in freezer containers.

Chives are perennials hardy throughout the continental United States, and the clumps grow bigger every year. Established chives start to grow very early in spring—they are usually already several inches high when the crocuses bloom. They are durable and easy to grow, needing virtually no maintenance.

The savory leaves have myriad uses in the kitchen. Chop and scatter them over salads, vegetables, meats, fish, or chicken, and add them to omelets, sauces, and soups. The flowers make pretty garnishes, and are quite ornamental in the garden. The plants do fine in containers, and you can dig and pot up clumps in fall for winter use indoors.

You must give them a cold dormant period before bringing them indoors, however, and the procedure is described under Bringing Garden Herbs Indoors, in Chapter Five.

Both types of chives grow best in full sun, but will also tolerate partial shade. A moderately fertile soil that is well drained is ideal for chives, but they will adapt to any good garden soil. Seeds are slow to germinate and tricky to handle, so start your patch with nursery plants or a division from a friend's clump. Set the plants 5 to 8 inches apart. After they bloom, cut back the flower stalks. To keep your chives growing vigorously, divide the clumps every three years.

You can cut leaves as needed from spring through much of autumn, whenever they are large enough—6 inches or so tall. When harvesting, cut back the leaf to 2 inches above the ground.

Coriander

Coriander's importance in Chinese cooking is evident in one of its common names, Chinese parsley. It is also widely used in Mexican cuisine, and is sometimes known as cilantro. Its botanical name is *Coriandrum sativum*. Both the leaves and seeds are used. The aromatic flavor of this herb defies description—it is part tangy, and part green, or "herby." The seeds taste sort of citrusy, and have a somewhat peculiar smell before they mature. You can use them whole or ground. In fact, coriander seeds have been in use throughout recorded history. Some were found in Egyptian pyramids. Today they help to season sausage and other foods.

The long taproot of coriander is edible, too, and tastes like the leaves but with a nutty quality.

Coriander is an annual that grows 2 to 3 feet tall. Its compound, divided leaves look a bit like those of flat-leaf parsley, only they are smaller and a lighter shade of green. The plants grow well in full sun or partial shade, in soil that is light and loose, moist but well drained, and reasonably fertile but not too rich in nitrogen. Too much nitrogen produces poorly flavored leaves. Coriander makes a good companion for caraway in the garden, for the two plants have complementary rooting patterns.

Sow seeds directly in the garden as soon as the danger of frost is past in spring. Direct-sowing works best; the long taproot makes coriander difficult to transplant unless the plants are young and small. In very warm climates it is better to plant in fall. Sow ½ inch deep, and when plants are a couple of inches tall thin them to stand 5 to 8 inches apart. Keep coriander carefully weeded, or mulch the plants to keep down weeds; this is especially important when the plants are young.

Coriander tends to bolt to seed in hot weather. Planting successions two to three weeks apart will extend the harvest of usable leaves. The plants may self-sow to produce a new batch of plants next spring.

Harvest individual leaves or sprigs as needed throughout the growing season. Young leaves have the best flavor. If you want to harvest seeds, pick the round seedpods when the leaves turn brown and seeds are mature, but before the pods burst open.

Corn Salad

This small annual plant has many names. Corn salad *(Valerianella locusta)* is the most common one in the United States, although the French name, *mache*, is also catching on. But you may also know it as lamb's lettuce, fetticus, field salad, or rapunzel (the latter derived, no doubt, from the plant's appearance in the fairy tale of the same name—Rapunzel was hunting for corn salad for her mother when the wicked witch caught her). The plant grows wild in much of the Northern Hemisphere. It has been domesticated, of course, and is very popular in France.

Corn salad is a small plant, with narrow, rounded, dark green leaves gathered into a rosette. It has a mild, nutty flavor that contrasts nicely with sharp-flavored greens. One popular way to serve corn salad is in a salad with beets, dressed with a vinaigrette. You can also cook it like spinach.

Like so many other salad greens, corn salad likes cool weather. But unlike other greens, some varieties of corn salad grow well in hot weather, too. You can plant in early spring for a late spring harvest, in summer eight weeks before the first frost for a fall harvest, or in early autumn for plants to winter over for an early harvest next spring. Gardeners in mild climates can grow it as a winter crop.

Small-seeded varieties generally do better in fall and winter, and large-seeded varieties hold up well in heat and are best for spring planting.

Direct-sow, ½ inch deep, or start transplants in containers. Seeds may take as long as two weeks to germinate, so be patient. Keep the soil evenly moist until germination occurs. When the seedlings have three or four leaves, thin the plants, and use the thinnings in salads. If you want to let the plants mature fully, space them 4 to 6 inches apart. If you will harvest them young, plants need only be a couple of inches apart. Seedling crops need not be thinned at all.

Corn salad is not difficult to grow, and not demanding in terms of soil. The compact plants are good for intercropping among larger vegetables such as broccoli, and are quite good-looking when planted among other salad greens. The plants grow slowly, and some may take as long as three months to reach full size. Small-seeded varieties may bolt in hot weather, so keep them moist. The flavor will not turn bitter in heat, but do harvest promptly when the plants mature, for the flavor will decline in overall quality.

Harvest seedling crops by simply cutting with a scissors. You can pick larger leaves as needed, or cut off the whole plant about an inch above the ground and it will send out new leaves. Cooks fond of baby vegetables can pick whole plants when the leaves are just a few inches long and use the plants whole to lend a decorative touch to salads.

If you are wintering over some plants for spring, protect them with cloches, hot caps, a cold frame, or a loose covering of straw.

Small-seeded varieties to grow in fall or winter include Blonde Shell; Broad-Leaved, which is perhaps the fastest to mature; Coquille; D'Etampes; Elan, which makes a good baby vegetable and is resistant to mildew; Verte de Cambrai; and Vit.

Some large-seeded varieties to plant in spring are Large-Seeded Dutch, which also does well in cool weather, and Piedmont.

Cress

The best-known cress is watercress, which is actually closely related to the nasturtium. It is possible to grow watercress without having access to a clear running stream, but there are land cresses that are easier to grow and have the same kind of zesty, peppery flavor. People have been eating cresses for centuries, and they remain versatile additions to gardens and kitchens today. The land cresses are among the easiest crops to grow. Use them to jazz up salads, soups, and sandwiches.

There are two main types of cress for the garden. The most commonly grown is the annual garden cress, sometimes called pepper grass. Garden cress (*Lepidium sativum*) is a small plant, with medium green leaves with rather feathery edges. One type, called curly cress (*L. sativum* var. *crispum*), has finely cut and curled leaves very like those of parsley. The plants are attractive in the garden, and so small that they can easily fit in a window box or modest-sized pot.

Grow garden cress in the outdoor garden as described below (sow every two weeks for a continuous harvest), or plant it in fall to winter over in the cold frame for an early spring crop. Garden cress is also easy to grow as a seedling crop on a windowsill in winter. Harvest with a scissors when the

seedlings are about 2 inches tall and have three leaves; they may reach this size in as little as ten days from sowing. You can also use garden cress seed for sprouts. The seeds are quick to germinate, and can be handled as directed in Chapter Six under A Crop of Sprouts.

Outdoors, you may wish to let a few plants go to seed and collect and save the seeds for future planting. The seed heads can also be dried and used in arrangements.

The other cress found in gardens is usually called upland cress. It is not closely related to garden cress—its scientific name is *Barbarea verna*. The plant is biennial but grown as an annual. It has a compact rosette of glossy, dark green compound leaves with rounded leaflets, and grows only about 8 inches high. Upland cress is slower to germinate than garden cress, and it is important to keep the soil evenly moist until the shoots push through the surface. Harvest begins six to eight weeks later.

Both cresses like cool weather, and can tolerate light frosts. What they do not like is heat; they bolt to seed rapidly in hot weather, and when the plants flower the leaves become too peppery hot to eat. Cresses are ideal crops for the autumn garden; sow them directly where they are to grow in mid to late summer, four weeks before the first frost. You can also sow them in early spring, as much as four weeks before you expect the last frost. Sow seeds ¼ inch deep.

Cresses thrive in full sun or partial shade, and neither is very fussy about soil. Both need plenty of moisture, but garden cress likes a lighter soil while upland cress prefers soil rich in organic matter. Thin the plants to stand 4 to 6 inches apart in beds, or the same distance apart in rows 1 foot apart.

Let the seedlings grow for ten days before thinning, and you can use the thinnings in the kitchen. Pinch out the growing tips to encourage the plants to grow bushier.

Pick individual leaves as needed after they are 3 or 4 inches long, or cut off the entire plant right above the ground for a cut-and-come-again crop. It will regrow several times. In cool weather you will be able to keep the plants producing for six to eight weeks.

Cucumbers

No other vegetable is as refreshing as a cucumber (*Cucumis sativus*). They don't offer much in the way of flavor, but their juicy, crisp texture can't be beat in a salad. Blended with yogurt in a raita, cucumbers make a cooling antidote to the fiery spiciness of curries and other Indian foods. Small-fruited varieties are perfect for pickling, and the very smallest are made into cornichons, those marvellous little French sour pickles.

It used to be tough to grow cucumbers because they are so disease prone. Cucumbers are subject to all sorts of blights, wilts, mildew, scab, mosaic, and numerous other bacterial and fungal ills. But multiple-disease resistance is bred into most varieties these days. If you tend to have disease problems in your garden, you should probably avoid the heirloom varieties that have less resistance.

Standard cucumbers need lots of space to spread out—the rambling vines can grow 8 to 10 feet long. But there are options for cramped gardens. You can train the plants to grow vertically, with the vines supported on grow netting or trellises, or you can grow bush cucumbers. The bush varieties produce full-sized fruit on short vines just 2 or 3 feet long, and grow happily in containers or small plots.

If maximum productivity is important to you, look for varieties that are gynoecious, having all female flowers (only female flowers bear fruit). Gynoecious plants are usually self-pollinating; those that aren't are sold along with a few seeds of male plants whose flowers will serve as pollinators.

Cucumbers need full sun and warm weather. They are unhappy when tempera-tures dip below 65°F, and don't do very well in cool, damp climates. To produce juicy, crisp-textured fruit, the plants need to grow steadily and fast. That takes fertile soil that is moist but well drained, and contains plenty of organic matter. Even moisture is critical, so water during dry weather, especially when the fruits are forming and enlarging. Mulch is often helpful.

Sow cucumbers directly in the garden when the soil temperature is at least 70°F and the weather is warm. The traditional method is to plant in hills 4 feet apart, in rows 6 feet apart. Plant eight or ten seeds around the top of each hill, and thin to leave the four sturdiest plants. Sow 1 inch deep. If you will train the plants vertically, space them 6 to 8 inches apart along the trellis. Bush varieties can be spaced 1 to 1½ feet apart in a bed.

Cucumber beetles, both spotted and striped, can be destructive. What's worse, they carry bacterial wilt, which can wipe out your plants. Cover young plants with floating row covers to keep pests off them. If necessary, spray or dust with rotenone or pyrethrum.

To grow the vines on a trellis or netting, fasten the stems to the support as they grow, with string, long twist-ties, or soft yarn. Tie loosely to avoid damaging the stems. Vertical growing not only saves garden space, but also makes it easier to find and pick the fruit.

Cucumber plants are shallow rooted, so avoid cultivating around them. You may notice that the leaves look limp on hot afternoons. Don't worry—they will freshen up again in the evening if the soil is moist.

Cucumbers are ready to pick in six to nine weeks, depending on the variety. Keep them picked to keep the plants producing. If even one fruit reaches full maturity the plant will stop bearing. For best quality pick the cucumbers while they are still deep green, firm, and solid. The fruit turns yellow when it ripens, so if you see that green color lightening toward yellow, pick the fruit at once. Older cucumbers have bigger seeds and a pithy texture, and can develop a bitter taste.

Good slicing cucumbers include Elite, Marketmore 80, Straight Eight (open pollinated), Slicemaster (gynoecious), and Early Pride Hybrid (gynoecious). If cucumbers tend to give you indigestion, try one of the "burpless" varieties, such as Burpless Hybrid, Sweet Slice Hybrid, Sweet Success (gynoecious), or Suyo Long.

Bush cucumbers for slicing include Bush Crop, Salad Bush, Spacemaster, Patio Pik, and Lucky Strike, which is recommended for northern gardens. Two bush varieties for pickling are Pickalot Hybrid (gynoecious) and Hybrid Bush Pickling.

If you want to make pickles, you might grow National Pickling (an old standard), Northern Pickling, Pioneer Hybrid, or Saladin (gynoecious). Another old pickling cucumber is West India Gherkin, which has been grown here since the 1800s. These fat little fruits look like tiny watermelons covered with spines, and the plant's leaves resemble those of watermelon, too.

For cornichons grow Small Paris, Fine Meaux, Vert de Massy, or the heirloom DeBourbonne. Pick when the fruits are the size of your little finger.

Want to try something a little more unusual in the cucumber line? Then consider Armenian Yard-Long, or China Long, with slender fruits up to 2 feet long; Lemon, or True Lemon, a round cucumber with light yellow skin and white flesh; or Crystal Apple White, which is, as its name implies, round and white.

Daylilies

You may wonder what the daylily (*Hemerocallis*), that paragon of the perennial garden, is doing in a book on kitchen gardens. But the flower buds of daylilies, as well as the tuberous roots, are edible. The buds make an interesting tempura, and can be used in stir-fries and other Oriental dishes (the Chinese call them golden needles).

You can use the tubers like Jerusalem artichokes—sliced and sautéed or added to stir-fries or salads.

Harvest buds for cooking the day before they would open, when they are still tightly closed but showing color. The best time to try cooking some daylily roots is when division of established clumps of plants in late summer or early fall leaves you with extra tubers and no place to plant them.

Daylilies are beautiful when massed at the back of the garden. (Dwarf varieties can go farther front.) Breeders have given us cultivars in an incredible array of warm colors from palest yellow to deep maroon, and a range of blooming times from early to late summer. Although each blossom lasts but a single day, the plants bloom for a couple of weeks, and planting early-, mid-season, and late-blooming cultivars can let you enjoy daylilies almost all summer long. One cautionary note: not all varieties do well in all locations, so buy plants from a trustworthy local nursery, or inquire of the mail-order nursery company about the suitability of plants for your area.

Daylilies are among the easiest flowers to grow. They will flower happily in full sun or partial shade, in any average garden soil. A moist but well-drained soil rich in organic matter is the optimum daylily medium. If you plant them in shade, their tall stems will bend toward the sun, but in warm climates where the summer sun is strong, the plants appreciate some shade in the afternoon.

In spring, anytime after the danger of heavy frost is past, plant dormant roots from the nursery. Wait a few weeks until all danger of frost is past to set out plants. Depending on the variety, space plants 1½ to 2 feet apart; the dwarf and smaller varieties can be planted at the closer spacing. Set plants at the same depth they were growing in the nursery container, with the crowns right at soil level.

Daylilies need little care after you plant them. Remove faded flowers to keep the plants looking their best, and cut back the flower stalks when blooming is finished. You need water only when the soil dries out. The roots spread each year, and eventually clumps of plants will become crowded and need division. Every three or four years, dig up mature clumps of daylilies in spring or early fall. Cut or pry apart each root clump into sections, each having at least three shoots. Replant the divisions at the same depth they were before, at the spacings recommended earlier for plants.

Dill

For some reason that is obscure, at least to me, the dried foliage of dill is called dillweed. In my book dill (*Anethum graveolens*) is anything but a weed. The tall, graceful plants with their feathery, blue green leaves and flat flowerheads of tiny greenish yellow flowers are handsome in the garden. The flowers attract bees, too. Dill's mild, rather tangy flavor adds a special quality to so many dishes. Dill leaves are outstanding with grilled salmon and other fish, and in potato soup and cheese sauce. Dill is used extensively in Scandinavian and Russian cooking.

The fine, delicate foliage unfortunately starts to look tattered when the flowerheads come into bloom. You can prolong the harvest of leaves by pinching off flowers as soon as you see them, but eventually the plants will bloom despite your best efforts. The best way to produce a continuous harvest of leaves is to make succession plantings every two or three weeks until midsummer.

Plant dill in full sun (it will tolerate some shade in the South), in moist but well-drained soil that is reasonably fertile and rich in organic matter. If the soil is rich enough the plants will self-sow, and new seedlings will pop up early the next spring.

The plants develop a taproot and do not transplant well, so sow seeds directly in the garden. Plant them ¼ to ½ inch deep, when the danger of frost is past. Thin the seed-

lings to stand 6 to 9 inches apart if you want to harvest seeds.

Dill is easy to grow and needs little care except for weeding. If your garden is in a very windy location, you may have to stake the tall, slender stems to keep them upright.

Pick leaves as needed, when you are ready to use them. Fresh dill leaves quickly go limp in the refrigerator. For long-term storage, freeze whole stems and cut off leaves whenever you need them. Dried leaves have far less flavor than fresh or even frozen ones, but if you do wish to dry them, spread them on a screen so they dry quickly.

Seeds are usually ready to harvest two to three weeks after the flowers bloom. Watch for them to turn light brown, but do not allow them to ripen fully or they will drop to the ground. Cut the seed heads with long stems. Then collect bunches of stems inside paper bags to dry the seeds, as described under Harvesting and Storing Herbs in Chapter Five.

Eggplant

Eggplant is the quintessential summer vegetable—it flourishes in hot weather and can't stand the cold. It belongs to the same plant family as tomatoes, potatoes, peppers, petunias . . . and deadly nightshade; botanically it is known as *Solanum melongena* var. *esculentum*. The chemical compound solanine, which makes nightshade poisonous, gives eggplant the bitter juice that can be drawn out by salting slices or chunks and letting them drain for an hour before cooking.

If you don't already think of eggplant as ornamental, think again. The star-shaped purple flowers are quite beautiful, and the fruits with their shiny, deep purple skin are attractive, too. There are also white-, red-, and green-skinned eggplants, and European varieties with white skin streaked or blushed with light rosy purple. Eggplant is pretty with pink or pale yellow petunias, with yellow marigolds, or in front of purple or yellow-podded pole beans.

The compact plants grow just 3 feet tall or less, and are at home in containers as well as garden beds or rows.

Eggplant plays a role in the cuisines of many nations. You will find it in Italian caponata and parmigiana, French ratatouille, Middle Eastern baba ghannouj, Greek moussaka, and an assortment of Indian dishes. Baby eggplant grilled with a brush-

ing of extra virgin olive oil and fresh herbs is a summer highlight around my house.

Give eggplant full sun, and well-drained soil containing plenty of organic matter. It will appreciate regular infusions of moisture, but does not fare well in soggy or heavy soil. The plants grow best in hot sum-

Baby eggplant is delicious, and doesn't have the bitter quality that larger fruits sometimes develop. The variety shown here is Pirouette.

mer weather, when the average temperature is from 70 to 85°F. They perform poorly in cool, damp climates and will refuse to set fruit when the temperature is below 60°F. The plants suffer when the mercury dips below 50°F and expire in frost.

Unless you live in a very warm climate, start seeds indoors ten to twelve weeks before your last frost date. They will germinate best in soil that is at least 70°F; 80°F is even better. Sow ¼ inch deep. Do not set out transplants until two or three weeks after the last frost, when the soil is warm and nighttime temperatures stay above 55°F. Don't be in too great a hurry to move plants outdoors; if the seedlings are exposed to cold the plants will not set fruit later on.

Set plants 1½ to 2 feet apart in all directions in a bed, or in rows 2 to 3 feet apart. Cover the young plants with floating row covers to keep off flea beetles.

Eggplant likes plenty of moisture, and mulch will slow its evaporation from the soil. Keep the growing area weeded if you don't lay a mulch. Unless your soil is very rich, feed four weeks after planting with fish emulsion and a seaweed fertilizer, or a product that combines the two.

The harvest season for eggplant is, unfortunately, rather limited. To extend it, pick the fruit before it matures fully and the plants will produce more. Young eggplants are tender, with smaller seeds, and they don't need to be salted and drained the way larger fruits do. You can pick standard eggplants anytime after they are 4 or 5 inches long, and baby eggplants when they reach 2 inches. In any case, pick them while the skin is still glossy; when it dulls the fruit is past its prime. When you cut open an eggplant the seeds should be light in color —if they are brown the vegetable is over-ripe.

There are lots of eggplant varieties to choose from. If you like baby eggplant, as I do, grow Slim Jim, Pirouette, Little Fingers, White Egg, or Easter Egg (the latter two are white).

Standard varieties, which produce large, oval fruit, include Black Beauty (a nonhybrid), Early Beauty, Early Bird, Dusky, and Prelane (a French variety). Florida Market does especially well in warm climates, and Agora performs well in the North.

Oriental or Japanese eggplants are long and slender—perfect for slicing. Japanese Purple Pickling bears small fruits. Orient Express is suited to cooler climates. Other good Oriental-type varieties include Ichiban, Millionaire, Pintung Long, and Tycoon.

Many people consider white eggplant the most delicious kind. The white-skinned fruits do have a mild flavor, and are interesting in the garden. Good varieties to try are Alba, Dourga, Chinese White, Osterei, and Long White Sword.

A few more varieties deserve special mention because they bear unusually beautiful fruit. Rosa Bianca is a lovely light shade of pinkish lavender; Bride and Pallida produce white fruits that are streaked (the former) or blushed (the latter) with light rosy purple; and Violette de Firenze is a delicate lavender sometimes with white stripes.

Endive and Escarole

These two greens add a snappy, bitter flavor and a nice crunch to tossed salads. They are grown like lettuce, but they need a longer season to mature (most varieties take 2½ to 3 months) and are hardier than lettuce. Botanically they are the same, both classified as *Cichorium endivia*, and both form loose heads. But endive has narrow, frizzy, finely cut leaves, while escarole has broader, flatter leaves. Both are a good source of dietary fiber. These plants have other uses besides salads. The Pennsylvania Dutch serve endive like dandelion, boiled and with a cooked sweet-and-sour bacon dressing. A classic Italian soup is made with escarole.

Gardening cognoscenti disagree about which plant is hardier, but both grow best in cool weather. You can plant them in very early spring, or to mature in fall. Gardeners in mild climates can grow endive and escarole in the winter. Farther north, some varieties are worth trying in a winter hotbed or insulated cold frame.

These plants are ideal for cool climates but they will grow in most gardens if you can keep them out of hot weather. Heat turns the flavor unbearably bitter.

Endive and escarole need full sun, and they are adaptable to any soil type, as long as the soil is moist. They can even tolerate acid soils where pines and azaleas thrive. The very best crops are grown in rich, fertile soils containing lots of organic matter. Humusy soil also retains moisture, which is especially important to keep spring crops from bolting in hot weather.

You can sow endive and escarole directly in the garden or start seeds indoors for transplants. For a spring crop, direct-sow ¼ inch deep, two to four weeks before you expect the last frost. Or start seeds indoors ten to twelve weeks before the last frost and set out transplants four or five weeks later. To extend the harvest start three or four plantings of a few plants at a time, three weeks apart.

Sow seeds for a fall crop in the garden or in a separate nursery area for later transplanting, twelve to fifteen weeks before you expect the first fall frost. Fall is the best time to plant in most areas, because the long, hot days of late spring and summer can goad the plants into bolting. The plants will tolerate a few light frosts in fall, which will actually improve the flavor. But cover any plants still in the garden if you are expecting more than a light frost. In cool climates where frost comes early, sow around the end of June to have plants ready to harvest before frosts get heavy in fall. In mild climates sow in fall for a winter crop.

No matter when you start endive and escarole, be absolutely sure you keep the soil moist until the seeds germinate and the little plants are a couple of inches high. Fall crops sown in summer will benefit from a bit of shade to keep the soil cooler until the seeds sprout.

Thin the plants to stand 1½ feet apart for most varieties, the same distance apart in all directions in a bed, or in rows 2 feet apart. Compact varieties such as Fin des Louviers can be spaced closer together. Wait to thin until the thinnings are big enough to use in a salad.

You can also grow endive to harvest when it is young and the leaves are only 4 to 6 inches long. Endive is a classic mesclun plant. If you plan to harvest the plants young, you can plant them closer together.

When setting out transplants, do not plant them too deep or the crowns may rot. Position the plants with the crowns just above the surface of the soil.

Endive and escarole don't usually have many problems with pests and diseases, although they may develop rot in cold, wet conditions. Fertilize once or twice during the growing season, sidedressing with compost or using a seaweed concentrate or fish emulsion.

Blanching the heads before harvesting blunts the bitter flavor and gives the leaves a creamier texture and color. You blanch plants by tying the outer leaves together with string or heavy rubber bands, or by inverting a flowerpot over each head (cover the drainage hole in the pot). Blanching takes about 2 weeks. Make sure the leaves are dry when you begin the blanching process; wet leaves may rot. If it rains during blanching, open up the plants to let them dry out, then retie or re-cover them.

If the first frost catches you unawares, you can dig the plants and replant them in tubs of soil in a basement or root cellar and then blanch them.

Following are some varieties to grow.

Batavian Full-Hearted, or Full Heart Batavian, is the best-known escarole. Its broad leaves with fluted edges are gathered into tight heads that need no blanching; the inner leaves blanch themselves to a creamy, buttery color and texture. Very hardy, it's a good choice for a fall or winter crop in appropriate conditions. Nuvol, an improved variety, can be grown for spring, fall, or winter harvest. Grosse Bouclee is a French variety.

Salad King is perhaps the most widely grown endive, with large heads of frilly, dark green leaves, slow to bolt. The heart blanches as the head matures. Green Curled, or Green Curled Ruffec, has crisp, deeply cut leaves. Fine Curled has even frillier leaves, and needs blanching if grown to maturity. It can also be grown as a seedling or cut-and-come-again crop. Fin des Louviers is similar but smaller, a good choice for gardens where space is limited.

Nina is another small endive, quick to mature. President is very hardy and recommended for fall crops. Traviata, or Scala, is a French endive with a large head of curly leaves and a heart that blanches nicely. Plants resist bolting.

Fennel

The delicate, feathery foliage of fennel (*Foeniculum vulgare*) is an asset to any garden, and garden designers are using the bronze-leaved form, which has leaves of deep coppery bronze, in ornamental gardens to provide a soft backdrop for flowers. The plants grow 3 to 4 feet tall, and can reach heights of 6 feet. The sweet flavor of fennel is like anise or licorice, but more mellow. Use the leaves to season grilled fish or chicken, tomatoes, sauces, and omelets. Their flavor is as delicate as their appearance and is easily lost to heat, so add fennel leaves at the end of cooking. The seeds are good in breads and cakes, in soups, and with beets. A tea or liqueur made with fennel seeds is said to aid digestion. In fact, fennel has been valued medicinally by the ancient Greeks, Romans, and medieval Europeans, as well as in China.

A variety of the species, *F. vulgare* var. *azoricum*, called Florence fennel, is grown for its sweet, succulent, licorice-flavored "bulbs," which are actually formed by the swollen overlapping leaf bases. Florence fennel is delicious raw or cooked, and is sometimes included in antipasto platters. Its leaves can be used as well as its stems.

Fennel has flat-topped umbels of tiny yellow flowers, similar to the flowerheads of dill. The flowers, like those of other members of the carrot or umbellifer family, attract butterflies.

Fennel is a perennial and has become naturalized in parts of California. But it is not hardy where winter temperatures drop below −10°F, so many gardeners grow it as an annual. The plants will often self-sow if you let some flowers go to seed in the garden.

Plant fennel in full sun, in well-drained soil of average fertility that is rich in organic matter. Fennel does best in sandy soil with lots of humus added, but it dislikes heavy clay. A near-neutral or slightly alkaline pH is best. Florence fennel performs best in a richer, moister soil.

Sow seeds directly in the garden (fennel does not transplant well) when all danger of frost is past, two weeks or so after your average last frost date. Plant them ½ inch deep. Keep the soil evenly moist until the seeds germinate, which usually takes about two weeks. When plants are a couple of inches tall, thin them to 6 to 8 inches apart. To extend the harvest of leaves, plant successions every two to three weeks right through summer until about the middle of August (September in warmer climates). For an early start next spring, let some plants self-sow, or plant seeds yourself in fall.

If you want to harvest fennel seeds, companion planting tradition says to keep the plants away from coriander, which may interfere with fennel's ability to set seeds. Companion planters also should not plant fennel near bush beans, caraway, kohlrabi, or tomatoes.

Sow seeds of Florence fennel in midsummer for a harvest in early fall. You can start cutting the stems as soon as they begin to swell, or wait until the bulbs mature about two-and-a-half months after planting. Blanch the bulbs by drawing soil up around the stem bases when they have swollen to an inch thick. Bulbs should be ready to harvest approximately ten days later.

You can cut leaves whenever you need them throughout the growing season. Fennel foliage loses most of its flavor when dried; for long-term storage, freeze whole stems as for dill, and clip off frozen leaves as needed.

If you want to harvest seeds you must take care to catch them as soon as they turn from yellow green to gray green. If you wait until the seeds turn brown they may fall to the ground before you get to them. Cut seed heads with stems attached and dry them in paper bags as directed under Harvesting and Storing Herbs in Chapter Five.

Garlic

Garlic *(Allium sativum)* is a perennial, but grown as an annual. Besides its universality in kitchens, garlic is popularly believed to possess the ability to ward off colds, and in the garden it can repel insect pests when used as a companion plant. Garlic is reasonably easy to grow, though a bit touchier than onions. A related species, elephant garlic *(A. scorodoprasum)*, is easier to grow and hardier. It has enormous cloves with a mild flavor—so mild, in fact, that it can be served as a cooked vegetable, and is especially good with a cream sauce. Elephant garlic can grow as a perennial in all but the coldest climates, and some corms can be left in the garden at the end of the season to start next year's crop.

Grow garlic and elephant garlic in full sun, in fertile, moist but well-drained soil. Bulbs develop better in light soil than in heavy clay. A sandy loam that contains lots of organic matter is ideal.

Like other onion relatives, garlic and elephant garlic need cool weather to get off to a good start. Plant garlic as early in spring as the soil can be worked, about four weeks before the last frost. The plants can stand a good deal of frost and even a light freeze. Elephant garlic can be planted with regular garlic in spring, or in fall (mulch it over winter). In warm climates plant both kinds in fall.

The plants can be grown from seed, but it is far easier to plant cloves. Set them pointed end up, with the tips 1 inch below the surface of the soil. Set regular garlic 3 or 4 inches apart, elephant garlic 6 inches apart. Keep the plants weeded, and water in dry weather. If any flower stalks appear, remove them.

Garlic matures three to four months after planting. It is ready to harvest when the tops turn yellow and droopy. When that happens, stop watering and push over all the tops. Three or four days later, dig the bulbs. In heavier soils it is helpful to loosen the soil first.

After you dig the bulbs, spread them out in a dry, shady spot to cure. If the weather is rainy, lay them on screens indoors. Let the bulbs cure until the tops are dry and the skin is papery crisp. Cut off the tops (unless you want to make a garlic braid), and cut off the roots near the base of the bulbs. Store the bulbs indoors in a cool, dry spot. Save a few bulbs to plant next year.

Scented Geraniums

These charming, small-leaved relatives of our common garden geraniums belong to the same genus, *Pelargonium*, but their leaves and flowers carry a broad range of scents. For example, there are geraniums scented like apple, apricot, cinnamon, coconut, nutmeg, ginger, lemon, lime, orange, peppermint, pineapple, rose, rose-lemon, rose-mint, strawberry, and musk. And there are more besides. The plants' small flowers are pink, white, or pale lavender, depending upon the species or variety. Like other fragrant plants, these little geraniums bring a whole new dimension to the garden;

brushing against the soft leaves releases their scent.

The perfumy flavors of the scented geraniums echo their fragrances, and work best in puddings or ice creams, in jellies, or as a garnish for cakes, salads, and fruit dishes. The flowers retain much of their original color and flavor when dried, as well.

Scented geraniums are tender perennials, and gardeners in warm climates can grow them as garden perennials. The rest of us have to grow them in pots to bring indoors in fall, or take cuttings at the end of the season to root indoors for next year's plants. You can also grow scented geraniums as houseplants on a bright windowsill, or in a light garden with the lamps turned on for twelve to sixteen hours a day.

To grow scented geraniums from seed, sow seeds indoors, ¼ inch deep, eight to ten weeks before the average date of your last spring frost. It is a good idea to soak the seeds for twenty-four hours before planting. The seeds germinate best in soil with a temperature of 70 to 75°F, and you may need to provide bottom heat by one of the methods described in Chapter Two.

Set out transplants or nursery plants after all danger of frost is past and the weather is warm. Space them 1 to 1½ feet apart.

Plant the geraniums in full sun (in warmer climates they will also tolerate partial shade), in soil that is well drained, of average fertility, and rich in organic matter. Good drainage is essential, for these plants do not like wet feet. As the outdoor season progresses, water only when the soil dries out.

To start plants for winter windowsills or next spring's garden, take cuttings in late spring or early fall. Cut vigorous young shoots about 4 inches long. Remove the bottom leaves, but make sure each cutting has at least three leaves. Let the cuttings air-dry overnight, then place them in a rooting medium (such as a mix of two parts potting soil to one part builder's sand), in bright light but not in direct sun. Provide bottom heat as for seeds until the cuttings root. You can root cuttings in individual pots, or root them in a flat and transplant to pots when roots have formed. The cuttings have rooted when a gentle pull on the leaves meets with resistance, and when new leaves begin to grow.

Hyssop

This plant (*Hyssopus officinalis*) has an aromatic, medicinal scent—it doesn't necessarily smell like something you would want to eat. But you can eat hyssop, both the leaves and the pretty violet flowers. The plant's strong, minty flavor is an interesting addition to green salads, fruit salads, tomato sauces, and poultry and lamb dishes. You can also make tea from the dried leaves or flowers. Oil from hyssop leaves is used commercially in making liqueur.

Hyssop is a most attractive addition to the garden. It grows about 2 feet tall, with rather small, narrow leaves. All summer and into fall the plants produce spikes of small violet flowers that attract bees and butterflies. Hyssop is a perennial hardy over most of the continental United States. It is lovely with feathery dill or fennel in the garden, or planted in back of pink-flowered dianthus or scented geraniums.

Full sun is best for hyssop, but it will also tolerate partial shade. Give it light and well-drained soil that tends toward dryness. Direct-sow in spring ¼ inch deep, later thinning plants to stand 1 foot apart.

Cut off spent flower spikes and prune occasionally if necessary to keep the plants shapely. Hyssop needs little maintenance other than that. You will need to renew the planting every four or five years, when the plants begin to lose their vigor. The easiest way is to dig up and divide the plants in spring or fall.

A similarly named plant also worthy of a place in the kitchen garden is anise hyssop. Anise hyssop is not very closely related to hyssop—it belongs to a different genus (its botanical name is *Agastache foeniculum*), although both plants are members of the mint family. The plants look quite different, too—anise hyssop grows 2 to 3 feet tall and has oval, toothed, grayish green leaves. However it, too, bears spikes of diminutive violet flowers in summer.

Both the leaves and flowers of anise hyssop possess a rather sweet licorice scent and flavor, and you can use them in many of the same ways as anise. Use them to decorate baked goods, and add them to beef stew, pickles, and Oriental dishes, especially those containing beef. The dried leaves make good tea.

Like true hyssop, this plant grows best in full sun and well-drained soil, but anise hyssop prefers a richer, more fertile soil. Anise hyssop is perennial and easy to grow, and may self-sow and increase its ranks.

Kale and Collards

These two vegetables are very similar, and so are their cultural needs. Both are non-heading members of the cabbage family, and both are classified as *Brassica oleracea*, Acephala Group. Kale has clumps of bluish green or grayish green leaves with curly, frilly edges. There are also some gorgeously colored ornamental varieties. Collards have smooth, dark green leaves. Both vegetables are very nutritious, rich in vitamins and minerals. Like their relatives, these plants grow best in cool weather. Collard greens are usually thought of as a southern crop, and they do tolerate quite a bit of heat, but they grow very well in the North, too, and can stand temperatures as low as 20°F. The flavor of both vegetables is sweetened and mellowed by exposure to light frost; they taste far better than the tough, cabbagey-tasting greens you find at the supermarket produce counter.

You can sow kale indoors, ½ inch deep, ten weeks before you expect the last spring frost, and transplant outdoors six to eight weeks later, or direct-sow four weeks before the last frost. For the best quality, though,

it is better to grow kale for fall harvest, and direct-sow ten to twelve weeks before you expect the first fall frost. In warm climates, direct-sow in fall to harvest in winter.

Direct-sow collards two to three weeks before the last spring frost, or get a head start indoors six to eight weeks before that. Or sow them ten to twelve weeks before the first fall frost.

Space kale plants 1 to 1½ feet apart in a bed, or in rows 2 to 2½ feet apart. Space collards about 15 inches apart in beds, or in rows 2½ to 3 feet apart.

Both crops grow best in full sun. Kale prefers a loamy soil containing decent amounts or organic matter and well supplied with—but not too rich in—nitrogen. Collards prefer a richer soil; in soils of modest fertility they will benefit from a monthly feeding with fish emulsion or another high-nitrogen fertilizer. Both plants need watering during dry weather. Kale needs little additional maintenance once it is established.

Harvesting can begin about six or eight weeks after the plants are in the garden, while the leaves are still young and tender. Pick the lower leaves of collards, and for the tenderest kale, pick the inner leaves (but do not pick the very central part of the plant, from which new leaves grow). Very young leaves can be used in salads, but for the most part, kale and collards are best as cooked vegetables.

Kale is quite hardy and can be harvested into winter in most gardens—even when it is covered with snow. Mulch thickly when the ground freezes, and kale will winter over in the North, and you can begin harvesting again in early spring. In warm climates you can pick kale all winter.

Ornamental kale is extremely winter hardy. The plants form rosettes of deep-green, fringed leaves flushed with violet red or creamy white in the center. As the temperature gets colder the color spreads out over more and more of the leaf surface, until eventually little of the green is left. The plants are highly decorative, and will hold up throughout the winter in many gardens. Although edible, the ornamental kales tend to be stronger flavored than conventional varieties, and you may prefer to use them strictly as ornamentals. Two good varieties are Coral Queen, which has rosy purple coloring, and Coral Prince, which has white coloring. There is also a miniature variety that makes a good container plant.

Some conventional kale varieties to grow are the traditional Vates Dwarf Blue Curled Scotch, a compact plant that performs well; Blue Siberian, another classic variety; Blue Surf; Konserva; Verdura; and Westland Winter. Winterbor Hybrid is very productive, and hardier than Vates; Snowbor, a similar variety, is also hardy and very quick to mature. A most interesting kale is Russian Red, or Red Russian, also known as Russian Kale or Ragged Jack. The leaves, which are flat and deeply cut rather than curled, are gray green in warm weather and turn red in the cold. This heirloom is the hardiest and most delicately flavored variety, and worth a try.

The most widely grown variety of collards is Georgia Blue Stem, which grows about 3 feet tall; Vates is another classic. Others include Champion, an improved Vates variety, and Hicrop Hybrid, which has good heat tolerance and retains its mild, sweet flavor in warm weather.

Kohlrabi

Although it is popular in Europe, kohlrabi (*Brassica oleracea*, Gongylodes Group) is still something of a rarity in American gardens. It is grown for its purple or pale green bulbs, which are actually swollen stems that form above ground level. The bulbs are best when harvested young—about 2½ to 3 inches in diameter. They have a mild, vaguely sweet taste rather like that of turnips, and a pleasantly crunchy texture. You can peel and eat the bulbs out of hand, like an apple, include them on a platter of crudités and serve with a dip, grate them into

COURTESY ALL-AMERICA SELECTIONS

Collard greens (shown here), like kale, are highly nutritious and taste sweeter after exposure to frost.

salads, sauté or braise them, or add them to soups. The plants' leaves are edible, too— you can cook them like spinach.

Grow kohlrabi in full sun, in moist but well-drained soil of reasonable fertility and rich in organic matter. Make sure the soil is adequately supplied with potassium; greensand, wood ashes, and granite dust are all good sources. Kohlrabi grows well in a range of soils, but fares rather poorly where the soil is quite heavy and dense.

Like the rest of the cabbage family, kohlrabi grows best in cool weather. Direct-sow about four weeks before the last spring frost, or ten weeks before the first fall frost. It is best to sow plants directly where they are to grow, because the young roots are very sensitive to disturbance. The plants can tolerate a few light frosts. In warm climates plant in fall for winter harvest. Sow seeds ¼ to ½ inch deep, and thin plants to stand 6 inches apart in all directions in a bed or 4 to 6 inches apart in rows 1 to 1½ feet apart. The plants need constant, even moisture; water during spells of dry weather.

The bulbs are ready to harvest in about six to nine weeks, depending upon the variety. To harvest, cut the stem a little below the bulb.

The two classic kohlrabi varieties are White Vienna, whose bulbs are actually pale green, and Purple Vienna, with bulbs of a dusty purple color. Kolpak and Grand Duke Hybrid are two other white varieties; Kolibri and Rapid are purple; all four mature faster than the Vienna types. An unusual kohlrabi is Gigante, which produces very large bulbs that are said to be mild and crisp despite their size, but which need 130 days to mature.

Lavender

Lavender carries with it a suggestion of Victorian times, of overwrought spinsters sniffing delicately at lavender-scented hankies to keep from swooning in moments of great agitation. The fresh, sweet fragrance of lavender is best known as an ingredient in perfumes and colognes, soaps, body lotions, talcum powders, and similar products. It is a classic contributor to potpourris and sachets, and has long been used to scent bed linens. But more and more people are discovering the culinary qualities of lavender flowers.

Lavender tastes like it smells, and is not pleasing to every palate. It is most often used in confections, and makes a memorable sorbet or ice cream. Lavender is also an interesting addition to fruit jellies and an unusual garnish for a fruit salad or compote. Lavender has been used in a tea to calm a nervous stomach, in a bath to soothe jangled nerves, and in poultices to treat headaches, muscle soreness, and aching joints.

Lavender is a rewarding addition to both flower beds and edible gardens. The leaves as well as the flowers are fragrant, especially when brushed against. In early to midsummer the little wands of purple flowers wave upon their slender stems. Lavender makes a charming edging along a path or the top of a stone wall, and in mild climates it can be grown as a low hedge.

It can also be grown in containers brought to a sunny spot indoors for winter and moved back outdoors in spring.

There are numerous species of lavender, most of them native to the Mediterranean area. The best and hardiest one for American gardens is English lavender, *Lavandula angustifolia*, which you may find listed in catalogs as L. spica, officinalis, or vera. English lavender is a bushy shrub 2 to 3 feet high, with slender gray green leaves and small spikes of tiny lavender purple flowers in early to midsummer. There are several cultivars derived from the species, including Hidcote, with deep purple flowers, Alba, which has white flowers, and the rosy pink–flowered Rosea.

As its Mediterranean origins suggest, lavender needs plenty of sun and a well-drained soil. Average fertility is sufficient; in rich soil the plants will be less hardy. Good drainage is essential. The pH should be in the neutral range to slightly alkaline; add lime if your soil is acid.

Lavender does not grow well in either the northern or southernmost parts of the country. It is reliably hardy only as far north as zone 6, where winter temperatures fall to −10°F (but should survive in zone 5 with a good winter mulch), or as far south as zone 8 or 9.

The plants are difficult to grow from seed, and it is best to purchase plants or rooted cuttings. Set out plants in spring when the danger of frost is past, or in fall. Space them 1½ to 2 feet apart, and position them at the same depth they were growing in their nursery containers. Lavender plants tend to grow slowly during their first year in the garden so don't give up on them. Clip back the stems to encourage bushier growth, and give the plants a good winter mulch. The plants will be more vigorous and free-blooming in their second year.

For use in the kitchen (and elsewhere) pick the flower spikes just before the buds open. If you want to dry them, remove the buds from the spikes and spread them on a screen rack in an airy location out of direct light.

Your lavender plants may lose their vigor after five years; if they do, take cuttings and start new ones. Take the cuttings in spring or late summer, cutting 3-inch side shoots with a "heel" from the main stem attached. Set the cuttings in moist builder's sand or another rooting medium in containers in a lath house, or in a shaded cold frame. Protect cold-frame cuttings during their first winter with a good layer of mulch. Move cuttings in containers indoors. Move the new plants to the garden the following spring, when the danger of frost is past.

Leeks

Leeks are nonbulbing relatives of onions that are grown for their thick white stems (which are actually the overlapping bases of their leaves). Leeks (*Allium ampeloprasum*, Porrum Group) have a milder, sweeter flavor than onions. With potatoes they make an incomparable soup, and are delicious in quiches and omelets, or prepared as a vegetable side dish. When preparing leeks you must cut off the roots and the coarse green tops—use only the white stalks. It is important to get all the dirt out from between the layers of the stalk—an easy way to do it is to slit the stems with a knife and rinse the soil out from between the layers.

In the garden you will also need to take special measures with leeks, to get the longest white stems. Leeks are also good companion plants in the garden. They are very hardy, but they do not do well in very warm climates.

Leeks need full sun, and loose, moist but well-drained soil with plenty of organic matter. They also like lots of nitrogen, so work in manure or cottonseed meal when preparing the soil. Leeks can follow beans in garden rotations, to take advantage of the nitrogen fixed in the soil by the legumes. Fertile soil will give you the largest leeks.

The plants need a long growing season—ninety days or so from transplanting. Keep the soil moist and the area well weeded throughout the time the plants are in the garden.

The traditional way to grow leeks is to plant them in a trench roughly 8 inches deep and 4 inches across. Loosen the soil in the bottom of the trench, and work in compost and composted manure. Set seedlings 4 inches apart in the trench and bury them deeply, covering the stems a couple of inches above the roots. If you prefer not to dig a trench you can instead plant at normal ground level and gradually hill up soil around the stems of the plants as they grow.

Start seeds indoors or in the cold frame, sowing ½ inch deep, four to six weeks before the last frost. Transplant the seedlings outdoors from two weeks before to two weeks after the last frost. The plants should be at least 4 inches tall when you transplant them. Don't rush transplanting—bigger plants will produce the best crops. Water after transplanting to help plants get established.

When the leeks are as thick as your little finger, add an inch of soil to the trench. Add another inch of soil every few weeks until the trench is filled. Timing is important; if you fill in the trench too early the plants may rot.

Leeks are ready to harvest anytime after the stalks are at least 1 inch in diameter. In fall, when the ground starts to freeze, you can dig and store them in a window well or outdoor storage cache, or in boxes of moist sand in the basement. Or cover the plants with 1 to 2 feet of loose mulch and leave them in the ground all winter. If you do not dig all the leeks in winter, be sure to get

The choice of lettuce varieties available to home gardeners continues to expand. Shown here is Sangria, a red-leaved butterhead type.

them out of the garden before the plants begin to grow again in spring. The plants are biennial and will bloom and go to seed in the second year, when they will be ruined for the kitchen. If some plants do go to seed, dry the flowerheads to use in arrangements.

There are surprisingly many varieties of leeks available to home gardeners. Some of the good performers are American Broad Flag, or Broad London, which is widely known; Musselburgh, another well-known variety, which is late to mature and easy to grow; Titan; Elefant; Varna; King Richard; Alberta; Pancho; Otina; and Argenta.

Lettuce

Lettuce (*Lactuca sativa*) is one of the best crops for home gardens. The diversity of lettuces is so great that there's a lettuce for every garden, no matter how small, no matter where you live. Even in the North you can grow lettuce in three seasons. There is far more to lettuce than the iceberg we see in the supermarket. We can grow leaf lettuces with frilly lime green foliage, smooth, deeply lobed leaves of rich green, or broad, wavy leaves overlaid with deep red or bronze. There are romaines and butterheads whose leaves are flushed with burgundy. There are varieties that produce compact little heads, perfect for container gardens and elegant individual salads. Breeders have developed cultivars with improved cold tolerance and heat resistance.

The key to success with lettuce is to plant the right variety in the right season. There are lettuces that grow best in spring or early fall and turn bitter in hot weather, some that hold up well in summer heat, and others that are bred to tolerate the growing conditions in autumn and the winter cold frame. The ideal climate for lettuce is cool and moist, but gardeners all across the country can grow beautiful lettuce by choosing varieties carefully and paying attention to growing conditions. In temperate and cool climates, grow lettuce in spring and fall. In warm climates grow it in winter.

Many lettuces are highly ornamental, and their compact size makes them quite versatile in the garden. You can plant lettuce as an edging, grow it with edible flowers or herbs, mix it with other salad crops, or plant a bed of nothing but different lettuces. You will be surprised at how pretty the garden looks. Imagine the blend of colors, from dark green to lime green to pale ice green to shiny red and deep burgundy. There are smooth leaves, lobed leaves, and frilly leaves. There are loose clumps of leaf lettuces, the tightly furled torpedoes of romaine, and soft, fluted butterheads.

Fast-growing leaf lettuce is a good interplant for big, slow growers such as tomatoes and cabbage. By the time the larger plants need the space, the lettuce is ready to harvest. Lettuce's shallow roots make it a good companion for vegetables with deep roots, like carrots.

There are four types of lettuce, and different varieties of each of those types have been bred to perform especially well in particular seasons. All four types of lettuce are grown basically the same way.

Looseleaf lettuce is the easiest to grow, and the most popular among gardeners. The leaf lettuces are the most diverse—there are many, many varieties in a host of leaf shapes, colors, and textures. Some leaf lettuces form very loose heads; others grow in rosettes. Leaf lettuces don't keep as long in storage as crisphead types, but more and more of them are showing up at farm stands and produce counters in supermarkets.

Butterhead lettuce forms a soft head of buttery, mild-tasting leaves that are soft rather than crisp and crunchy. Boston is the most familiar variety in the market, but others are better for home gardens. Butterheads have dark green outer leaves and creamy ivory centers. They are very sensitive to extreme temperature fluctuations, and grow best in a very fertile, moist but well-drained soil that is rich in organic mat-

ter. They do well in the North, where days are short in spring and early fall.

Romaine, or cos, grows in slender, upright heads of long, overlapped green leaves with very crunchy midribs in the lower portion. Crisp, hearty romaine is the lettuce used in Caesar salad. It is easy to grow, and richer in vitamins than crisphead lettuces. Romaine adapts to hot, dry conditions and handles temperature swings better than the other kinds.

Crisphead lettuces are best known in the form of the ubiquitous supermarket iceberg (which, incidentally, is not truly the variety Iceberg). The plants form large, round, solid heads of crisp leaves. This is the most difficult lettuce to grow at home; it needs rich soil, cool weather, regular fertilizing, and plenty of moisture. In hot, dry weather the plants will probably not head up properly. Iceberg is the least nutritious kind of lettuce (it contains the most water), but it stores and ships well, which explains its popularity with commercial growers.

All lettuces are essentially cool-weather crops, and have traditionally been planted in spring. While most lettuces will grow well in spring and in early fall, when conditions are similar, breeders have given us varieties particularly well suited to other times of year. Some lettuces that do particularly well in spring and early fall are Black-Seeded Simpson and Red Sails (leaf types), Four Seasons (a butterhead), Ballon (a romaine), and Green Ice, Ithaca, and Reine des Glaces (crispheads). Bolt-resistant, heat-tolerant varieties that hold up well in summer heat include the romaines Apollo, Rosalita, Romulus, and Little Gem (which is good for baby lettuce); and the butterheads Buttercrunch, Kagran Summer and its improved version Orfeo, Butter King, Mignonette, Vista, and Sangria. Many leaf lettuces also perform well in summer, including Grand Rapids, Oak Leaf, Ruby, Red Sails, Salad Bowl, and Slobolt. Short-day varieties that stand up to the cold, wet environment of the winter garden in mild climates or the insulated winter cold frame farther north include the leaf variety Red Grenoble; the butterheads North Pole, Arctic King, Brune d'Hiver, and Red Montpelier, which can be used for baby lettuce; and the romaines Rouge d'Hiver and Winter Density. You can also now buy (for a price) seeds of a few European varieties that can be forced into early growth in a cold frame or tunnel in very earliest spring. These varieties mature quickly. Leaf lettuce will also grow indoors in winter.

Lettuce grows in either full sun or partial shade. For the best growth, plant it in light-textured, fertile, moist but well-drained soil. A sandy loam to which plenty of leaf mold or compost has been added is an ideal growing medium for lettuce.

Lettuce for spring crops can go into the ground as soon as the soil can be worked. Direct-sow from four weeks before to two weeks after the date you expect your last frost, when the nighttime temperature stays above 25°F. Or start seedlings indoors four weeks before you plan to set them out. Lettuce needs light to germinate. Outdoors, sow about ⅛ inch deep; indoors, scatter seeds on top of the germination medium and just press them in lightly. If you broadcast seeds in a flat indoors, thin the tiny plants to stand 2 inches apart a couple of weeks later. Handle the plants carefully when transplanting; lettuce seedlings are delicate.

It is important to harden-off lettuce thoroughly before moving it to the garden in early spring; when hardened, lettuce plants can survive temperatures in the twenties. Harden seedlings by cutting back on watering and putting the seedlings in a cool place for two or three days. Then harden them off as described in Chapter Three.

To extend the harvest make several small sowings of leaf lettuce two to three weeks apart instead of planting all at once. Another way to prolong the harvest is to direct-sow outdoors the same time you set out seedlings that were started indoors.

Sow summer lettuce in mid to late spring. Remember to use heat-resistant varieties. It may be difficult for the seeds to germinate if the weather is hot and the soil is very warm. One way around the problem is to pretreat seeds indoors in summer. Place the seeds on a damp paper towel, roll up the towel, put it in a plastic bag that has a few holes slit in it, and refrigerate overnight to encourage germination. Plant in partial shade, or cover the planting area and, later, the plants with shade netting during the hottest part of the day if you are at home. Keep the soil moist and when the plants are a few inches tall, mulch to help conserve soil moisture. In light soils, sow summer lettuce ½ inch deep.

Eight weeks before you expect the first fall frost it is time to sow fall varieties. In areas where winters are mild, make succession plantings every three weeks from early fall through winter.

When seedlings are 3 or 4 inches high, thin leaf lettuce to stand 8 or 9 inches apart, head lettuce a foot apart. If you are planting in rows, make them 14 inches apart for leaf lettuce and 1½ feet apart for heading varieties. Use the thinnings in salads.

Another secret to growing good lettuce is to keep it growing at a fast pace. Good soil and ample moisture are part of the answer. Regular fertilizing helps, too. Feed plants every three weeks during warm weather with fish emulsion or seaweed fertilizer. Water whenever the soil starts to dry out, but do not let the soil get soggy; the plants' lower leaves will rot if the soil is too wet. And watch out for slugs and earwigs, which love the succulent leaves.

Pick the outer leaves of leaf lettuce anytime you need them after they are 4 or 5 inches long. Or cut off the entire plant an inch above the root crown when it matures, about six to eight weeks after planting. Either way, the plants will produce more leaves.

Cut butterhead lettuce when the heads are fully developed, from seven to ten weeks after planting. Handle butterheads very carefully to avoid damaging the tender leaves. Crisphead is cut when the large heads are solid; they mature about thirteen weeks after planting.

As fall progresses, be mindful of frost. Lettuce can tolerate light frost, but you will need to protect plants from heavy frosts. You can leave lettuce in the garden without protection all during fall if the temperatures drop slowly—the plants will adapt gradually to the colder weather. But a sudden frost will kill them, so cover with loose mulch or hot caps at night if an early frost is predicted for your area.

There are far too many lettuce cultivars to describe here. Check seed catalogs for descriptions of the varieties recommended below.

Good looseleaf varieties include Black-Seeded Simpson, Grand Rapids, Green Ice, Lollo Rossa, Oak Leaf, Royal Oak Leaf, Baby Oak, Red Sails, Red Fire, Ruby, Salad Bowl, Red Salad Bowl, and Slobolt.

Some romaine types to try are Ballon, Parris Island Cos, Rosalita, Rouge d'Hiver, Valmaine, and Winter Density.

Recommended butterhead varieties include Arctic King, Brune d'Hiver, Buttercrunch, Kagran Summer, Morgana (a baby lettuce), Merveille des Quatres Saisons (Marvel of Four Seasons), North Pole, Red Montpelier, Sangria, and Tom Thumb (good for baby lettuce).

Crispheads to grow are Gemini, Great Lakes, Green Ice, Minetto, New York (also called Wonderful), Ithaca, and Reine des Glaces.

Growing Lettuce Indoors

To grow lettuce in the indoor garden, concentrate on leaf types, which mature faster than heading varieties. If you will grow the lettuce on a windowsill, wait until late winter to plant it, when the days are growing longer. Start the seeds in a relatively cool place, where the temperature is 60 to 65°F. A medium of equal parts potting soil, peat moss, and vermiculite, or a blend of two parts soil, one part builder's sand, and one part crumbled compost would be good for lettuce. Scatter the seeds on top of

the moist medium and press them in gently; do not cover. When the seedlings have developed at least one set of true leaves, transplant to individual 6-inch pots, or 6 inches apart in a flat.

An unobstructed east or west window should provide adequate light for windowsill plants. Or grow them in a light garden, with the lamps 6 to 8 inches above the tops of the plants and lit for fifteen hours a day. For lettuce to make its best growth indoors it needs cool temperatures, between 50 and 70°F. Consider the temperature when choosing a place to grow the lettuce.

Fertilize every couple of weeks with a liquid seaweed fertilizer or, if the plants are not in a frequently used living area, fish emulsion. Keep the soil evenly moist but not soggy. Check the plants daily for signs of rotting or pests. If you find decaying leaves, remove them immediately and cut back on watering. If you spot aphids, whiteflies, or other pests, take appropriate measures as suggested in Chapter Two.

Lettuce will, of course, grow more slowly indoors than outdoors, but you should be able to start picking about seven or eight weeks after planting. Pick individual leaves from the outside of the plants so the plants continue to grow. Some varieties to try indoors are Black-Seeded Simpson, Grand Rapids, Green Ice, Oak Leaf, and Salad Bowl. You might also try one of the European forcing varieties that are bred for short-day conditions and lower light levels.

Marigolds

Marigolds are ubiquitous in the gardens of America, loved for their sunny yellow, orange, mahogany red, and white flowers. Organic gardeners esteem the plants because their roots exude a substance that is toxic to nematodes, making marigolds outstanding companion plants. All gardeners are familiar with marigolds, but not all gardeners know that some varieties are edible. If you want to grow marigolds to eat you must choose varieties carefully—most marigolds don't taste good at all.

Several varieties of marigolds are recognized as edible. The best known are two signet marigolds (*Tagetes tenuifolia*, sometimes listed as *T. signata*), Lemon Gem and Tangerine Gem. Both are bushy, mounded plants with ferny foliage, growing to 1 foot tall. They bloom abundantly all summer long. Lemon Gem has small, single, yellow flowers with a lemony scent and flavor. Tangerine Gem has orange flowers with the same flavor; its name describes the color, not the taste. Lulu is another marigold with a citrusy taste. It grows 8 inches tall and has single yellow flowers. Other edible varieties include Little Giant (orange), Paprika (red and yellow), and Climax (yellow).

You can use marigold petals in the same way as calendulas, to color and flavor rice dishes, soups, chowders, and pasta. Try them in tea sandwiches, or sprinkle them over salads. For winter use, dry petals individually and grind them to powder.

The edible marigolds are compact plants that are well suited to the front of the garden, and the smaller varieties make good edging plants. Or plant marigolds next to a sidewalk or driveway, or grow them in pots and window boxes.

Marigolds are easy to grow if you can give them plenty of sunshine, and well-drained soil of average fertility. The plants are half-hardy annuals that grow best in warm weather and love the heat.

It is unlikely that your local garden center will carry the edible varieties as started plants; plan on starting them from seed. Sow indoors, ¼ to ½ inch deep, six to eight weeks before you expect the last frost. Move plants out to the garden after all danger of frost is past. Or direct-sow a couple of weeks before the last frost date. In the warmest climates, sow marigolds in fall for winter flowers. Space plants 6 to 9 inches apart.

Marigolds do not require very much maintenance during the growing season. Pick off faded flowers to keep the plants blooming. Water only when the soil dries out, and weed as necessary. A monthly feeding with a seaweed or other liquid fertilizer will give the plants an extra boost.

Marjoram

Marjoram, or sweet marjoram, belongs to the same genus as oregano; its botanical name is *Origanum majorana*. Its small, oval leaves have a smooth, aromatic scent and flavor. The plants are small, seldom much more than a foot tall, and bushy, best placed in the front of the garden. The tiny white flowers emerge from unusual round knot-like buds that gave rise to an old name for the plant, knotted marjoram. Do not, however, confuse this plant with pot marjoram, *O. onites*, which does not taste as good.

The subtle flavor of marjoram is somewhat similar to that of oregano, but milder and less aggressive, giving this delightful herb a host of uses in the kitchen. Use it in tomato sauce, to season roasted meats, poultry, and mushrooms and other vegetables, in herb butters and sauces, and in omelets, salad dressings, and soups. I especially like a combination of marjoram and thyme, or with basil and bay leaves.

Marjoram is a perennial but is not hardy except in the warmest parts of the United States. Most of us must grow it as an annual. It is easiest to purchase new plants each year; the seeds germinate slowly.

However, if you prefer to grow your marjoram from seed, sow indoors four to six weeks before the average date of your last spring frost. The seeds germinate best in the presence of some light; press them lightly into the soil but do not cover them. Keep the medium evenly moist. Set out the seedlings, or plants from an herb farm or garden center, when all danger of frost is past and the soil is warm.

Give marjoram a location in full sun, in fertile, light, well-drained soil rich in organic matter. It prefers a neutral to slightly alkaline pH. Space plants 6 to 8 inches apart in the garden.

Keep the growing area carefully weeded throughout the season, and water only during prolonged dry spells. Pinch back the plants before the flowers open in mid to late summer, to maintain the best shape. In mild climates you can cut back the plants to 1 inch above the ground and they will regrow and produce another good harvest.

Because the leaves are small, harvest by snipping stems as needed and stripping off the leaves. At the end of the season, before the first frost, cut the plants back to the ground and air-dry the stems in bunches, or the individual leaves on screens, as described under Harvesting and Storing Herbs in Chapter Five. Marjoram holds its flavor better than a lot of other herbs when it is dried, and will retain a much greener color than the marjoram you buy in the supermarket.

Mints

Few things are more refreshing than a glass of iced mint tea on a summer day. Mints have the ability to cool and invigorate us from the sluggishness we feel in hot weather, a quality that comes from the menthol in their leaves. Mints are widely used to flavor all sorts of sweets, and personal-hygiene products like toothpaste and mouthwash. They appear in the cuisines of many countries, particularly those of the Middle East. And mint also plays a role in some quintessentially American preparations, like the mint julep. Candied mint leaves make an interesting garnish for a dark-chocolate cake; you can prepare them as described for flowers in the section on Feasting on Flowers in Chapter Four. Mint has a long and distinguished history; it was well known to the ancient Greeks, and shows up in the tale of Baucis and Philemon, and other classical myths.

The genus *Mentha* is large and varied, and a few of its best known members will represent it here. I have space enough to describe only a few mints, but you could easily have an entire garden of nothing but mints. Most of them are perennial and produce spikes of tiny pink, white, or pale purple flowers sometime in summer.

Spearmint, *M. spicata*, grows about 2½ feet tall; its lance-shaped leaves are glossy, wrinkled, and rich green. This is the most versatile mint in the kitchen. It is a traditional accompaniment for lamb and for peas, and is used to make jelly and all sorts of desserts.

Peppermint, *M. × piperita*, grows to 3 feet tall, with smooth, green leaves and purplish stems. Its flavor is stronger than spearmint's, and it is used primarily in desserts, especially in combination with chocolate, and for tea. A cup of peppermint tea is an old-fashioned remedy for an upset stomach. A variety of this species, orange mint, *M. × piperita* var. *citrata*, has a tangy, citrusy flavor and *tastes* somewhat like oil of bergamot *smells*.

Apple mint, *M. suaveolens*, reaches a height of about 4 feet, and its toothed, oval, downy leaves have a rather sweet, fruity flavor. A cultivar whose leaves are variegated with white, *M. suaveolens* 'Variegata', is known as pineapple mint because its scent is reminiscent of that tropical fruit.

Corsican mint, *M. requienii*, is a tiny, creeping plant with minuscule round leaves. It has what many people consider the true mint taste, and was the original flavoring ingredient in crème de menthe.

Mints are spreading, often invasive plants that can be as annoying in the garden as they are delightful in the kitchen. They travel by means of underground runners and will take over the garden unless you contain their ambitious roots. The best trick I know of for containing mint is employed by Bernard Currid, the gardener in charge of the herb garden at the Brooklyn Botanic Garden. He grows mints in the BBG herb garden in bottomless square wood boxes about 1 foot deep. You can also plant mint in large containers and sink the pots into the ground if you wish. Or make a barrier with sheets of metal.

When designing a garden with mints,

then, the best approach is to plan blocks or large clumps of mint. The more vigorous ones—peppermint, spearmint, and apple mint—can be grown as groundcovers if their roots are not confined. Mow or cut back the plants when they start to bloom, and as needed, to keep them looking good.

Corsican mint does not spread as rapidly as its cousins, and its diminutive size suggests different uses for this plant in the garden. Its tiny leaves are pretty between the paving stones or bricks in a path, and charming spilling out of soil pockets in the side or top of a stone wall. Corsican mint is also well-suited to rock gardens.

If you practice companion planting you will certainly want to grow some mints in your garden—they are considered wide-spectrum bug repellants.

Most mints can be grown from seed, except for peppermint, which is sterile and produces no seeds. But mints hybridize freely with one another and it is difficult for commercial growers to keep the seeds pure. The most common methods of propagation are root division and cuttings, and as a gardener your best bet is to purchase young plants. The common types of mint are sold in many garden centers, and herb farms and mail-order herb nurseries sell a wide assortment, often twenty or more different kinds. If you have a friend with an established planting, you can take your own cuttings or divisions in summer—they root easily in moist soil.

Mints are very easy to grow—too easy, in some gardeners' opinions. They are best in partial shade, although full sun is also acceptable in cool and temperate climates. Mints are not terribly fussy about soil, but the ideal growing medium is a moist soil of average fertility that contains some—but not a lot of—organic matter.

Plant anytime in spring, or plant cuttings and divisions when you take them in summer. Set plants 1 to 2 feet apart, except for Corsican mint, which should be planted closely. Cut back the plants as needed to keep them from looking weedy, and water during dry weather. You will not need to do a whole lot of weeding after the plants are established. In late fall, cut the plants back to the ground. In the extreme North, mints benefit from a winter mulch.

Every five years or so, dig up the mint patch, divide the roots, and throw out the old, woody plants. Replant the younger roots from the outer areas of the bed. This kind of regular division will keep the plants vigorous and under control.

If you grow mint in containers, where it will do quite well as long as you give it plenty of water, you will have to divide and replant every year to keep the pots from becoming overcrowded. You can also root some cuttings to grow in pots indoors in winter. Put the pots in a south or east window, or in a light garden.

Pick fresh leaves or cut stems as needed, throughout the season. You can also dry or freeze mint for long-term storage.

Mushrooms

See Chapter Six for information on growing mushrooms.

Mustard

This leafy member of the cabbage family, with its zippy flavor, is easy to grow and nutritious, and has a variety of uses in the kitchen. If you have never grown mustard (*Brassica juncea*), consider putting it in your garden this year. You can use the leaves in salads when they are young, or sauté older leaves or simmer them slowly in broth. Mustard adds zest to stir-fries and soups, too. The greens contain lots of vitamins A and C, and minerals. Some varieties, like the feathery Mizuna, are quite handsome in the garden when displayed against flowers or brightly colored vegetables.

Like other brassicas, mustard thrives in cool weather, although some varieties are tolerant of heat. You can plant in spring or early fall, and the plants grow quickly to harvest size; you will be able to start picking leaves just six to eight weeks after sowing.

Give the plants a spot in full sun. Mustard is not fussy about soil, but the ideal soil is fertile and moist. Sow spring crops two to four weeks before you expect the last spring frost. If you plant a heat-tolerant variety you can make several succession plantings two weeks apart. To get an earlier start, you can sow seeds indoors six to eight weeks before the last frost and move seedlings out to the garden four to six weeks later. Sow ¼ to ½ inch deep.

Unless you choose a heat-tolerant variety, it is better to plant for fall harvest, sowing directly in the garden six weeks before the average date of the first fall frost. The flavor of most mustard greens becomes nearly incendiary in summer, and it is generally easier to get greens of good quality in the cooler weather of autumn. The plants will tolerate light frost, and in fact, a touch of frost will sweeten their flavor.

Thin the plants to stand 4 to 6 inches apart in rows 1 to 1½ feet apart, or 6 inches apart in all directions in a bed.

Keep the plants evenly moist throughout the growing season. Mulch is helpful, especially for spring-planted crops; by holding moisture in the soil, mulch can help the plants delay bolting in hot weather. When the plants bloom their flavor is ruined, so immediately pick off any flower stems that do appear. Also, the flowers will self-sow if you let them go to seed, and volunteer plants can become a nuisance. On a positive note, though, mustard flowers are edible, and add a touch of bright yellow to salads.

Mustard is seldom troubled by pests, but floating covers will keep flea beetles and other insects off of young plants.

Pick individual leaves as you need them, or cut the whole plant at once.

There are numerous varieties of mustard available to home gardeners. Some of the Oriental mustards are covered under Chinese Cabbage and Other Oriental Greens; several more are discussed below.

Mustards with various degrees of heat tolerance include Southern Giant, the mild-tasting Fordhook Fancy, and Green Wave, which has curly, deep green leaves that are perfect for southern-style greens. Tendergreen, or mustard spinach, has tender mild leaves and edible flowering stems. For pungent, spicy flavor try Florida Broadleaf or Southern Giant Curled. Mizuna has pretty, feathery, fringed leaves of light green, and can be grown as a cut-and-come-again crop. The mild leaves of Osaka Purple bear a purplish tint and are veined in purple; use them as cooked greens or raw in a salad. Red Giant is both cold tolerant and bolt resistant, a good crop for early spring or fall, with mild-flavored, crinkly dark red leaves.

Nasturtiums

The great gift of these colorful flowers is their ability to grow in poor soil where many other plants would fail. Nasturtiums are easy to grow, produce their bright, warm flowers all summer long, and are edible, too. Both flowers and leaves have a sweetish, peppery watercress flavor that can perk up any number of dishes. After removing the pistils, which are often bitter, use the flowers in tossed salads, or as a garnish for tuna, chicken, or potato salads, soups, and pasta. Chop the flowers or leaves and add them to butter or cream cheese to spread on sandwiches, or blend them into dips. The immature flower buds can be pickled and used as a substitute for capers.

Nasturtiums have round, deep green leaves and rather large flowers with wide, flaring petals, elongated throats, and traditionally, long spurs. The flowers come in a range of warm colors: deep mahogany, cherry red, orange, rich gold, scarlet, salmon, and cream.

There are two kinds of nasturtiums with different growing habits. The traditional climbing or trailing type (*Tropaeolum majus*) has long stems that can grow to 8

Alaska nasturtium has green and white varie-gated leaves.

feet. You can train them to climb a fence or trellis if you fasten the stems to the support as they grow. Or let the plants ramble over a slope or bank, or let them trail from hanging baskets. The other kind of nasturtium is

the dwarf plants that grow just 1 to 1½ feet tall. Plant dwarf varieties as edgings, or to carpet a bare spot with their leaves and flowers. Or grow them in containers.

Plant nasturtiums in full sun, if possible; they will also tolerate partial shade, but will not flower as exuberantly. In warm climates, though, the plants perform best with a bit of light shade in the afternoon. Give them well-drained soil of average fertility; they will even bloom in poor soil. But they won't do well in very fertile soil; in rich soil nasturtiums produce lots of leaves but few flowers.

Direct-sow when the danger of heavy frost is past, a week or two before the average date of the last spring frost in your area. Nasturtiums do not transplant very well, and it is best to sow them right in the garden. Gardeners in warm, frost-free climates can sow nasturtiums in fall for winter flowers. Plant seeds ¼ inch deep, and cover the seeds carefully with soil—they need darkness to germinate. Space climbing/trailing varieties 2 to 3 feet apart, dwarfs 1 foot apart.

Nasturtiums bloom all summer long and need little care. Water them only when the soil dries out. Keep an eye out for aphids, which love nasturtiums, and take appropriate measures if necessary.

The following cultivars are all pretty, reliable, and good to eat. Empress of India, an heirloom climber/trailer with rich red flowers contrasted against deep green foliage, is very handsome in the garden. Glorious Gleam is a traditional favorite, with large, fragrant, multicolored flowers on stems about 6 feet long. Semi-Tall Double Gleam is similar, but its trailing stems grow to just 3 feet. Whirlybird is a dwarf series growing about 1 foot tall by 1 foot wide, with spurless flowers in a nice range of colors and carried above the leaves. You can buy mixed colors or individual colors of mahogany, cherry rose, scarlet, orange, salmon, gold, or tangerine. Dwarf Jewel is also available in single or mixed colors. Alaska is a dwarf growing to 1½ feet tall, whose leaves are variegated with white.

A close relative of the nasturtium that also bears edible flowers is the annual vine known as canary creeper (*Tropaeolum peregrinum*). The easy-to-grow vine climbs to a height of 8 feet, and produces small, bright yellow flowers that are rather similar to nasturtiums but exotically fringed. Canary creeper was named for the flowers' color, but they remind this gardener of a flock of little birds perched among the lobed leaves. Grow canary creeper next to a fence or trellis, in full sun or partial shade, in well-drained soil. The flowers bloom late in summer and continue through the first frosts. Use them like nasturtiums in the kitchen.

Okra

Okra, without which a gumbo would not thicken, is grown for its seed pods, which are green (or a rather surprising purple red in one variety), ribbed, pointed, and up to 9 inches long. The pods contain a mucilaginous sap that is released when they are cut open. But you can enjoy okra for qualities other than its gluey juice. Young pods can be rolled in cornmeal and fried, or dipped in batter for a delicious tempura. The pods are crunchy and tasty.

Okra (*Abelmoschus esculentus*) contributes its beautiful flowers to the garden composition, and a close look at them reveals okra's relationship to hollyhocks, hibiscus, and mallows. The blossoms of okra are creamy or light yellow, with deep red centers. Standard varieties can grow up to 7 feet tall, and are attractive plants for the back of the garden. Dwarf varieties grow closer to 3 feet high, and are better positioned in the middle ground of the bed or border. The dwarfs are easier to work with when designing an edible garden with visual appeal.

This is a warm-weather vegetable, and grows best when temperatures average 70 to 85°F. Okra likes lots of sun, and struggles in a cool, damp climate. It cannot stand any frost. The plants grow best in soil that is fertile and well drained, with a substantial percentage of organic matter. Sandy soil is fine as long as sufficient nutrients are present.

Sow okra directly in the garden in spring,

Okra likes plenty of heat and sun, and produces lovely flowers somewhat similar to hibiscus, to which it is related.

1 inch deep, a week or so after the last frost, when the soil has warmed to at least 60°F. It is best to direct-sow; okra roots do not like to be disturbed. Thin plants when they are a few inches high. Space dwarf varieties 10 inches apart in all directions in a bed, or in rows 2 to 4 feet apart. Space standard varieties 1½ feet apart in beds, or slightly closer together in rows 4 to 6 inches apart.

Okra is a heavy feeder, and will benefit from a monthly feeding with fish emulsion or a fertilizer that combines fish emulsion and seaweed. A light mulch will keep the soil from crusting over. Water only if the soil dries out an inch or two below the surface.

The first pods are ready to harvest as soon as two months after seeds are sown, so okra is not only a plant for southern gardens, despite its preference for heat. Harvest the pods when they are just a few inches long, and still tender; larger, older pods become tough and fibrous. If pods are allowed to mature fully the plants will stop producing, but if you harvest often the plants will keep flowering. Harvest pods every few days, cutting the rather thick stems with a sharp knife. Many people develop an allergic reaction after touching okra plants; wear gloves when harvesting to prevent any problems. Okra does not store too well, so use the pods promptly.

There are a number of okra varieties from which to choose, most of them open pollinated. Clemson Spineless is probably the best known, a good performer with pods that can grow up to 9 inches long, if you let them. Perkins Mammoth Long Pod is a medium-sized heirloom variety growing to 5 feet tall. Another medium-sized variety is the hybrid Annie Oakley, which does well in the North. Dwarf Green Long Pod grows just 3 feet tall; a similarly sized variety is Lee, which is best in southern gardens. The most unusual okra, which lends an exotic air to the garden, is the dwarf Burgundy, with pods and stems of deep wine red, and blossoms of creamy yellow.

Onions

Onions (*Allium cepa*) are among the earliest crops to go into the garden, and they are easy to grow if you know the secret of success. The secret is to plant a variety that will grow and produce in the number of daylight hours your area receives. Onions are day-length sensitive; some will only form bulbs where the days are relatively short in summer, that is, in the southernmost parts of the United States. Other onions need medium or long days, and most of these will succeed in gardens farther north than Atlanta, although gardeners in the northernmost United States should plant long-day varieties.

Some varieties are grown for their mature bulbs. Very large, sweet onions, like Bermuda and Spanish types, do not usually store well over a long period, and are best used fairly soon after harvest. Smaller onions with a strong flavor are generally the best keepers because they have the thickest skins.

Some onions (*A. cepa*, Aggregatum Group) form bunches of small, underground bulbs and are usually pulled for scallions before they mature fully.

You can grow onions from seeds or from small bulbs called sets. Seeds take longer, and are usually started indoors. But there is a vastly greater choice of onion varieties available in the form of seeds than sets. In fact, most onion sets are simply labelled "yellow," "white," or "red." Whether seed-grown or set-grown onions perform better in the garden is a matter of debate. Some gardeners claim that onions grown from sets are more susceptible to disease, while others contend that sets produce more reliably than seeds.

If you buy sets at your local garden center, choose those that are ½ to ¾ inch in diameter. Plants grown from large sets tend to bolt to seed and have thick necks; they are best used as scallions. Small sets take a long time to produce large onion bulbs.

Onions grow best in full sun, in light, well-drained soil that is loamy or sandy, reasonably fertile, and rich in organic matter. Onions do not perform well in very acid soil, or in heavy clay soil unless you first work in lots of organic matter. If your soil is extremely dense, build raised beds to grow your onions. Prepare the soil by working in a few inches of compost, some composted manure, bonemeal or rock phosphate for phosphorus, and wood ashes to add potassium and keep the pH level up.

Sow onion seeds indoors, ½ inch deep, four to six weeks before you want to set the plants out in the garden. Bunching onions, the kind you grow for scallions, can be planted out as early as six weeks before the last frost. Bulbing onions can go out a week earlier. The seedlings should be about ½ inch in diameter when they go outdoors. If you prefer, you can direct-sow onions as soon as the soil can be worked, four to five weeks before the last frost.

Onion sets, too, can be planted as soon as the soil is ready to work. Plant them so that just the pointed tips poke through the soil. If you are growing scallions, plant sets with their tips ½ inch below soil level, to produce longer white stems. In heavy soil plant more shallowly, leaving the top third of the bulb exposed.

Space the sets or plants 2 inches apart for scallions and 3 to 4 inches apart for bulb onions. If planting in rows make them 1 to 1½ feet apart.

Onion plants need cool temperatures when they are young, while the tops are growing. Later in the season when the bulbs are maturing, more warmth is beneficial. Onions need lots of water while the plants are becoming established and making their early growth. Although they appreciate even moisture throughout the growing season, they can get by with less as the bulbs mature. Just try not to let onions get too dry—if the soil becomes very dry the onions will develop a stronger flavor.

Keep the onion patch well weeded throughout the season.

Cultivate regularly between plants to keep the soil loose (be careful not to damage developing bulbs). Mulch the plants when the tops are 2 to 3 inches high, to slow the growth of weeds and conserve soil moisture.

If you notice any flower stems popping up as the onions grow, pick them off right away. When onions send up flower stems the quality of the bulbs is ruined.

Sometimes bulb onions appear to be lift-ing themselves out of the soil as they grow. If any bulbs become partly uncovered, don't cover them with soil; instead, cover them with straw or other loose mulch. If the bulbs are left exposed they may develop sunscald.

Onion leaves are edible, like chives, and you can snitch a few during the season for use in the kitchen. The young flowers are edible, too; if any appear on your plants you can use them in a salad or float them in bowls of soup.

Harvest scallions when the leaves are no more than 10 inches tall. For mature bulbing onions to use fresh or store over winter, let the plants grow until the tops fall over. If some tops are still standing when most of the rest have fallen, push them over yourself. A week or two later, when the leaves are brown and dried up, dig the onions with a garden fork. Let them cure outdoors for a week to toughen the skins before you store them. If the weather is uncooperative, cure them indoors. Store onions in a cool, dry place.

Some good short-day onion varieties to grow in the South are Burgundy, Granex, Sweet Winter (which will winter over even farther north), Texas Grano, 502, Vidalia, and White Bermuda.

Long-day and mid-season varieties to grow in the rest of the continental United States include Buffalo, Italian Red Torpedo, Ruby, Ailsa Craig, Bermuda White Hybrid, Burpee Sweet Spanish, Downing Yellow Globe, Early Yellow Globe, Norseman, Northern Oak, Owa, Red Giant, Southport Red Globe, Southport White Globe, Stuttgarter, Sweet Sandwich, and Sweet Slice.

For small onions to pickle or boil, grow Barletta, Crystal Wax Pickling, Pompeii, Purplette, or Snow Baby.

Welsh onions establish perennial clumps the second year from sowing. If you leave a few onions in the ground after harvesting, the bulbs will multiply, the clump will spread, and you will have scallions year after year without doing any new planting.

Welsh onion varieties include Red Welsh and White Welsh.

Other bunching onions to grow for scallions include Evergreen Long White Bunching (the hardiest), Beltsville Bunching (do well in summer), Hardy White Bunching, He-Shi-ko, Red Bunching, Summer Bunching, White Lisbon, and White Spear.

Oregano

It's hard to imagine spaghetti sauce or pizza without oregano. In the kitchens of America cooks rely on this spicy-flavored herb to season Italian-type dishes. But oregano has many virtues besides its affinity for tomatoes. It is a fine addition to omelets and salad dressings, and very tasty with beans, eggplant, sweet peppers, and zucchini.

For kitchen gardeners, the first step in getting a good crop of oregano is to grow a plant with plenty of aroma and flavor; not all oregano plants are created equal. *Origanum vulgare*, a plant known as both oregano and wild marjoram, is a species that grows wild on hillsides in the Mediterranean area. It grows vigorously in the garden and produces rather pretty pink flowers in summer, but its flavor is disappointing from a cook's point of view. Still, it is often found on the market, especially in seed form. For the best flavor plant Greek oregano, *O. heracleoticum*, also listed as *O. vulgare* spp. *hirtum*. Insuring that you grow the kind of oregano you want can be a tricky proposition. The oreganos look a lot alike, especially when they are small. And seeds and plants can be mislabelled, or not labelled at all with any name other than oregano. Here's what you can do.

First, start with plants. Seeds are slow and difficult to germinate, and plants grown from seed may have little flavor. Second, buy plants from a reliable mail-order supplier who will tell you which species you are buying and ship you the species they promised. Or buy plants at a local garden center or herb farm where you can examine them before you bring them home. Rub a leaf or two—gently, you don't want to damage the plant, especially if you decide not to buy it—to find out if a good, strong scent is released. If the leaves are not fragrant, do not buy the plant.

Oregano grows from about 1 to 2 feet tall, with oval leaves and small spikes of little purple or white flowers in late summer. As its Mediterranean origins suggest, oregano loves the sun, and grows best in a light, well-drained soil of average fertility. It prefers a neutral to mildly alkaline pH. If the soil is moist and rich, your oregano will have an insipid flavor.

Set out plants when all danger of frost is past in spring, two weeks or more after the average last frost date. Space plants 6 to 8 inches apart and plant them at the same depth they were growing in their containers.

Commercial growers usually propagate oregano from root divisions or stem cuttings, and you can get plants this way, too, if you have a friend with a healthy stand of flavorful plants. Make root divisions in spring, or take stem cuttings anytime during the growing season, and keep the soil moist until they root.

Oregano needs little care after it becomes established. You will not have to fertilize it, and it can tolerate some drought, although it does appreciate water during prolonged dry spells. A few weeds pose little threat to the vigorous plants, so it won't be disastrous if you neglect to pull a weed here or there. The plants are perennial but not hardy where winter temperatures drop below −10°F. Northerners can grow oregano as an annual, and gardeners in more temperate climates may want to give the plants a winter mulch.

Harvest oregano by cutting sprigs or stems as needed anytime after the plants are well established in the garden and more than about 6 inches high. Clipping the stem tips serves to prune the plant and encourage it to grow bushier.

Pansies, Violas, and Johnny Jump-Ups

These three pretty flowers are all perennials that are usually grown as hardy annuals. All are edible and, although their flavor is quite bland, rather like very mild lettuce with a faint hint of mint, they are a beautiful addition to the salad bowl. Or use them to garnish a bowl of dip or a platter of fruit and cheese at a party.

Pansies (*Viola* × *wittrockiana*) have long been favorites in spring flower gardens. They love cool weather and can be planted with bulbs, as garden edgers, and in pots and windowboxes. They take up little space and will fit into the smallest gardens. The plants are either annual or biennial and grow 6 to 9 inches tall. Pansies can be had either with or without the distinctive dark clown face markings, and they are sold in practically all garden centers. The vast color range includes red, rose, maroon, pink, lavender, true blue, dark blue, violet, purple, orange, gold, yellow, creamy white, and a purple so dark it appears black. They are outstanding in the spring garden, and will bloom well into summer if you clip off dead flowers regularly and give the plants even moisture. Warm-climate gardeners can plant pansies in fall for winter flowers.

Violas or horned violets (*V. cornuta*) are very similar but can often be grown as perennials, bloom later in the season, and do not have clown faces. Their cultural needs are like those of pansies, but they can take more heat and are hardy enough to winter over in cool and temperate climates with a good mulch. The color range is similar to that of pansies though not quite as extensive, encompassing blue, dark blue, wine red, apricot, yellow, and white.

Johnny jump-ups (*V. tricolor*) are charming miniature versions of pansies with purple, white, and yellow petals marked with black. These cheerful little plants self-sow and come back year after year. They can grow to about a foot tall. Their stems tend to ramble a bit, but the flowers are so delightful that the rather weedy habit seems a reasonable trade-off. Some cultivars are available in several different color combinations and also a pure yellow. Look for them to be listed under the name of miniature violas in seed catalogs.

Start seeds of any of these plants indoors in winter, eight to ten weeks before the last frost date. Sow the fine seeds shallowly—about ⅛ inch deep—but make sure they are covered with soil; they need darkness to germinate. Set out plants in early spring when the danger of heavy frost is past. You can also plant garden-center plants at this time. Space the plants 5 to 8 inches apart. To get an earlier start for pansies, sow them outdoors in midsummer and winter over the plants in a cold frame or under a thick mulch. Remove the mulch when the threat of serious frost is gone.

The plants prefer full sun but also grow and bloom well in partial shade. Give them moist, fertile soil rich in organic matter. Keep the soil evenly moist throughout the season and pinch off faded flowers promptly to prolong the blooming period.

The best selection of pansies, violas, and Johnny jump-ups I have seen is in the catalog of Stokes Seeds (see Appendix), but most seed and nursery companies carry at least a few pansies.

Parsley

This most familiar of herbs is ubiquitous as a garnish in restaurants, and usually goes back to the kitchen with the empty plates. That's too bad, because parsley is well worth eating—it contains more vitamin C than oranges and is an effective breath freshener. In addition to its generous helping of vitamin C, parsley also serves up protein, vitamin A, several B vitamins, calcium, iron, phosphorus, potassium, and magnesium. Its flavor goes with just about anything except sweets, and one of its primary gifts is an ability to blend the flavors of other seasonings in a dish. Parsley can be eaten raw or cooked, in salads, soups, sauces, butters, omelets, and quiches, and with fish, meat, and poultry. Large quantities of parsley go into tabbouleh, that piquant Middle Eastern salad, and you can even dip sprigs of parsley in batter and fry them as tempura.

Parsley is a biennial growing from 6 to 8 inches tall. In the second year it sends up flower stalks that can reach 2 feet or more and offer little in the way of ornamental value. The dark green, compound, divided leaves are flat in Italian or flat-leaf parsley (*Petroselinum crispum* var. *neapolitanum*), and tightly curled in curly parsley (*P. crispum* var. *crispum*). Parsley is not harmed by light frost, and with a good mulch should stay harvestable through much of the winter, even up North. In the garden, parsley is attractive in the foreground, and curly parsley is also quite handsome as an edging plant. The dark green color of the leaves goes with any other color in the garden, foliar or floral.

Parsley can be very tricky to grow from seed; seeds germinate quite slowly, usually requiring two to three weeks and sometimes taking as many as six. To improve the chances of succeeding with seeds, soak them in warm water for twenty-four hours before sowing, and water with hot water as needed to keep the soil evenly moist until the seeds sprout. Sow ¼ inch deep, indoors about eight weeks before you expect the last spring frost, or directly in the garden as soon as the soil can be worked, three to four weeks before the last frost. The seeds must have darkness to germinate, so make sure they are completely covered.

Set out transplants or nursery plants anytime after the danger of heavy frost is past.

Although parsley will grow for two years, it is best to start with new plants annually. The flavor of the leaves turns rather bitter in the second year when the plants bloom. You may want to leave a few second-year plants in place and let them self-sow. But in my experience self-sown crops have never been sufficient to supply my needs. I think it's best to plant every year. Start seeds in pots indoors in early summer or buy new plants from the herb farm later in summer to grow in a light garden in fall and winter.

Parsley will grow happily in either full sun or partial shade. The ideal soil is fertile, moist but well drained, somewhat light in texture (a sandy loam is perfect), and rich in organic matter.

Once established the plants are easy to grow, but do keep them weeded. The only serious pests I've ever encountered were several caterpillars of the black swallowtail butterfly, which turned half my parsley into bare stems in a single afternoon. (They also posed a dilemma, because I didn't want to destroy them. In the end I found some alternate host plants growing wild in the neighborhood and escorted the caterpillars to a new cafeteria.)

Harvest sprigs of parsley as needed anytime after the plants are big enough. Parsley is best used fresh—it loses so much flavor when dried that it's really not worth the trouble. If you want to store it for longer than a few days, freeze it. To keep parsley fresh in the refrigerator, stand the stems in a glass of water and cover the leaves with plastic wrap or an inverted plastic bag.

Peas

There are several kinds of peas (*Pisum sativum*) available to gardeners today, and many varieties within those types. Traditional garden peas, sometimes called English peas, are grown for the plump, sweet peas that form inside the pods; the pods themselves are tough and stringy, and are discarded. Garden peas come in early varieties, which are ready to harvest about fifty to sixty days after planting, and main-crop varieties that mature a bit later and produce a heavier crop. Some French peas produce a greater number of smaller, tender, very sweet peas inside the pods; these are known, descriptively enough, as *petits pois* (little peas).

Essential to Chinese cookery is the snow pea, or sugar pea (*P. sativum* var. *macrocarpon*), whose sweet, edible pods are picked while they are still flat, and the peas inside are still tiny.

A cross between the two is the sugar snap pea, introduced to the market in the late 1970s, which has both a crisp, sweet, edible pod and sweet, tender peas. You can harvest sugar snap peas either before or after the peas have swelled inside the pods, and still eat pod and all. After the pods are past their prime you can still shell and use the peas. The original Sugar Snap pea has a string along the edge of the pod that should be removed before cooking, but stringless varieties are now available. Sugar snaps are delicious served raw with a dip, or steamed, with a little butter. Or try combining them with new potatoes in a cheese sauce laced with dill. Fresh from the garden sugar snap peas are, for me, one of the highlights of the year—the quality of the just-picked peas just cannot be maintained when the peas sit in the supermarket or even the local farm stand. The sugar in all kinds of peas starts to change to starch as soon as the pods are picked. For the best flavor, pick the peas when you are ready to eat them.

The white blossoms of peas are also edible, as are the young leaves and tendrils; they add a delicate, mild flavor to salads and an interesting decoration to a bowl of soup.

Peas are a cool-weather crop and can go into the garden in early spring, three to four weeks before the last frost, or in midsummer for a fall harvest. In the southernmost climate zones, peas grow best as a winter crop. Do not plant spring peas too early—they need a soil temperature of 50°F to germinate properly. Seeds can be treated with the fungicide captan to increase their durability in cold, wet soil, and treated seeds will germinate in soil as cold as 40°F. Some seed companies routinely treat their pea seeds and some do not; if you want untreated seed, ask for it. I would much rather wait an extra couple of weeks to plant and avoid the fungicide. Companies that do not treat their seed, or that offer a choice between treated and untreated seed, say so in their catalogs.

Peas need lots of moisture to sprout; soaking them in water for twenty-four hours before planting is generally helpful. Roll the seeds in a legume inoculant powder before you plant, to improve their nitrogen-fixing ability and increase yields.

Give your peas a spot in full sun (although they will tolerate partial shade), in soil that is reasonably fertile but not too rich in nitrogen, light, and well drained. Sandy soils with a high organic matter content are ideal for peas. Peas also prefer soil that is not too acid; wood ashes can both add potassium to the soil and slightly raise the pH.

Most peas need to be supported, whether the vines grow 2 to 3 feet tall, or 6 to 7 feet tall. You can plant them in a single row in front of a trellis or grow netting, or in double rows with the support running between the rows. Lower-growing "bush" peas need only a 3-foot support. Some companies sell collapsible wire grid fending to support the smaller varieties. If you do not want to plant in rows you can instead group the peas around tripods or teepee frames.

Sow peas ½ to 1 inch deep in heavier soils; 1 to 1½ inches deep in very light soils or when planting in summer for a fall crop. Thin if necessary so the plants stand 2 inches apart. Make rows 1½ to 2 feet apart for the so-called bush varieties, and 3 to 4 feet apart for tall varieties (to allow room for the supports). Put supporting devices in place at planting time; waiting until the vines are big enough to need them may result in damaged plants.

To extend the harvest, make two or three succession plantings ten days to two weeks apart, or plant both an early and a main-crop variety. Peas will tolerate light frost in fall, but get them picked before you get a heavy frost. The flowers are damaged by frost.

Peas need regular moisture, especially when the plants are blooming and pods are forming. But they are very sensitive to standing water, and prolonged spells of cold, wet weather may cause them to rot. The plants are also susceptible to mildew, so water at the root zone rather than from overhead to avoid the wet foliage that could lead to problems.

The best growth occurs when temperatures average 60 to 65°F. When the weather is too hot, the flowers will drop without setting pods, and the pods already formed will not develop properly.

When the harvest begins, keep a close eye on the pods. Pick often—even every day—to keep the plants producing. Harvest garden peas about three weeks after flowering, when the pods are plump but still firm and green, before they start to shrivel or turn yellow. Snow and sugar snap peas can be picked sooner. Take care when picking. The slender stems are surprisingly tough, and if you yank the pods you may damage the vines and decrease their productivity. If harvesting proves difficult, use scissors to snip the stems.

An early crop of peas that is finished producing by early summer can be followed in the garden by a warm-weather crop.

Early varieties of garden peas include Improved Laxton's Progress and the similar Knight, Spring, Sparkle, Patriot, Little Marvel, Alaska, Maestro, which resists disease, and Daybreak and Bounty, both of which freeze exceptionally well. All of these varieties grow from 1½ to 3 feet tall, and most of them are good for freezing as well as fresh use.

Low-growing main-crop peas include Olympia; Wando, the most heat resistant, recommended for warm climates and late planting; Lincoln, which tolerates heat and disease; Green Arrow; and the unusual Novella, whose semileafless vines have tendrils that interweave to make the plants self-supporting. Some tall-growing main-crop varieties are Alderman, or Tall Telephone, and MultiStar.

If you want to grow *petits pois*, try Giroy, Petit Provençal, Precovil, Triplet, or Waverex.

The sugar snap clan includes the original Sugar Snap, which grows tall, as well as the shorter, earlier Sugar Ann, Sugar Bon, Sugar Mel, and Super Sugar Mel. Sugar Daddy is stringless and freezes well.

Some good snow pea varieties are Dwarf Grey Sugar; the somewhat taller Mammoth Melting Sugar; Oregon Sugar Pod II, an improved, disease-resistant form of a popular West Coast variety; Blizzard; and Snowflake.

Peppers

Peppers contain lots of vitamin C—more than oranges, in fact. If you let them ripen to their full red or golden color the vitamin C content reaches its peak. Peppers contain sizable quantities of vitamin A, too. Gardeners can grow these vitamin-rich vegetables in several forms. Bell peppers (*Capsicum annuum*, Grossum Group), with their blocky shape and mild flavor, are most common. Green peppers are simply picked immature; all bell peppers turn yellow or red eventually. Some bell peppers develop a wonderfully sweet flavor when they ripen fully. Sweet frying (banana) peppers have a long, tapered shape, and are delicious in sausage-and-pepper sandwiches or cooked with scrambled eggs. Chili peppers (*C. annuum*, Longum Group) come in a host of sizes and several shapes. They range in pungency from the mildly hot Anaheim, which is ideal for Mexican *chilis rellenos* (stuffed peppers), to the fiery jalapeño and the downright incendiary cayenne.

Pepper plants are compact, growing to about 2½ feet tall, and very productive for their size. They are good candidates for small gardens and container culture.

Peppers are not really hard to grow if you can give them the conditions they need, but they are persnickety in their environmental demands. Peppers need warm weather—they cannot stand any frost, and suffer when the temperature dips below 50°F—but the weather must not be *too* warm—they do not

192 *The Year-Round Vegetable Gardener*

like temperatures much above 90°F. Peppers also require constant, even moisture and high levels of humidity. If these conditions are not met the plants will sulk, dropping their blossoms without setting fruit. The ideal temperatures for peppers average between 70 and 75°F during the day and 60 to 70°F at night. In warm climates they are best grown in fall or winter.

Peppers don't do well in very windy locations, either, and may need a windbreak if your garden is subject to frequent wind.

Peppers need full sun, and light, well-drained, somewhat sandy soil that contains plenty of organic matter. They are very sensitive to the amount of magnesium in the soil. If a soil test shows your soil to be low in this mineral, give it a boost with some dolomitic lime, or a solution of epsom salts (one tablespoon to a gallon of water).

Sow seeds indoors, ¼ inch deep, six to seven weeks before you expect the last spring frost. The seeds need warmth to germinate—75 to 85°F. Set out seedlings in the garden two to three weeks after the last frost, when the soil temperature is at least 60°F at a depth of a few inches, and night-time temperatures no longer drop below 55°F.

Harden-off seedlings carefully before you transplant them outdoors; follow the directions given in Chapter Three. Set out only the sturdiest, stockiest plants. Spindly, lanky seedlings will never produce well.

Set bell and sweet peppers 1½ to 2 feet apart in rows 3 feet apart, or 15 inches apart in all directions in a bed. Hot peppers can be placed 1 to 1½ feet apart in rows or beds. Water immediately after transplanting. Keep the area well weeded for the first few

Peppers grow best in warm weather, and can be tricky for gardeners in cool, northern climates. But several varieties, including Gypsy Hybrid, shown here, were bred to perform well in northern gardens.

Not for the faint of heart, Super Cayenne chili pepper, shown here, is the hottest of the hot.

weeks, until the plants establish themselves in the garden. Then lay down a mulch.

A constant supply of moisture is important for peppers to make their best growth, especially during flowering and fruit formation. Feed the plants monthly during the growing season with a balanced, all-purpose fertilizer that is not too high in nitrogen.

Although peppers are susceptible to a host of pests and diseases, they are not usually troubled severely, especially if they are rotated through the garden on a four-year cycle. Sunscald of the leaves is the most common problem, and if you live where summers are very hot, covering the plants with shade cloth during the hottest part of the day should help to prevent it.

In the South, plants may stop producing when summer reaches its peak. But if you give them lots of water they may begin to bear again in fall when the weather cools off.

Pick peppers anytime after they are big enough to use, while they are immature and green, or after they change color. If you want to pickle chili peppers, or dry them to make a wreath or string, let them ripen completely before harvesting. It is a good idea

to cut the fruit from the plants with a sharp knife instead of picking them, to be sure the plants' rather delicate roots are not disturbed in the process. At the end of the season, when you expect the first light frost, pick all the peppers remaining on the plants.

You can freeze peppers without blanching them first, although they are best used for cooking after they have been frozen. Handle very hot chili peppers with care in the kitchen. Wear rubber gloves to avoid irritating your skin, and remove the seeds and white membranes before using the peppers.

A tremendous number of bell peppers are available to gardeners. Some of the many varieties that will eventually turn red are Bell Boy, Bell Tower, the classic California Wonder, Ace and New Ace, which mature early, the Earlibird series of hybrids, each bearing the name of a songbird, and Yolo Wonder, another classic. Gypsy, North Star, and Galaxy do well in northerly climates, while Bell Captain is recommended for the South. Vidi has an elongated shape that is popular in Europe. Golden Summer and Yellow Belle ripen to yellow; Ariane turns an unusual (for peppers) orange. Purple Belle and Purple Beauty turn from green to deep purple before they finally ripen to red. Chocolate Beauty turns an interesting shade of deep brownish red.

Park's Pot Hybrid produces medium-sized bell peppers on small plants that are perfect for containers.

Sweet frying peppers include Cubanelle, Sweet Banana, Italia, Italian Gold, Red Bull's Horn (Corno di Toro Rossa), and Ultra Gold.

For pickling try the small, rounded Sweet Cherry or Large Sweet Cherry.

Which chili peppers to plant depends on how hot you like them. Anaheim is among the mildest, and Ancho or Poblano, which is used in chili powder when dried, is also relatively mild. Among the hottest of the hot are Serrano, Jalapeño, and the absolute hottest, Long Red Cayenne and Super Cay-

enne. Super Chili Hot falls somewhere between Jalapeño and Cayenne varieties. Tam is a milder version of Jalapeño that is still plenty hot. Tabasco is also quite hot, and is used in the fiery sauce of the same name. Zippy Hybrid, Hungarian Wax, and Hungarian Rainbow Wax are all medium-hot. A relative newcomer is Mexibell, which is a hot bell pepper.

Garden Pinks

The flowers in the genus *Dianthus* are among the most wonderful in the kingdom of flowers. Most of them are easy to grow, they bloom with abandon in a range of lovely red, rose, and pink shades (white, too), and some are among the most exquisitely scented of all flowers, with an intoxicating, sweet-spicy, clovelike fragrance. The highly scented species and varieties are best for the kitchen garden. The flowers taste like their scent, at once spicy and perfumy. You can use pinks in sorbet or ice cream, or as a garnish for soups, fruit salads, cakes, and puddings. Or chop the flowers and blend with butter to spread on muffins. The white base of the petals is usually bitter and should be removed before you use the flowers in the kitchen.

Good dianthus to grow in the kitchen garden include the perennial cheddar pinks (*Dianthus gratianopolitanus*) and grass pinks (*D. plumarius*), and clove pinks or carnations (*D. caryophyllus*), which are rather touchy and are grown as annuals in most parts of the United States. If you decide to grow clove pinks, look for smaller, hardier varieties and avoid the large, often faintly scented florist carnations. Garden pinks are delightful in the front of the garden, and their grassy, grayish green leaves are a beautiful counterpoint to the rosy flowers. They harmonize nicely with purple, blue, white, and light yellow colors in other herbs, vegetables, and flowers. Garden pinks are also at home in rock gardens and containers.

Grow pinks in full sun, in light, well-drained soil of average fertility, with a neutral to slightly alkaline pH. They may not survive in either very cold or very warm climates. It is easiest to purchase plants to set out in spring, around the date of the last frost. Or sow seeds indoors, ⅛ inch deep, about four weeks before the last frost date and move plants outdoors when they are several inches tall. Or direct-sow in spring

Garden pinks are truly delightful in the garden. If you want to enjoy them in the dining room, too, plant the most fragrant types.

or early summer, when the soil has warmed to about 70°F. Space plants 8 to 12 inches apart.

When transplanting, do not plant too deeply; set the crowns even with the soil surface.

Plants for Kitchen Gardens 195

The plants are short-lived and need to be renewed every two or three years. Divide mature plants in spring, or take cuttings in midsummer when the plants have finished blooming.

Water pinks during dry weather. Cutting them back after they've bloomed often encourages them to flower a second time.

Radicchio

Italian chicories that form tight, dark red heads of piquant, bitter-flavored leaves in fall are generally known in the United States by their Italian name, radicchio. Although these plants are varieties of chicory, *Cichorium intybus*, they look different from other chicories and are handled differently, so we will consider them separately.

Radicchio is quite a beautiful vegetable, and adds a colorful highlight as well as its distinctive flavor to salads.

Plant radicchio in full sun, in fertile, moist but well-drained soil rich in organic matter. Plant from late spring to midsummer to harvest in autumn. If you live in a warm climate where winter temperatures do not drop below 10°F, plant radicchio in fall for a winter harvest. You can sow directly where the plants are to grow, or start seeds indoors or in a nursery area and transplant to the garden when seedlings are about four weeks old. If direct-sowing in hot summer weather, it is vital to keep the soil moist for seeds to germinate. Like other chicories, radicchio is essentially a cool-weather plant and may need a bit of pampering to get off to a good start in summer.

Thin plants to stand 6 to 8 inches apart in beds; if planting in rows, make the rows 1½ feet apart.

Traditionally, radicchio has needed special care to form its heads. First, let the bitter green leaves grow all summer (you can cut a few leaves when they are just a few inches long and enjoy their milder flavor). When the weather turns cool in fall, about a month before you expect the first frost, cut back the top growth to 1 inch above the crown. The plants will resprout and form the tight red-and-white heads, which are ready to harvest six to eight weeks later. A touch of frost enhances the color, but heavy frost will damage or kill the plants unless you protect them. Newer varieties do not need this special treatment, but the old classic radicchios do.

If you forget to cut back your radicchio, all may not be lost. The green leaves will be killed by freezing temperatures, but the new head may form anyway, underneath all the frozen foliage. Before you toss the plants on the compost heap, check to see if you might have some heads to harvest after all.

Most radicchios mature in 2½ to 3 months from seed.

Verona Red, or Rouge de Verone, perhaps the best-known radicchio, produces softball-sized heads of burgundy red with pronounced creamy white veins. Sow in late spring and cut back the leaves in early fall. Very hardy, where winters are not too severe you can cover Verona Red with mulch and leave plants in the garden all winter.

Treviso Red, or Rossa di Treviso, another classic, has elongated heads of burgundy veined with white; summer leaves are green and very bitter. It's not quite as hardy as Verona Red, and will not winter over as well.

Castelfranco, another heirloom, has tender, moderately bitter leaves streaked with red, gold, white, and green, and does not need to be cut back to produce heads. Less hardy than other varieties, harvest this one before frost, or cover plants at night when frost is expected.

Early Treviso matures quickly and is sown in midsummer when the daylength begins to decrease. Giulio needs no cutting back, is bolt resistant and thus good for spring planting. Augusto is similar but a bit larger, very frost tolerant, and a good variety for winter growing. Medusa is an early-maturing, medium-sized variety to plant in late spring or summer in the North, or fall in the South. Silla matures faster than any of the others, producing small heads on bolt-resistant plants that stand up well to summer heat; it's a good choice for small gardens and succession planting.

Radishes

Most of us are familiar with the small, round, red-skinned radishes that are found in every supermarket and salad bar. These are typical of the small early radishes that are among the fastest-maturing vegetables in the garden, ready to harvest in as little as three weeks. But there are other kinds of radishes, too. Early and mid-season varieties are the small, pungent globes and cylinders used to add snap to salads. The large, late-maturing daikon and winter radishes are mostly mild flavored (except for Round Black Spanish and Long Black Spanish, which are zestier) and are used in stir-fries, tempura, and soups, or as cooked vegetables, or pickled. They are called Winter Radishes not because they mature in winter, but because they keep well in winter storage. All of them share the botanical name *Raphanus sativus*.

Early varieties can also be grown indoors in winter, if you can give them enough light and temperatures around 60°F.

Radishes are among the easiest vegetables to grow, and the early varieties are especially versatile in the garden. Because they grow so quickly and take up so little space, early radishes are often interplanted among larger, slower-growing plants. You may find it easier to simply stick radishes here and there among the other plants in the garden instead of putting them in rows or beds by themselves. The larger-rooted winter varieties, though, take up more space and are better planted in groups.

All radishes grow best in cool weather, with temperatures averaging 60 to 65°F, and they can take some light frost, but they will grow in practically any American garden. In warm climates plant them in fall or winter, or grow mid-season varieties that can stand more heat.

Plant radishes in either full sun or partial shade. They grow best in loose, light, moist but well-drained soil that is free of stones, rich in organic matter, and not too high in nitrogen. Too much nitrogen encourages the plants to produce luxuriant leaves and puny roots. Loose soil is particularly important for the large-rooted winter radishes, some of which grow 1½ feet long or more.

Direct-sow early varieties as soon as the soil can be worked in spring and has attained a temperature of 40°F or higher, about four to six weeks before the last frost date. To extend the harvest make several sowings ten days apart. You can start planting early radishes again in late summer for fall harvest. Sow ½ inch deep, and thin plants when they are an inch tall to stand 3 inches apart in all directions in a bed, or 2 to 3 inches apart in rows 10 to 12 inches apart.

Sow mid-season varieties in mid to late spring, ¾ inch deep. You can plant successions every ten days until midsummer. Thin plants to 4 inches apart. If planting in rows, make them 12 to 15 inches apart.

Sow winter varieties ten weeks before you expect the first fall frost. In southern gardens, sow anytime in fall to harvest in winter, or for an early crop, plant 8 to 10 weeks before the last spring frost to harvest in early spring.

Keep the soil evenly moist until seeds germinate. After the plants are up, water when the soil begins to dry out. Radishes need moisture in order to grow quickly, which produces the crispest, best-tasting roots, but too much water promotes leaf growth rather than root development.

Mulch your radishes if you are so inclined; otherwise they should require little maintenance. They may be attacked by root maggots, but the use of floating row covers should keep the flies from laying their eggs in the vicinity.

Early varieties are sensitive to daylength,

and tend to bolt to seed in summer more because of the long days than the hot weather. When radishes bolt the roots develop an unpleasantly hot flavor, but you can let them bloom and harvest the crunchy seed pods, which make an interesting addition to salads. You can also stir-fry or pickle the pods.

Harvest early radishes before they exceed an inch in diameter; if you let them get too big they tend to turn pithy and hot. Pull mid-season varieties whenever they are large enough to use. Leave winter radishes in the ground until after the first frost, which will mellow and sweeten their flavor. You can store winter radishes in a window well or other outdoor storage area, as described in Chapter Five.

There are many, many early radishes from which to choose. Small, round radishes with red or red-and-white skins include Cherry Belle, Cheriette, Champion, Scarlet Globe and its variations, Saxafire, Fluo, D'Avignon, and the nonhybrid Sparkler. Easter Egg produces round roots in assorted colors of red, pink, lavender, and white. Plum Purple is an unusual purple, and Snow Belle is round and white. Valentine has white-skinned roots with red flesh. French Breakfast is a classic nonhybrid that has been in cultivation since the nineteenth century. White Icicle has cylindrical, white roots.

Mid-season varieties include Comet, Red Devil, and Red Pak.

Some of the large winter radishes are both cold tolerant and bolt resistant, and can be grown either as late or mid-season crops. April Cross, Summer Cross, and Omny all fit this category.

Munich Bier is a large-rooted radish that is planted with other winter radishes in midsummer to harvest in fall. This is the variety that is served in German beer gardens, sliced and lightly salted.

Long Black Spanish and Round Black Spanish are two winter radishes with black skin, crisp white flesh, and a lively flavor.

Many of the Oriental winter radishes, the daikon types, have a milder flavor and long, tapered roots. Try China Rose, Chinese White, Chinese White Celestial, Miyashige, or Tokinashi.

Rosemary

Rosemary (*Rosmarinus officinalis*) has long been part of myth and legend. It was said to have the power to keep away evil spirits, and to improve the memory. It is a traditional symbol of remembrance, friendship, and love, and was often included in brides' bouquets. Rosemary adds a fresh note to potpourris and sachets, and is invigorating in the bath.

But in the kitchen rosemary holds a unique place. Its unusual flavor is predominantly piney, with a spicy-sweet undertone. Both the leaves and flowers are edible. Rosemary complements lamb (try it in a mustard sauce for roast lamb), pork, fish, poultry, and wild game, peas, carrots, mushrooms, and potatoes. It will liven up sauces and soups, and a bit of rosemary is a delicious addition to minestrone soup.

Rosemary is a shrub that seldom grows more than 5 or 6 feet tall, and is only half hardy; it usually does not survive temperatures below 10 or even 20°F, especially not without a thick mulch. The plant has grayish brown bark on its woody stems, and very narrow—needlelike—leaves ½ to 1½ inches long and dark green. Gardeners in warmer climates will enjoy rosemary's lovely sky blue flowers in summer. There are also cultivars with white and pink flowers, and one with a creeping habit that can be grown atop a stone wall, in a rock garden, or as an aromatic ground cover in warm climates. A single rosemary plant, neatly clipped and shaped, can serve as the focal point of a small formal garden bed.

Those of us in cool and temperate climates must grow rosemary in a big pot and bring it indoors over winter. The plant can be difficult to manage in a container, but the results are worth the effort. A potted rosemary plant makes a charming accent on a deck or patio. Because it loves the heat, it will thrive on a stone terrace or next to a stone wall. Rosemary can also be trained as a topiary in a simple shape like a standard (a ball of foliage atop a straight, long stem).

The plant is native to the Mediterranean area. Not surprisingly, it will take all the sun you can give it, and prefers a light, well-drained soil of average fertility with a pH near neutral. If your soil is acid add lime or wood ashes to raise the pH.

If you are growing rosemary in a container, choose one with ample space for the plant's roots; remember, rosemary is a shrub and has a more extensive root system than many herbaceous plants of the same size. A well-drained medium is especially critical for container-grown rosemary. The plant cannot tolerate standing water, and its roots will rot if the soil or potting mix is too wet.

Pick leaves or sprigs whenever you need them, after the plant is big enough. If you are pruning a large specimen to a formal shape, use the clippings in the kitchen. For long-term storage you can dry the leaves, or freeze sprigs and remove leaves as needed.

If you have a potted plant indoors during cold weather, place it in a south-facing window. Rosemary appreciates humidity, so mist the plant each day or set it on a pebble tray.

Sage

The genus *Salvia* is large and varied—it includes over 700 species. Cooks are most familiar with culinary sage, *S. officinalis*, whose aromatic leaves are such an important part of poultry stuffings. Flower gardeners are well acquainted with the ornamental salvias with their flower spikes of flaming scarlet or rich violet blue. Several sages combine both ornamental and culinary qualities, and can be grown for their decorative edible flowers.

Culinary sage grows from 1½ to about 3 feet tall, depending upon the variety. The plant is a shrub and develops woody stems with age. Sage has oblong gray green leaves with a puckered, pebbly texture. In summer there are small white, purple, or pink flowers that are aromatic like the leaves. Interesting cultivars include Purpurea, which has purple leaves; Aurea, which is golden leaved; Icterina, which is variegated with gold; and Tricolor, with leaves variegated in green, purple, and creamy white. The species form of sage is hardy in most of the continental United States, except for the very coldest and warmest climates, where it must be grown as an annual. The purple and variegated varieties are less cold hardy and may not survive where winter temperatures fall below −10°F. All sage should get a good winter mulch in gardens that experience winter temperatures below zero.

Sage is a classic ingredient in poultry stuffings and sausages, but it has a host of other uses, too. The flavor complements lamb, pork, and wild game, and you can also use sage to flavor cheese, omelets, vegetables, and breads. It is difficult to describe the taste of sage. It is a combination of aromatic, tangy, and bitter, and to many palates is at its best in young, fresh leaves. The flowers are also edible, and can be candied as described under Feasting on Flowers in Chapter Four.

Pineapple sage, *S. elegans*, is a delightful plant growing to 3 feet tall, with pineapple-scented leaves and flowers of brilliant scarlet. Use them in jams and jellies, float them in iced tea or punch, or use them to garnish puddings, chicken salad, or fruit salad.

Clary sage, *S. sclarea*, is a biennial growing to 3 feet tall, with pink or purple flowers and very large, heart-shaped gray green leaves. The entire plant has a very pleasant aromatic balsam scent. Clary makes an interesting substitute for culinary sage, and its flowers are edible as well as its leaves. You can also make tea from the dried leaves or flowers.

Sage will grow from seed, but will take a long time to reach harvestable size, and the cultivars will not grow true from seed. Clary sage, however, is relatively easy to grow from seed. Sow in spring when the danger of frost is past, ½ inch deep. Keep the soil moist until the seeds germinate.

Start culinary and pineapple sage with young plants from a nursery or herb farm. Commercial growers generally propagate their plants from cuttings or layerings of older plants, and you can use these methods, too, to renew established plantings. Take stem cuttings in spring and root them outdoors, or take them in fall and root them in pots indoors over winter. Or layer the plants in spring or in early fall by bending the tips of several stems down to the soil, holding them in place with U- or V-shaped pins or pegs, and covering the stem with soil a few inches from the tip; the tip of the stem should not be covered. The following spring, cut the stem right behind the soil mound, and plant the rooted stem tip where you want the new plant to grow.

If you will be growing sage as an annual and will have only young plants you can space them 6 to 9 inches apart. Mature plants need 1½ to 2 feet between them. Clary and pineapple sage can go about 1 foot apart.

Sage is not particularly fussy about soil as long as it is well drained. A soil that is rich in organic matter and of average fertility should be fine for sage. In dense, poorly drained soil, sage will be less cold hardy than in lighter soil; the roots will be more likely to rot. Plant sage in full sun, and keep the soil moist for the first couple of weeks, until the plants are established in the garden. Thereafter you need water only during dry spells. Some gardeners like to cut perennial sages way back in spring to prevent the plants from flowering and going to seed. In any case, the plants start to lose their vigor after a few years as they grow woody, so plan on putting in new plants about every three years.

Pick individual leaves whenever you need them throughout the growing season. If you want to dry sage for winter use, dry the leaves in an oven or microwave as de-

scribed under Harvesting and Storing Herbs in Chapter Five. The leaves may discolor if they dry too slowly.

Shallots

This onion relative produces clumps of small, brown-skinned bulbs with purplish flesh. Their flavor is oniony, but milder, sweeter, and without the sharpness of most onions. Shallots (*Allium cepa*, Aggregatum Group) are widely used in French cooking, and they lend a touch of sophistication to omelets, soups, and other dishes. Try them sautéed with mushrooms and a bit of thyme, to accompany a steak or roast.

Shallots are expensive to buy in stores, but very easy to grow. You simply plant individual bulbs that multiply into clumps of six or more. They are perennial in mild climates, and gardeners there can simply leave some bulbs in the ground to winter over and start next year's crop. Farther north, save some of the harvest to plant next spring.

Give your shallots full sun, and moist but well-drained, fertile soil. They may rot if the soil is soggy. Like most onions, shallots can tolerate some light frost. They can be grown just about anywhere in the continental United States.

In warm climates plant the bulbs in fall; elsewhere plant a week or two before the average date of the last spring frost. Plant with the pointed tip upward, deep enough so that the tip just protrudes from the soil. Set the bulbs 6 inches apart in all directions in a bed, or 4 to 6 inches apart in rows about 9 inches apart.

If you choose to mulch your shallots, wait until about a month after planting, when several shoots are up. The bulbs need about one hundred days to mature, and need to be kept weeded and moist throughout the season.

You can dig some shallots before they are fully mature, if you wish. But leave the rest of the crop in the ground until the tops turn dry and brown, and fall. If you are getting close to your first fall frost and the tops have not yet started to wilt, stop watering the plants. Dig the bulbs carefully and, if weather permits, let them cure outdoors for several days to toughen the skins. You can store shallots for several months in the same place you store onions and garlic.

A number of mail-order seed companies sell shallot bulbs. The best selection is offered by Le Jardin du Gourmet (see Appendix), which in addition to the standard type offers French gray shallots, and frog's leg shallots, which are much larger.

Sorrel

Sorrel *(Rumex acetosa)* was at one time used medicinally, and probably with good reason. It is quite high in vitamin C and also contains minerals. The light green leaves have a pleasant, tart, lemony flavor that is welcome in salads and soups, and simply marvellous in a sauce for grilled or broiled fish. The leaves are arrow-shaped and grow in a rosette on slender stems. They are delicate in texture and do not store well; it is best to pick sorrel when you are ready to use it.

The plants are perennial and usually produce for three or four years, but they can also be grown as annuals. Moist, nitrogen-rich soil that contains lots of organic matter is ideal for sorrel. The plants thrive in full sun in cool climates, or partial shade elsewhere. Sow directly in the garden in mid-spring, when the soil temperature is at least 60°F, or in fall. Plant seeds ¼ inch deep. Thin plants to stand 8 inches apart in a block. You probably will not need to grow an entire row of sorrel.

The plants may bolt in summer, but if you pick off the flower stems they should produce more usable leaves in fall. Pick outer leaves individually or, if you prefer, cut the whole plant. Established plants provide one of the earliest harvests from the spring garden.

Spinach

When I was a kid most of us tolerated spinach only because it was Popeye's amazing strength-building food. A hefty helping of spinach may not create an instant bulge in your biceps (or forearms), but it is among the most nutritious of vegetables. The leaves are loaded with vitamin A, and rich in vitamin C and iron, too. Spinach is good both raw and cooked. You can add it to a tossed salad or toss it with sliced mushrooms and crumbled bacon for a spinach salad. Spinach can be steamed, stir-fried, or creamed, or added to casseroles, soufflés, and crêpes.

The most familiar kind of spinach *(Spinacia oleracea)* is the type with heavily savoyed—crinkled—leaves. But there are also semi-savoyed and smooth-leaved varieties that are far easier to wash. The plants produce a good harvest and don't take up much space, so they are good for small gardens.

Spinach grows best when the days are short and cool, and is planted in spring and for fall. Traditionally other greens have been grown in summer as spinach substitutes—amaranth or tampala, New Zealand spinach, Malabar spinach, and orach or mountain spinach most often—but some of the bolt-resistant spinach varieties hold up surprisingly well in hot weather.

You can plant spinach in full sun or partial shade. Its shade tolerance makes it a good interplant for taller crops that will cast shadows over it. Give it well-drained, sandy soil that is rich in organic matter and not too acid. Spinach needs a pH of 6.0 or higher—6.5 to 7.5 is best.

Direct-sow in early spring, three to four weeks before the last frost, when the soil temperature is at least 35°F, and preferably 40 to 50°F. Sow ½ inch deep, and firm the soil to be sure the seeds, which are irregularly shaped, make good contact with it. Thin plants to stand 5 to 6 inches apart in all directions in a bed, or 3 to 4 inches apart in rows 1 to 1½ feet apart. For an extended harvest, make several succession plantings ten days to two weeks apart. Sow fall crops about nine weeks before the first fall frost. Sow thickly in summer because the seeds do not germinate well in warm soil. In the warmest climates, where the temperature does not often fall below 25°F, plant spinach in fall to harvest in winter. Gardeners farther north can also plant in fall, mulch the plants to winter them over, and harvest in early spring.

The best-quality leaves are produced when the plants grow quickly, so they need even moisture all season long. In very sandy soil, feed monthly with fish emulsion or another nitrogen-rich fertilizer. Keep the area well weeded, too, for weeds will compete with spinach's shallow roots for moisture and nutrients. Spinach is notoriously prone to an assortment of mildews, blights, and other diseases, although many of the varieties currently on the market have some degree of tolerance or resistance. Read catalog descriptions carefully.

Harvest can begin about two months after planting. You can either pick individual outer leaves as they become big enough to use or cut off the whole plant an inch above the base and new leaves will grow. Spinach freezes well.

Smooth-leaved spinach varieties include King of Denmark; Sputnik, which grows well in spring, summer, or fall; Wolter, a disease-resistant Dutch variety; Space; and Olympia, which is slow to bolt. Semi-savoys include Hybrid No. 7, Melody, Avon, Indian Summer, and Tyee, which is disease tolerant, bolt resistant, and also good for fall crops or wintering over. Vienna is tolerant of several diseases and produces good crops. Some particularly bolt-resistant varieties are Broad-Leaved Summer, or Round, with smooth leaves; Broad-Leaved Prickly Seeded; Italian Summer, a semi-savoyed type; and Nordic, a smooth-leaved Dutch variety. If you like to grow open-pollinated vegetables to save your own seeds, try the classic Bloomsdale Longstanding, or Cold-Resistant Savoy, which is good for fall and winters over well.

Squash

Squashes are true all-Americans, natives of the New World. They come in a great range of shapes and sizes, all of which are divided into two large groups: summer squash and winter squash. Summer squash has soft, tender skin; it is picked before it is mature, and is eaten skin and all. This group includes the many varieties of zucchini, crookneck varieties shaped something like little bowling pins with curved necks, and scallop squashes that look sort of like fat little Frisbees with scalloped edges. Summer squash is delicious sautéed, steamed, baked, or grilled. Tender young zucchini cut into sticks is a welcome addition to a platter of crudités. Some varieties make delectable—and cute—baby vegetables.

Winter squash takes longer in the garden and is allowed to mature fully. It develops a tough shell, is harvested in fall, and can be stored over winter. Winter squash has golden orange flesh that is sweet tasting and rich in vitamin A. It is usually baked. Buttercup, butternut, acorn, and hubbard are the best-known types of winter squash.

Squash blossoms are edible, too, and becoming increasingly popular. The plants produce separate male and female flowers, and rely on insects to transfer the pollen. The female blossoms produce the fruit, and can be recognized by the small swelling at their base, which will turn into the squash if the flowers are pollinated. The male flowers do not have this bulge, and they are the ones to eat. You can stuff them with a cheese or meat filling, or dip them in batter and fry them. There is now a variety on the market—Butterblossom—which produces mostly male flowers.

Squash is easy to grow if you can give it rich enough soil, but the sprawling vines do take up a lot of space in the garden. There are, however, more and more bush varieties being introduced (actually they have shorter vines rather than a true bush form), and they are better suited to small gardens than the rambling kinds. You can also save space by training vining varieties to grow vertically on a trellis or other support, but you must support the heavy fruit of winter squash by tying a cloth sling around each one so the stems don't snap.

Both summer and winter squash need full sun and soil that is fertile, moist but well drained, and rich in organic matter. Given good soil and plenty of water, the plants will produce with abandon. If your neighbor grows zucchini you probably won't have to; gardeners with successful crops are always looking for ways to unload their excess.

The squash clan craves warm weather and the plants cannot tolerate any frost. They do not transplant well and are best sown directly in the garden, 1 inch deep, two to three weeks after the last frost, when the soil temperature is at least 60°F. Gardeners in areas where the warm growing season is short will have trouble getting winter squash to mature—some need over one hundred days—and may have to start plants indoors. In this case, sow four weeks before outdoor planting time, in individual peat pots to minimize root disturbance during transplanting.

The traditional way to plant squash is to pile up soil into small hills 2 to 3 inches high. Space hills for bush varieties 4 to 5 feet apart, and 6 to 8 feet apart for vining varieties. Plant six seeds in the top and

Acorn is the most popular type of winter squash. The variety shown here, Cream of the Crop, produces creamy white skinned fruit on semi-bush plants.

sides of the hill, spacing them evenly apart. Thin later on to leave the healthiest, sturdiest two or three plants in each hill.

You can also plant squash in beds, spacing summer squash 2 feet apart in all directions, and winter squash 3 to 4 feet apart.

For best growth, keep weeds out of the growing area and keep the soil evenly moist. Mulching is a good idea—it helps keep weeds down and slows the evaporation of moisture from the soil. Mulch also keeps the developing squash from contact with the soil, which can sometimes cause rotting. If your soil is not highly fertile, feed the plants once a month with fish emulsion or an all-purpose organic fertilizer.

If pests tend to be a problem in your area, cover young squash plants with floating covers. The squash vine borer is a notorious pest that can wipe out a crop in a matter of days. The caterpillar chews its way into the base of the stems, and the plants wilt very suddenly. Other insects spread disease among the plants, so prevent them if you can.

If borers do attack, you may be able to save the plants by slitting the damaged stems with a sharp knife and removing the caterpillars. Cover the cut stem with dirt so it doesn't dry out. Or apply rotenone around the base of the stems.

Summer squash is ready to pick as quickly as forty-two days after planting, although most varieties take between fifty and sixty days. For baby vegetables, pick while the fruit is still very small, even with the flower still attached, if you wish. Summer squash should have tender skin that is easy to pierce with your fingernail. Zucchini is best when it is 4 to 7 inches long and 1 to 2 inches in diameter. I like it best when it is 4 or 5 inches long—it is deliciously tender and the seeds are quite small. If you let your zucchini get a foot long the quality will just not be as good. It is worth the trouble of harvesting every day or so to catch the vegetables in their prime.

Harvest crookneck squash when the fruit is about 4 inches long, and scallop squash when it is about 4 or 5 inches across. Keep all summer squashes picked to keep the vines producing more.

Winter squash is treated differently. Its quality is poor if you pick it too early—the flesh will be mushy or watery, and the flavor will be insipid. To give winter squash as much time to mature as possible, harvest as close to the first serious frost as you dare. This is always a judgment call, but the fruit will tolerate a few light frosts, which will in fact improve its flavor. Just be sure when you harvest that the shell is so hard that you cannot make a dent when you press with your fingernail.

Cut the fruit from the vine with a sharp knife, leaving at least 3 inches of stem attached. Handle carefully to avoid bruising or otherwise damaging the squash—it is tough but not indestructible. Except for acorn, winter squash should be cured by placing it in a warm (75 to 85°F), dry place for a week before you put it into storage. If weather conditions are right you can simply leave the vegetables outdoors. Store all winter squashes except for acorn in a warm, dry location as described in Chapter Five. Acorn squash keeps best in a window well or other cool, moist storage area.

There seem to be endless numbers of squash varieties on the market, with new ones appearing every year. Among zucchini, Ambassador and Aristocrat are well known and widely grown. Super Select is another good variety. Seneca Milano is very early, and Spineless Beauty has no annoying spines on its stems. Black Beauty and Raven are very dark green, Greyzini is grayish, and Gold Rush and Butterstick Hybrid are a surprising golden yellow. Green Magic and Burpee Hybrid Zucchini are two bush varieties. Seneca Gourmet is especially good for baby vegetables. Gourmet Globe and Ronde de Nice are globe-shaped instead of cylindrical.

Yellow crookneck squash varieties include Early Summer Yellow Crookneck, Butter Swan, Sundance, Dixie Hybrid, and Seneca Crookneck.

Goldbar and Seneca Butterbar are two straight yellow squashes. Early Prolific Straightneck Hybrid grows on a bush-type plant.

If scallop squash is for you, there are several choices. Patty Pan is the traditional white-skinned variety. Yellow Bush Scallop and Sunburst both have golden yellow skin, and Sunburst's bright green tip makes it especially striking as a baby vegetable. Scallopini has pale green skin and produces an early harvest. Peter Pan is also green, and recommended for baby vegetables.

Cocozelle is a dark green bush squash with light green stripes; it takes longer to mature than most other varieties.

Sun Drops produces small, oval yellow fruit on compact plants. It is ideal as a baby vegetable—pick the fruit while it is very small, while the flower is still attached.

Several Lebanese squashes, including Kuta Hybrid and Ghada, are now on the market. They produce pale green, oval fruit that is renowned for its flavor, and can be used like winter squash when fully mature. For use as a summer squash, pick when small.

Acorn is the most widely grown kind of winter squash. The ridged, round fruit tapers to a point at one end. Table Queen and Royal Acorn are two traditional dark green–skinned varieties; Table Ace and Autumn Queen are also green, on bush-type plants. Three acorns with creamy white skin are Fordhook Acorn, Swan White Acorn, and Cream of the Crop, which is semi-bush. Jersey Golden Acorn has yellow skin and makes an interesting baby vegetable.

The most unusual squash, spaghetti squash, has been appearing in more and more supermarkets. On the outside spaghetti squash looks pretty uninteresting—it is oval, fat, and round, with smooth, light yellow skin. But inside this squash is like no other. After cooking, its fibrous flesh can be separated into long strands that resemble spaghetti. In fact, it is delicious served with spaghetti sauce. But you can also serve it buttered with perhaps a dash of nutmeg or cinnamon. You will find it listed in some catalogs as vegetable spaghetti.

Delicata, another unusual winter squash, yields small oblong fruit with pale green shells striped in darker green, and sweet orange flesh. Sweet Dumpling is similar but even smaller, with each fruit about the right size for a single serving.

Buttercup is a sweet-flavored variety that produces fruit with a round but slightly flattened shape rather like a drum. Other buttercup types are Sweet Mama, Honey Delight, and the compact All Seasons.

The other most familiar group of winter squashes are the butternuts, which have round bottoms and big, thick necks. Good varieties include Early Butternut Hybrid, the widely grown Waltham Butternut, Zenith Hybrid, and Burpee's Butterbush, which is a bush type.

The biggest, weirdest looking winter squash is hubbard, which is shaped like a somewhat cortorted giant football and has a thick skin that's covered with warts. Hubbard squashes store particularly well and have sweet, golden flesh. Blue Hubbard is a most peculiar dusty blue color and looks rather unearthly; Golden Hubbard has reddish orange skin.

Tarragon

The first secret to growing good tarragon is to plant the right kind. There are two: French tarragon (*Artemisia dracunculus* var. *sativa*) and Russian (*A. dracunculus*), and both are sometimes sold either as French tarragon or just plain tarragon. The plants are similar in appearance but it is important to distinguish them; French tarragon has a far superior flavor. That flavor is aromatic and rather like licorice in the fresh leaves; when dried the taste mellows and sweetens. I find that I prefer the flavor of dried tarragon leaves in certain dishes.

Tarragon is heavenly in chicken salad and indispensable in béarnaise sauce. It is also outstanding in salad dressings, omelets, vinegars, butters, and sauces, and excellent with fish.

How do you tell the two types of tarragon apart? First of all, if you see tarragon seeds you can be sure they are of the Russian type; French tarragon does not produce seeds and must be propagated by vegetative (asexual) methods. The plant's appearance differs, too. French tarragon has small, lance-shaped leaves of deeper green, and is a smaller plant, reaching about 2 or 2½ feet when mature. Russian tarragon is bigger and coarser, growing to as much as 5 feet, with longer leaves. You will not be able to judge mature size when you buy a young plant, obviously, but if you find later in the season that you bought the wrong variety, find a different source next year.

Tarragon needs well-drained, fertile, crumbly soil with a fairly light texture and a pH near neutral. A sandy loam rich in organic matter is ideal. The plants will not perform well in acid, very wet soils; they will be less hardy and may develop root rot. Full sun is best for tarragon, but it will do tolerably well in partial shade. The plant is hardy to a temperature of about −20°F, and grows best where it experiences at least some freezing weather in winter.

Plant in spring when the danger of frost is past, at the same depth the plants were growing in their nursery containers. Set plants 1 to 2 feet apart.

You can also grow a young tarragon plant in a container indoors, in a soil mix with excellent drainage. Light can come either from a sunny window or fluorescent fixtures in a light garden. Tarragon does need a lot of humidity to grow well indoors, but is prone to mildew in damp, stagnant air. Set the pot on a pebble tray and mist the plant daily, but run a small fan in the room to keep the air moving.

Tarragon needs to be divided often to retain its vigor and maximum flavor. You can divide plants in spring, when the new growth appears. If you prefer to start new plants from cuttings, take tip cuttings from young shoots in spring in cool and temperate climates, or autumn in warm climates.

Keep tarragon well watered, and water during dry weather. The plants almost never bloom in American gardens, but if any flower stems do appear on your plants, pick them off. No matter where you live, your tarragon will appreciate a good winter mulch. If your garden is in an exposed location, protect tarragon from cold winter winds by setting up a windbreak.

Pick leaves as needed throughout the growing season. In fall, before the first frost, cut back the stems and hang them upside down in bunches, out of direct light, to air-dry. Handle the leaves carefully when harvesting and preparing for drying—they are easily bruised.

Thyme

No kitchen garden is complete without at least one kind of thyme, but deciding what kind of thyme to grow and what kind you are buying can be problematic. The genus *Thymus* is large and confusing, and the multiplicity of names for each type are a taxonomist's nightmare. Thymes are more often mislabeled and misidentified than just about any other garden plants.

But the plants themselves, whatever they are called, are easy to grow and have myriad uses in the kitchen. Thyme is excellent with poultry and in poultry stuffings, with meats and fish, cheeses, and vegetables, especially mushrooms. Add it to omelets, quiches, and crêpes, soups, seafood chowders, butters, and salad dressings. One of the French *fines herbes*, thyme plays a part in many French dishes, and is also important in Cajun and Creole cookery. For herbalists, thyme has a host of medicinal uses: the leaves contain an antiseptic oil.

The thymes are small plants, with little leaves and tiny flowers of pink, lilac, or white. The flowers are edible as well as the leaves, and make a charming, delicate garnish. In the garden they attract bees.

Thymes are perennials with a creeping habit, whose lower stems turn woody with age. From the travelling horizontal stems grow slender, vertical green stems with small oval leaves of dark grayish green. The plants are native to the Mediterranean region, and they are evergreen in warm climates.

Their modest stature makes thymes perfect for rock gardens, edging garden beds, and bordering paths and walkways. They will tumble over small rocks and low edgings, and will spill over a stone wall when planted in pockets of soil along the top. You can also grow them in pots both indoors and outdoors. Low-growing types like creeping thyme can be used as ground covers or planted between paving stones.

Common thyme, *Thymus vulgaris*, which you may also see listed as English or French Thyme, is the best known of the clan and the classic culinary thyme. It grows 6 to 12 inches tall, and in midsummer minuscule white or pale lilac flowers congregate around the tips of the stems. The species has dark green leaves, the cultivar Aureus has golden leaves, and the foliage of Argenteus is variegated in green and white and appears silvery from a distance.

Lemon thyme, *T. × citriodorus*, has a lemony scent and taste. It grows to about a foot tall, with oval leaves that are a bit wider than those of common thyme, and pale lilac flowers. Two noteworthy cultivars are Aureus, with golden leaves, and Silver Queen, which is silvery.

Creeping thyme, *T. serpyllum*, hugs the ground and forms a thick mat. This species is often misidentified and frequently confused with other species of similar appearance.

Most seed catalogs and garden centers carry common thyme, but herb specialists carry dozens of different kinds. You will find various European thymes, thymes with variegated, reddish, golden, or silver foliage, and thymes scented like caraway, nutmeg, or oregano.

Thymes are sun lovers, but they will tolerate partial shade as well. Give them warm, light, loose soil tending toward dryness and—most important of all—well drained. In wet soil the plants are susceptible to fungus. Average fertility is fine, and a near-neutral pH is best.

You can start species thymes from seed; sow indoors, 1/8 to 1/4 inch deep, eight weeks before the last frost. Keep the medium evenly moist until the seeds germinate. Move the young plants outdoors a couple of weeks after the last frost, or whenever the soil has warmed to 68°F or more. Space plants 6 to 10 inches apart.

Commercial growers propagate thyme by cuttings, layering, or division, and these methods work for home gardeners, too. Thyme needs to be renewed every three or four years to keep the plants vigorous and productive, and these techniques are good ways to keep your patch going. Division is the easiest of the three, and you can do it in mid to late spring. Dig the plant carefully (the roots can go surprisingly deep into the soil), retaining as much of the soil around the roots as you can. Cut apart the root ball into several smaller sections, and replant the sections in the garden. Water thoroughly after replanting.

Take tip cuttings about 3 inches long from vigorous young shoots in mid to late spring or even in summer. Do not use the older woody stems for cuttings. Root the cuttings in moist sand or a light soil mix, and transplant them to the garden when they have developed roots.

Young shoots can be layered in spring or summer. The procedure is described under Sage, earlier in this chapter.

Thyme is easy to grow and usually needs little care during the growing season. Spider mites sometimes take up residence among the leaves, but they can be removed with insecticidal soap.

In areas where winter temperatures are likely to drop below 10°F, give thyme a thick winter mulch to prevent frost heaving that could damage the crowns. Thyme is reliably hardy to −10 or −20°F (zone 5).

Pick sprigs whenever you need them throughout the growing season, or cut back the whole plant to about 2 inches above the ground and it will regrow. Thyme air-dries easily.

Tomatoes

Tomatoes are the pride and joy of many a gardener. Everybody, it seems, grows tomatoes, even if they grow nothing else. Tomatoes are the most widely grown vegetable in America with good reason: there is simply no comparison between juicy, flavorful ripe tomatoes fresh from the garden and the pale, solid, bland-tasting specimens sold in supermarkets. Tomatoes were not meant to be harvested by machines, packed in boxes, and shipped across the country to sit in a bin in the market. To enable them to withstand such treatment, breeders have developed firmer, thicker-skinned fruit, some with flat sides to facilitate packing, and commercial growers harvest before the tomatoes are ripe and sometimes treat them with ethylene gas to ripen them artificially. No, the quality of supermarket tomatoes does not even approach that of the home-grown crop. The best way to get "real" tomatoes is still to grow them yourself.

Tomatoes today come in an incredible array of sizes, and a number of colors, shapes, times to maturity, and growth habits. All of them belong to the same species, *Lycopersicon lycopersicum*. There are huge beefsteaks, marble-sized cherries, and every size in between. There are pink, orange, and yellow tomatoes. There are meaty, pear-shaped varieties good for processing into sauce, paste, or juice. There are compact plants that grow happily in hanging baskets or flowerpots, and tall vining plants that can get to be 6 feet tall in a good year. Some of the old favorites and heirlooms that have been hard to find have become more accessible in recent years. Marglobe and Rutgers, two old-timers that are still favorites of many gardeners (like my dad, who swears by Marglobe), are now available in improved forms that are more productive and disease resistant than the originals. European varieties are available, too. There is even a seed company that specializes in tomatoes—Tomato Growers Supply Company (P.O. Box 2237, Fort Myers, FL 33902). Their 1991 catalog lists 179 tomato varieties.

To extend the harvest season you can plant early varieties, which mature fifty to sixty-five days after transplanting, mid-season varieties, which are ready in sixty-six to seventy-nine days, or late varieties, which take eighty to ninety days.

You will see the words *determinate* and *indeterminate* in catalog descriptions, and you may also find references to patio tomatoes. Determinate plants grow 1 to 1½ feet tall, stop growing when their fruit is set, and produce their entire crop over a very short period of time. These varieties are a good choice for small gardens, and for gardeners who want to can or otherwise process the harvest. Early varieties are good for short-season areas. You can also grow determinate tomatoes in a large container, such as a 5-gallon plastic bucket with drainage holes punched in the bottom.

Indeterminate tomatoes keep growing and producing fruit until they are killed by frost in the North, or succumb to late blight in the South. The plants can reach 4 or more feet tall and the harvest continues for many weeks. Indeterminate tomatoes can also be trained to grow vertically; pinch out all the suckers and fasten the main stems to supports as described in Chapter One.

Smaller plants sometimes called patio tomatoes have been bred especially for container growing. They bear smaller fruit than standard-sized plants except for cherry tomatoes. Plant them in a well-drained potting mix, water whenever the soil feels dry (every day in hot weather), and feed every other week with a liquid fertilizer.

One drawback to tomatoes is their susceptibility to a number of bacterial and fungal diseases, but the majority of varieties have some degree of resistance or tolerance to one or more of them. Capital letters following the variety name, or included in the name, indicate the diseases to which that variety is resistant or tolerant. *A* indicates alternaria blight, *F* stands for fusarium wilt (there are two kinds, so you may see two Fs, or F1 and F2), *V* is verticillium wilt, and *T* is tobacco mosaic virus. Nematodes also attack tomatoes, and can carry and spread diseases; resistance to them is indicated by the letter *N*.

Start tomato seeds indoors four to eight weeks before the average date of your last spring frost. Sow ¼ inch deep in a moist growing medium. Set the containers in a warm place; seeds germinate best when the soil temperature is 70 to 75°F. They need lots of humidity, too, so place the containers in a propagation unit that has a plastic cover, or put them in a plastic bag to maintain humidity. When shoots appear, remove the bag or cover and give the seedlings all the light you can. Place them on your sunniest windowsill, or in a light garden. Plants that do not get enough light will grow tall and lanky, with the leaves far apart on the stems. They will never perform as well in the garden as sturdy, compact plants.

When plants develop their first or second set of true leaves, thin them to stand 3 to 4 inches apart in a flat, or to leave one plant in each individual pot or cell. Prepare the seedlings for life outdoors by carefully hardening them off as described in Chapter Three, for about ten days.

Transplants can go out to the garden two to four weeks after the last frost, when nighttime temperatures no longer drop below 55°F.

Gardeners who live where the growing season is long and warm can sow directly in the garden when the soil is warm—at least 60°F. Water well immediately after sowing.

If you buy transplants at the garden center instead of growing your own, look for stocky little plants with a good green color. Resist the temptation to buy plants already in bloom—they will have difficulty making

the transition to the garden. Also steer clear of tall, lanky plants, which are weak and will never perform well.

Tomatoes need full sun—at least six hours a day—and fertile, moist but well-drained soil that is rich in organic matter. Phosphorus and calcium especially must be in good supply. Phosphorus is needed for good flower and fruit production. And calcium, along with adequate moisture, is important in preventing blossom-end rot, a scaly brown patch that can develop on the bottom of the fruit. Work plenty of rock phosphate into the soil the autumn before planting, and if a soil test shows a calcium deficiency, add lime.

In the garden, determinate tomatoes supported by stakes can be spaced 1 to 2 feet apart, indeterminate plants 1½ to 2½ feet apart. If you will support the plants with cages, set them 3 feet apart. Rows should be 3 feet apart. If planting in a bed, set the plants 2 to 3 feet apart in all directions, depending on their means of support. If you will train indeterminate tomatoes to grow vertically on a trellis, you can plant them 1 foot apart. Put supports in place when you set out transplants, to avoid injuring roots later on.

Set plants at least 2 inches deeper than they were growing in their containers. Or set each plant in a trench almost horizontally and bury the stem to just below the bottom leaves. Roots will grow from the buried part of the stem, giving the plant additional support and increased capacity to absorb water and nutrients. The tops of trench-planted tomatoes will straighten out and grow upward.

Give the new transplants cutworm collars if cutworms are a problem in your garden. Keep the plants well weeded and watered as they establish themselves in the garden.

In fact, tomatoes need constant, even moisture all season. If the soil is too wet the roots will rot, and if it's too dry the plants will stop producing. If the soil is allowed to dry out and then becomes very wet, the flowers can drop and the fruit may crack.

Also, uneven moisture combined with lack of calcium encourages blossom-end rot.

If the leaves of your tomato plants curl it means the plants are too wet—good drainage is important.

Tomatoes grow better in many gardens when they are given 2 to 4 inches of loose mulch. In addition to helping hold soil moisture, mulch also keeps dirt from splashing up onto the fruit during rainstorms.

When you water, water deeply. Frequent light watering encourages shallow roots and weaker plants. Water at the base of the plant, not from overhead; wet leaves invite disease. Make a shallow depression in the soil around the base of each plant to catch and hold water.

Fertilize with a good all-purpose fertilizer when the plants set fruit, and monthly thereafter for the rest of the season. Don't overfeed or give plants too much nitrogen, or you will get lots of leaves and not much fruit.

Tomatoes are sensitive to both cool and hot weather, preferring average temperatures of 70 to 75°F. If the temperature falls below 55°F the blossoms may drop. They may also drop in very hot weather, so gardeners in southern regions may want to give the plants some shade during the hottest part of the day.

Aphids and whiteflies may attack tomatoes, but can be controlled with insecticidal soap. Handpick or use rotenone on beetles or tomato hornworms. If you smoke, never do it around your plants, or work among the tomatoes after smoking without first washing your hands. Keep all fallen leaves and other debris picked up throughout the growing season to help minimize the possibility of disease. Clean up thoroughly after the harvest is complete, too.

Tomatoes are damaged by even the lightest frost, although if you protect them from the first fall frost as described in Chapter Five you will probably be able to harvest for a few more weeks. If a severe frost is predicted, pick any tomatoes still on the plants. Or pull up the plants and hang them upside down in a dark shed or closet. Mature tomatoes will ripen. Green tomatoes that are full size and beginning to turn yellow can be ripened indoors. Wrap them individually in newspaper or put them in a dark place. Immature green tomatoes can be cooked in a number of ways.

In a book of this size it is impossible to list all the tomatoes on the market, let alone attempt to describe them. Below are just some of the many varieties available; consult your favorite seed catalog for descriptions and additional selections. Disease resistance codes are given where available.

Some early determinate varieties are Bush Beefsteak, Sub Arctic Maxi (good for cooler climates), Earlirouge VF, Johnny's 361 (beefsteak), Pilgrim VF, and Summerset VF. Indeterminate early varieties include Champion Hybrid VFNT, Early Girl Improved Hybrid VFF, Marmande (a French heirloom), Early Cascade VF, and Dona (a French variety).

Determinate mid-season varieties include Burpee's Big Boy Hybrid, Carnival Hybrid VFFNTA, Celebrity Hybrid VFFNTA, Floramerica Hybrid VFFA, Marglobe Improved VF, Mountain Pride VF, Spring Giant Hybrid VFN, and Supersonic Hybrid VF. Some indeterminate tomatoes for mid-season are Better Boy VFN, Big Pick VFNT, Jet Star Hybrid VF, Bonny Best (an heirloom), Carmello (a French variety), Ramapo Hybrid VF, and Super Fantastic Hybrid VF.

Late determinate varieties include Cal-Ace VF (good for dry climates), Caro Rich (orange, and very rich in vitamin A), Homestead 24F (good for the South), Rutgers Improved VF, and Super Bush Hybrid VFN (which needs no support). Many beefsteak tomatoes are late-season indeterminate varieties, including Beefmaster VFN Hybrid, Beefsteak, Brandywine (open pollinated), Burpee's Supersteak Hybrid VFN, Crimson Cushion, Pink Ponderosa, Red Ponderosa, and Super Beefsteak VFN.

Long Keeper was bred for storage, and is of better quality than the usual supermarket tomato.

If you want to grow pear-shaped tomatoes, try Bellstar, La Rossa, Milano, Nova, Red Pear, Roma VF, or San Marzano.

Dwarf and small-fruited determinate plants that are suited for container growing include the early varieties Burpee's Pixie Hybrid and Pixie Hybrid II, Gem State, Tiny Tim, Toy Boy VF, and Whippersnapper; and the mid-season varieties Gardener's Delight or Sugar Lump, Small Fry VFN Hybrid, Patio Prize VFN Hybrid, and Lunch Box VF. Basket King Hybrid and Red Robin produce early and grow well in hanging baskets; Florida Basket is a mid-season hanging basket variety.

Small-fruited indeterminate tomatoes to harvest in mid-season include Heartland, Cherry Flavor VFFNT Hybrid, Sweet 100, and Sweetie, which is open pollinated.

If you want to try yellow tomatoes, consider the indeterminate varieties Garden' Peach, Golden Boy Hybrid, Golden Queen, Jubilee, Lemon Boy VFN Hybrid, Yellow Cherry, Yellow Pear, and Yellow Plum. Or try Chello Yellow, a semideterminate yellow cherry tomato.

Orange Queen and Caro Rich are two orange varieties. Pink Cherry is a pinkish red cherry tomato. Pink Grapefruit is a most unusual yellow flushed with pink.

Turnips

If you detested turnips (*Brassica rapa*, Rapifera Group) in your younger days, some of the newer, smaller-rooted varieties may change your mind. You may be surprised at the mild, sweet flavor. Both the leaves and roots of turnips are edible. Some varieties are grown for their nutritious, pungent leaves, which are rich in vitamins A, C, and E, as well as calcium, iron, and potassium. One kind of turnip is grown for its flowering stems and goes by the name of broccoli raab.

Turnips mature quickly—some in as little as thirty-five days—and grow best in cool weather. Traditionally they were planted in early spring, or in summer for fall harvest, because hot weather ruined the flavor and texture of the roots, turning them woody and bitter. Storage varieties of turnips are still grown this way. But some turnips, called summer turnips, can stand up to some heat, and can be planted in spring for summer harvest, or in summer for fall harvest. They can tolerate a bit of light frost. These summer turnips are small and tender, with a mild, sweet flavor. They are easy to grow and make good baby vegetables if you pull them when they are the size of radishes. Unlike larger rooted turnips, these summer varieties will not keep well in storage. Gardeners in warm climates can grow them in spring or fall.

Plant turnips in full sun, in fertile, loose soil that is free of stones, moist but well drained, and rich in organic matter. Work in rock phosphate a season ahead of planting to insure a good supply of phosphorus.

Direct-sow a few weeks before the last frost date, when the soil is at least 45°F, and make succession plantings every three weeks all through spring. For fall, plant eight to ten weeks before you expect the first frost. Sow seeds ¼ inch deep.

Thin the plants to stand 3 inches apart in all directions in a bed, or 2 to 3 inches apart in rows 6 inches apart. Use the thinnings in salads. If you tend to have insect problems in your garden, lay down floating row covers after sowing the seeds.

Water deeply once a week during dry weather, and mulch to help conserve moisture and keep roots cool.

One of the most popular turnips is Purple Top White Globe, whose roots are white on the bottom where they are underground, and purple on the top which is above ground. Similar varieties are Royal Crown, DeNancy, which is French, and De Milan,

another French variety that is a rosier color on top. Tokyo Cross is very early to mature, as is Market Express, whose white roots are wonderful as baby vegetables. White Lady, Snowball, and White Egg are all white. Presto grows very fast, and is used for pickling in Japan. Scarlet Queen and OhNo Scarlet resemble radishes, with red skin and white flesh. Golden Ball has yellow flesh. All Seasons adapts to spring, summer, or fall gardens.

If you love turnip greens, try growing Seven Top, All Top, or Shogoin in cool weather.

Sweet Violets

Sweet violets (*Viola odorata*) possess a sweet fragrance that has long been appreciated in perfumery. They have a similar flowerly flavor that can add interest to deli-

Turnips can be surprisingly sweet and mild if you harvest them young. The best-known variety, Purple Top, has roots that are white below ground and purple on top, where they are above ground.

cate desserts and other dishes. Violets are delightful when candied; you can use them fresh to float in punch or a chilled fruit soup, or scatter them on top of fruit salad or ice cream.

The sweet violet is a small plant with deep green heart-shaped leaves, that in spring bears dainty, quiet little flowers of purple or white on stems just 6 inches tall. There are cultivars in various shades from light purple to deep violet, white, and rosy red to pink. The smaller, single-flowered varieties are easiest to candy; for instructions see Feasting on Flowers in Chapter Four.

Species violets grow wild in woodlands

and meadows, and their natural habitats offer clues to the conditions violets like in the garden. Give violets partial shade and rich, moist soil with plenty of organic matter. The plants spread readily by means of underground runners, as well as seeds dropped from nonornamental seed-producing flowers hidden under the leaves, and can be planted as a groundcover. Violets can become invasive, but I count myself among the gardeners for whom the charm of the flowers is worth the effort needed to keep them under control in the garden. If you pull up unwanted volunteers, you can use violets to edge a shady part of the kitchen garden.

It is easiest to grow violets from nursery plants or divisions or offsets taken from established plantings. Seeds need stratification (a cold treatment) before they will germinate. If you want to grow violets from seed, sow them in a container of damp soil and place the container in the refrigerator for several days. Then put the container in a closet or other dark place until the first shoots appear, anywhere from one to three weeks later. When they do, move the container to a bright windowsill or light garden.

Set out seedlings or nursery plants around the date of the average last frost in spring. Space them about 6 inches apart. If you already have an established clump of violets that you want to use for groundcover, you can dig and divide clumps in summer after the plants have bloomed, or in early fall. Or you can lift the small offsets that grow at the ends of the underground runners and replant them someplace else if you wish.

Violets will bloom for you year after year with practically no care, and who could ask more of any garden flower?

APPENDIX

Sources of Seeds, Plants, and Supplies

The following companies are some of the best mail-order sources of seeds, plants, tools and equipment, and natural fertilizers and pest controls. Many are small compa- nies and must charge for their catalogs, so check with them before ordering one unless the catalog is listed below as free.

Seeds and Plants

Bountiful Gardens
Ecology Action
5798 Ridgewood Rd.
Willits, CA 95490

W. Atlee Burpee & Co.
Warminster, PA 18974
Catalog free.

Comstock, Ferre & Co.
263 Main St., Box 125-0125
Wethersfield, CT 06109

The Cook's Garden
P.O. Box 535
Londonderry, VT 05148
(802) 824-3400
$1 for catalog.

Fungi Perfecti
P.O. Box 7634
Olympia, WA 98507

J.L. Hudson, Seedsman
P.O. Box 1058
Redwood City, CA 94064
$1 for catalog.

Le Jardin du Gourmet
P.O. Box 75
St. Johnsbury Center, VT 05863
(802) 748-1446

Johnny's Selected Seeds
Foss Hill Rd.
Albion, ME 04910
(207) 437-4301
Catalog free.

Nichols Garden Nursery
1190 North Pacific Hwy.
Albany, OR 97321
(503) 928-9280
Catalog free.

Park Seed Co.
Cokesbury Rd.
Greenwood, SC 29647
(803) 223-7333
Catalog free.

Pinetree Garden Seeds
New Gloucester, ME 04260
(207) 926-3400
Catalog free.

Seeds Blüm
Idaho City Stage
Boise, ID 83706

Shepherd's Garden Seeds
30 Irene St.
Torrington, CT 06790
(203) 482-3638;
in California (408) 335-5311
$1 for catalog.

Stokes Seeds Inc.
Box 548
Buffalo, NY 14240
(416) 688-4300
Catalog free.

Well-Sweep Herb Farm
317 Mt. Bethel Rd.
Port Murray, NJ 07865
(201) 852-5390
$2 for catalog.

Tools, Equipment, and Supplies

Gardener's Supply
128 Intervale Rd.
Burlington, VT 05401
Catalog free.

Gardens Alive!
Natural Gardening Research Center
Hwy. 48, P.O. Box 149
Sunman, IN 46041
(812) 623-3800
Catalog free.

Indoor Gardening Supplies
P.O. Box 40567
Detroit, MI 48240
(313) 668-8384

The Kinsman Company
River Rd.
Point Pleasant, PA 18950
(800) 733-5613
Catalog free.

The Natural Gardening Company
217 San Anselmo Ave.
San Anselmo, CA 94960
(415) 456-5060

The Necessary Catalogue
Necessary Trading Co.
8320 Salem Ave.
New Castle, VA 24127
(703) 864-5103
$2 for catalog.

Walt Nicke Co.
36 McLeod Lane, P.O. Box 433
Topsfield, MA 01983
(508) 887-3388
Catalog free.

Ringer
9959 Valley View Rd.
Eden Prairie, MN 55344
(800) 654-1047
Catalog free.

Index

Agriculture Department, U.S.
(USDA), 21, 58, 109
air circulation, 21
in cold frames, 118
for indoor gardens, 126–27
light gardens and, 44
allelopathy, 31
anise, 31
anise hyssop, 169–70
see also hyssop
annuals, 19, 60, 68
cutting back, 120
deadheading, 81
winter-flowering, 120
aphids, 71, 76
in cold frames, 118
controlling, 89, 118, 128
indoors, 128
arugula, 20, 32, 131–32
extending harvest of, 72–73,
78
harvesting, 96, 132
planting, 60, 92, 132
as seedling crops, 69–70,
132
ashes, for maggot control, 74
asparagus, 20, 31, 45, 74, 132–
134
companion planting, 33
diseases and pests of, 134

fertilizing, 53, 133, 134
forcing, 120
harvesting, 72, 133–34
planting, 19, 60, 133
preparing beds for, 108, 133
watering, 87
asparagus chicory, 155
autumn gardens, 16, 93–114
benefits of, 93–94
cleaning up, 114
extension of season for, 94–
95
frost protection for, 111–12
harvesting, 94–99, 101
harvesting and storage of
herbs in, 101–4
maintenance of, 109–10
mulch for, 107, 110
natural storage and, 104–7
planting, 107–9
soil preparation for, 113–14
in temperate climates, 108
vegetables for, 97
watering, 110
weeding, 110
window well storage and,
105

baby vegetables, 25, 80, 81
see also specific vegetables

bacteria, in soil, 39
basil, 29, 31, 32, 134–35
deadheading, 90
growing indoors, 129, 135
planting, 59, 60, 70, 92, 135
uses of, 134–35
beans, 31, 45, 53
baby, 80
diseases of, 52
harvesting, 81, 82–83
planting, 59–60, 70
succession planting and, 91
watering, 87
see also specific varieties
bean sprouts, 123–24
beds:
intensive, 23
raised, 21, 48, 148
soil composition and, 48
beebalm, 29, 61, 140
beets, 20, 29, 45, 53, 140–41
baby, 80
companion planting, 31, 141
forcing, 120
harvesting, 81, 117, 141
pests of, 141
planting, 61, 69, 91, 92, 99,
108, 141
storage of, 105, 141
thinning, 76, 141